Suzy Chiazzari is a well-known lecturer and practitioner of colour therapy. Her love of Mediterranean cooking and a life-long interest in health prompted her investigation into the relationship between colour and food. Her work with colour and holistic healthcare has been featured in many publications and she has made several professional television appearances. She is the author of three books including *The Complete Book of Colour*, also published by Element.

by the same author

Colour Scents
The Complete Book of Colour
The Healing Home

Nutritional Healing with COLOUR

SUZY CHIAZZARI

ELEMENT

Shaftesbury, Dorset • Boston, Massachusetts
Melbourne, Victoria

This edition first published in the UK in 1999 by
Element Books Limited
Shaftesbury, Dorset SP7 8BP

Published in the USA in 1999 by
Element Books, Inc.
160 North Washington Street
Boston, MA 02114

Published in Australia in 1999 by
Element Books and distributed
by Penguin Australia Limited
487 Maroondah Highway, Ringwood, Victoria 3134

Cover illustration photographs © RSA Photography
Cover design by Slatter-Anderson
Plate photographs by Iain Bagwell
Design by Roger Lightfoot
Typeset by Footnote Graphics, Warminster, Wilts
Printed and bound in Great Britain by
J W Arrowsmith Ltd, Bristol

British Library Cataloguing in Publication
data available

Library of Congress Cataloging in Publication
data available

ISBN 1 86204 310 8

Contents

A Note on Conversions

The units used in the recipes in this book are given in the order metric, imperial, and American. The conversions are practical ones for kitchen use; precise ones are given below.

In British use, dry spoon measures are heaped or rounded, and in American use they are level: all dry spoon measures are given here as rounded to prevent confusion. Liquid spoon measures are also different, but this is not significant for very small amounts.

Units of measurement

American

1 tbsp = 3 tsp = $\frac{1}{2}$ fl oz = 14.785ml
1C = 8oz/8 fl oz = 16 tbsp = 237ml
1 liquid pint = 16 fl oz = 28.88 cu. in. = 0.473 litre

Imperial

1 pint = 20 fl oz = 34.68 cu. in. = 0.568 litre

Oven temperatures

Description	Centigrade	Fahrenheit	gas mark
very cool	110	225	$\frac{1}{4}$
	130	275	1
cool	150	300	2
warm	160	325	3
	180	350	4
medium	190	375	5
fairly hot	200	400	6
	220	425	7
hot	230	450	8
very hot	250	475	9

Introduction

The Relationship Between Food and Colour

I have always taken delight in colour and in food. Growing up in a tropical environment in Durban, South Africa, I was fortunate in sampling a wonderful range of fruit and vegetables which were delicious, nutritious and bursting with colour energy. After paying my relatives in Italy several visits I developed a taste for Italian country cooking, and having moved to England I still take great pleasure in preparing and eating fresh natural food.

One day a few years ago I was looking at my dinner plate when it occurred to me that the different colours of the vegetables might have a special meaning. Could it be that they were a sign of the nutrients in the food, and that the more colourful the meal, the more nutritious it was? As a colour therapist and food enthusiast, I decided to learn more about traditional views of nutrition, and other more esoteric ways of looking at food. Not only did I investigate the links between the colours of natural fresh foods and their nutritional content but I also considered the significance of their colours from a holistic viewpoint, since our minds and spirits need nourishment as well as our bodies. This book is a result of my researches and independent thinking, and it presents to you a way of integrating what I have learnt simply and effectively into your everyday life.

Colour energy is not a physical force that disappears when we close our eyes: it exists in its own right, and the quality of the light vibrations we take into our system at every moment has a profound effect on our mental, emotional and spiritual well-being, whether we are awake or asleep, sighted or blind. (Blind people are very sensitive to colour vibrations and some can even differentiate between different colours through touch – my research revealed cases of sighted people in Russia who had been taught to do this in a surprisingly short time.)

The colours in food reveal important information about its actions on us, and all the aspects of its healing qualities – physically, emotionally and mentally. The natural colouring of fresh fruits, flowers and vegetables can be divided into three groups, corresponding directly to the three primary colours found in sunlight – red, green and blue-violet, which provide the perfect balance of light energy that creates the right environment on our planet to support life. Each group contains certain chemical and energetic qualities which have specific beneficial actions upon our system and which form the basic groups of the Colours for Life Diet.

Light Energy

Light energy is essential for human beings, because our good health is dependent not just on a balanced metabolism but also upon the ability of our bodies to draw in and circulate vital light energy through our energetic system. Light energy from the sun is essential for life on earth, and every colour vibration which is part of natural sunlight has certain life-giving properties.

In traditional Chinese medicine light energy is known as *chi*, and it is believed that this life-force flows through the cosmos and through every living thing. Ancient Chinese medical practitioners were the first to recognize the importance of the daily flow of energy through our systems, and of how *chi* circulates around our bodies through a network of invisible lines – or meridians – which are closely linked to our nervous system. When *chi* flows uninterrupted through our energy system we are connected to the life-force current and we are full of energy, but if this light energy is blocked the effect soon influences our physical body and we feel 'washed out' or 'off colour'.

Chi is made up of two opposing but complementary forces, which the Chinese call yin and yang. Yang represents masculine energy, which is moving, stimulating and hot coloured. The complementary feminine force is yin, which is still, pacifying and cool coloured. Yin energy is light and moist, and relates to the shorter wavelengths of light; yang energy is dense and dry, and corresponds to the longer wavelengths. When there is a balance between yin and yang in our system, harmony reigns. Therefore, we can, accepting the wisdom of traditional Chinese medicine, base a diet on the principle of the balance of yin and yang to help us select foods that create energetic harmony between our body, mind and spirit. Different tastes, for example, can be classified on the scale of yin–yang; the most yang are salty in flavour, while the most yin are sweet.

I find the principle of yin and yang helpful particularly when relating the colours of food to their nutritional and healing qualities in the Colours for Life Diet. Red- and orange-coloured foods have more yang energy, so they are more stimulating and warming, while blue foods are more yin and therefore lighter to digest and more cooling. Green food has a balance of yin and yang, and this is why a diet rich in green salads, vegetables, fruit and herbs is excellent for our health. Green food also contains a good deal of fibre, some of which maintains a healthy digestive tract, ensuring any excess fibre passes through our system. (This means that when you follow the Colours for Life Diet you can eat as much green food as you like, without worrying about putting on weight.) It is no accident that many plants are green, for this colour vibration is found in the middle of the visible colour spectrum, and although green foods form the first food group they correspond to the second primary colour of light. The wavelength of the green ray is neither long nor short and it has neither a warming nor a cooling action. This gives it a unique function in maintaining harmony.

Light Energy and the Three Colour Groups of Food

From ancient times until quite recently we lived close to nature and its cycles, and we were able to read the signals in the world around us: sailors and farmers could predict the weather by the colours of the sky, and the shapes and hues of herbs gave traditional healers essential information regarding their healing uses; much of this knowledge was contained in sayings, passed down from one generation to the next. I remember my grandmother, who taught home economics over fifty years ago, telling me that we should always have at least three colours on the plate. Unfortunately because tips like this have been dismissed as old wives' tales their meanings have been lost and so we have also lost the underlying wisdom.

Understanding colour can help us rediscover how to read nature's signs.

Phytonutrients in the natural world

In the plant kingdom, harmony is achieved by keeping the atmosphere on earth clean and healthy so that life can flourish. We can also view plants as a microcosm, reflecting the patterns of the cosmos. The plant kingdom is specifically able to keep us in perfect health because through three basic colour groups it contains a mixture of the three primary light vibrations. As health is a state of harmony, in order to be healthy we require a balance of the basic nutrients embodied in the main colour groups of plants. Eating too much of any particular colour group and not enough of another will result in disharmony and imbalance of biological and metabolic functions. If this imbalance is not corrected our bodies will weaken and we will fall ill.

In the last few years conventional scientific research investigating phytochemistry, the chemistry of plant products, has begun to support this strong health connection between the colours of food and their nutritional value that colour therapy has long recognized. Analysis of the pigments colouring plant foods confirms that multicoloured meals are not just good-looking but positively good for you because each colour is linked to a different phytochemical with particular health benefits. As a result well-known health-care organizations such as the Bristol Cancer Centre actively use this knowledge in their patients' treatment.

White and light green vegetables such as potatoes and lettuce, for example, are rich in vitamin C, which strengthens our immune system and our resistance to infection. Dark green vegetables such as spinach and broccoli provide carotenoids, which can help to ward off heart disease. Red, orange and yellow vegetables, especially tomatoes, contain antioxidants which fight the effects of ageing and can protect against cancer. Pigments generally influence the acidity levels in the food as well, so that red and bright pink coloured foods are much more acidic than those coloured blue. Blue food is more alkaline and has a pacifying effect on our system. (*See* chapters 6 and 7 for more details about the specific healing properties of certain foods.)

We should eat a variety of fresh food from each of the three colour groups. This not only ensures our body systems function properly, but will also protect us against illness caused by adverse genetic and environmental factors. Happily, nature provides us with the colour code that ensures we can get all the physical and energetic nutrients we need for health and vitality.

Green
The light-reacting pigment chlorophyll gives plants the green colour we usually associate with them, and it is the medium through which most plants harness their energy from sunlight. Chlorophyll absorbs light from the red and blue ends of the spectrum, thus maintaining an energetic balance within the plant itself, and is the most important colour group. Fresh green foods from the plant kingdom have a natural ability to cleanse and balance our metabolism so that we can be healthy too.

Red
Some foods have carotenoid pigments, which also absorb light for photosynthesis. These are found in the many brightly coloured fruits and flowers that make up the plant world's second family of colour, and which corresponds to the red ray. More than 60 varieties of carotenoid compounds have been isolated, ranging from lemon yellow to tomato red, and so durable are the colour pigments of carotenoids that even when consumed by animals they end up colouring animal foodstuffs such as egg yolks and butterfat. The longer wavelengths of red, orange and golden-yellow have stimulating and warming qualities and this is reflected in the food of these colours.

Pink–purple
The third family of colour in the plant world is made up of the anthocyanidin pigments. These range from the palest pink through red to bright purple. Their brilliant hues are contained in solution in the plant's cell sap. An important pigment in this third group is violanin, which gives flowers, fruits and vegetables their characteristic purple colouring. The violet wavelength in sunlight has a quick rate of vibration and a high frequency, which makes food of this colour very fortifying but much less physically stimulating than the red varieties.

Phytochemicals

Perhaps the most important of the phytochemical nutrients found in plants is the group called flavonoids (sometimes called bioflavonoids), of which over 4,000 have now been identified. These provide a rainbow of different coloured foods which have antioxidant, anti-inflammatory and collagen-stabilizing properties and have been proved to actively prevent heart disease. Unlike vitamin C, which protects the watery parts of the body, and vitamin E, which protects fat-based compounds, flavonoids protect from a wide variety of toxins in both the watery and fatty parts. Flavonoids can be divided into two groups, anthoxanthins and anthocyanidins.

Anthoxanthins are pale in colour and produce mostly yellow foods such as potatoes and yellow-skinned onions. Within this group is naringenin, which gives grapefruit its distinctive colour. Naringenin has been given to transplant patients, since it actively suppresses the immune system, thus diminishing the risk of rejection. Also in the anthoxanthin group are the isoflavones, which help balance hormones and are associated with reduced risk of prostrate and breast cancer. A rich source of these is soya beans. Anthocyanidins (also known as anthocyans) are responsible for the red, blue and purple colours of foods such as berries, beetroot, cranberries, bilberries and black grapes, and have a powerful antioxidant effect. Many of these foods have been used for hundreds of years as traditional remedies.

A meal rich in colourful fruits and vegetables may contain up to a gram of these important flavonoids and this may be as significant to our health as vitamins and minerals. Some of the phytochemicals are as powerful as vitamin C; medicinal plant research by J Masquelier in 1980 found that anthocyanidins can be 50 times stronger than vitamin E. Combining flavonoids with other antioxidants proves even more powerful and this combination is likely to have a profound effect on our health and to slow down the ageing process. Samantha Christie, a nutrition researcher and the author of *Anthocyanidins – Key Members of the Flavonoid Family*, concludes: 'For a broad spectrum of effect eat a variety of colour in natural foods – from yellow/orange carotenoids found in sweet potatoes, carrots, tomatoes, and melons, to the blue/violet pro-anthocyanidins in berries and grapes. Drink berry juice and red grape juice (diluted due to its high sugar content) and red wine in preference to white.' I would add to this last point that drinking red wine is more important for meat eaters than for vegetarians.

The discovery of flavonoids is a very important reminder that the nutritional benefits of wholesome foods go well beyond the familiar. We must all now recognize that plant foods contain other more subtle yet much more powerful properties related to colour.

Phytonutrients and their corresponding colours

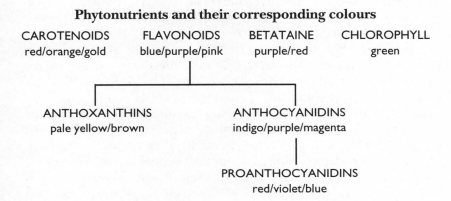

CAROTENOIDS
red/orange/gold

FLAVONOIDS
blue/purple/pink

BETATAINE
purple/red

CHLOROPHYLL
green

ANTHOXANTHINS
pale yellow/brown

ANTHOCYANIDINS
indigo/purple/magenta

PROANTHOCYANIDINS
red/violet/blue

Following the Colours for Life Diet

When sunlight falls onto the coloured pigments in plant cells the energy of the sunlight is stored and used for growth so that the plant flourishes. If we eat the plant when it's freshly picked the light energy remains active and provides us with energetic ingredients that keep us healthy on a more subtle level. In order to make sure you are receiving a balance of colour energy into your system, it's essential to eat *fresh* natural food from all three groups. The more food has been tampered with by processing, the more the light energy is lost and the more difficult it becomes to ensure you have a balanced diet. Processed food may be artificially coloured, but no matter how much colouring is added this vital energy can never be replaced.

Just as eating food which is devitalized and over-processed severely impairs your health, so eating very stimulating foods such as meat, fish, tea and coffee dulls the palate and means you may end up having to season your food heavily. When you return to more natural ways of eating, your palate becomes more sensitive to the taste of the food itself. This means you should season your food lightly – with just a few herbs and spices.

When you eat plenty of fresh natural food every day, there is no need to go on any 'conventional' diet: you can eat as much as you like. The Colours for Life Diet will ensure you assimilate the goodness you need while eliminating all the toxins and excess you don't require, so your body maintains its correct weight and you glow with good health. It is fully compatible with special diets, such as the food-combining diet (Hay diet), Fit for Life (for arthritis), the Bristol diet (for cancer), and more general ones, such as the Mediterranean diet (to prevent heart disease).

Traditional diets based on a high consumption of meat, rather than decreasing the appetite, heighten the desire to eat more, and in Westernized countries the amount of food we eat often far exceeds our physiological requirements. It is ironic that the people of wealthy nations, who gorge themselves on meat, suffer from many diseases unknown in poor areas of the world, where people live on a high-fibre vegetarian diet. By reducing the amount of flesh we consume we will find it easier to achieve a diet which prevents us from being overweight and which is better suited to our sedentary lifestyles. However, the Colours for Life Diet does guide meat and fish eaters as well as vegetarians.

In this book you will learn to correct the colour energy imbalances that can cause disease, by choosing food and drink with certain colour frequencies that will aid the free flow of vital energy around the body. Together we will also discover how deep breathing and a positive mental outlook affects our ability to absorb cosmic nutrition.

Eating is essential to life as breathing, and when you are relaxed and able to enjoy good food, you create inner balance and a strong body. A little extra one day can be counteracted by a little less the next, and you will develop a healthy attitude to food. It is the aim of this book to help you find your own balance so that your diet provides you with all the goodness you need to keep healthy in body and mind. By showing you a new perspective on eating I hope you can share my enthusiasm for eating freely, colourfully and joyously.

1 | Holistic Nutrition: Nourishing Mind, Body and Soul

The minute we say the word 'diet', our stomach muscles tighten as we conjure up a host of negative images: controls, restrictions, measuring, doing without, hunger, pain, worry. It's unfortunate that we now usually associate 'diet' with feelings of guilt and discomfort, only thinking of dieting as something we do when we want to lose weight. Diet comes from the Greek word *diaita*, which means 'mode of living', encompassing a whole way of life and implying the provision of sustenance to every part of our being, and originally a diet was thought of not as something relating only to our body but as a much broader concept which included the health of our mind and our spirit.

So how did our own notions of diet ever get so out of hand? The answer is to be found in our surroundings as well as in what we eat. The dream of modern technology was to make life easier for us, and to leave us with maximum relaxation and leisure time. Unfortunately the opposite has happened. The wonders of modern technology have brought with them a host of unforeseen problems that affect every aspect of our lives. Modes of transport, communication systems and manufacturing technology continue to change at an alarming, disorientating rate. As the speed of these developments accelerates, the natural world and humankind can't adapt fast enough to keep up with the changes, putting enormous pressure on our once balanced systems.

High levels of stress, bad diet with unhealthy fast foods, little exercise, poor living and working conditions and pollution have steadily been pushing our bodies and minds to crisis levels. We are rapidly losing control of our own lives and we urgently need to take back our power and responsibility for our own well-being.

In order to provide for dietary needs, we need to break our old unsuccessful habits and thought patterns, to assert our individuality, to heighten our aspirations and to make the most of our creative energies. If we constantly describe ourselves as 'couch potatoes', or constantly think and talk about dieting (worrying about cellulite or our 'spare tyres'), we are only fuelling the obsessive behaviour which encourages overeating. By concentrating on our defects we undermine our self-esteem, which is the very thing we need to build in order to become healthy individuals. We should try to think positively and to create a way of living which nurtures and nourishes our being at all levels. Then we will be better equipped to replace darkness and disease with harmony and light.

Our diet today should remain true to the Greek ideal and should not be an isolated part of our health programme. Food and water may provide the main source of nourishment for our physical body, but we need other forms of nourishment too. Our soul needs nourishment from love, while our spirit is nourished by light and air. If we get plenty of fresh air, love, natural light, clean water and energetic food, these cosmic nutrients can combine to make up a complete diet, providing us with a new mode of living which will bring us good health, longevity and peace of mind and spirit.

The sooner we recognize that illness is the final result of disharmony in our *entire* system – body, soul and mind – the sooner we will improve our quality of life. We have to re-educate ourselves to concentrate on promoting good health rather than on the treatment of disease. This is the basis of holistic health, which involves our whole mode of living. Only when we have peace of mind, and are in touch with our loving soul, can we have a healthy body. In order to develop a new mode of living suitable for our needs, it will be helpful if we learn to view ourselves in a different way.

By studying the cosmic forces that surround us we can learn about the cosmic forces within us. Each of us is a mirror image of the universe; that is, a microcosm which reflects the macrocosm. There are references to this idea in many religions, and the Bible in particular states that man was made in the image of God. As we do not live in isolation from the universe, so the human body cannot be separated into individually functioning parts.

The Seven Cosmic Rays of Light

It is commonly believed that our universe appeared out of a swirling mass of energy that held the potential for all life. We each have our own ideas of how this cosmic soup divided into the dark, the receptive feminine yin force, and the light, the active and complementary yang force, but we all agree that neither total lightness nor total darkness was able to sustain life and there was needed a third and balancing force in which it could flourish. That third force, or trinity, was colour.

Just as nitrogen, oxygen and argon are the primary elements of the air we breathe, so the three primary colours of light from which all other colours are formed are red, green and blue-violet. These are the primaries used by colour healers, who relate them to the ways in which energy can be absorbed from sunlight.

The primary colours of light are different from the primary colours used to make up artists' pigments and paints. When the three primary pigment colours – red, yellow and blue – are mixed together, they create black: this method is known as the subtractive method of mixing colour. (We normally use these pigment primary colours when considering the colours of objects in our surroundings – the external colours of foods, the colours in a dining room or of our tableware.) However, when the three primaries of blue-violet, red and green light are projected in the additive method of mixing colour, they create brilliant white light.

The primary colour red links to the masculine force, which is yang, warm and magnetic in nature, while blue-violet is the colour energy that corresponds to the feminine force and is cool and electrical in nature. Red is the longest wavelength and has the slowest vibration and it has a warming or energizing quality. Blue-violet is the shortest wavelength and has the highest vibration and this has a purifying quality as well as bringing feelings of contentment and upliftment. These are the two opposing and complementary forces in nature. When the red and blue-violet light combined, a cohesive and balancing force came into being and this is nature's healing colour: green.

By mixing each of the three primary colours together we can create three secondary colours: yellow, turquoise and magenta. Together with the primary colours, these secondary colours make up the six cosmic rays found in pure sunlight. (Isaac Newton separated the blue and violet to create the commonly accepted seven rainbow colours.) Red, magenta and yellow can be grouped together as the warming 'magnetic' colours, while turquoise, blue and violet are cooling 'electrical' colours. Green has a balancing and normalizing quality which is considered bipolar, and is neither hot nor cold. It is through all of the primary and secondary colour rays that we are imbued with life-force energy.

Imagine the universe being pervaded by these rays – each travelling in rhythmic waves. As these light vibrations slow down, they turn into sound vibrations. Every colour has a corresponding sound, and every sound a matching colour. As the sound waves slow down they become fixed into different sound wave patterns, which hold certain chains of atoms and molecules together. Thus matter is formed.

Each form of matter is a vibrating mass of particles which in turn gives off its own sound and light vibrations. All life is connected because all matter is made up of atoms and molecules, which are held together by rhythmic electromagnetic vibrations. These vibrations hold the formations of atoms and molecules together in certain patterns, but when these cohesive vibrations are disturbed the forms and shapes of these particles can be broken down.

Like the electromagnetic field that surrounds the earth, we are surrounded by light vibrations in an envelope of pulsating colours, sounds and aromas. These sound and light vibrations flow between all living things, the rocks, the plants, the animals and birds, humankind. In this way we are all connected to one another, and the harmony or disharmony of our colours and sounds spreads out around us like ripples in a pond. The whole universe is a magnetic field of positive and negative charges which is vibrating and producing electromagnetic waves. Our physical form is a field of continually moving energy, circulating through cells, tissues, muscles and organs.

Light and sound waves interact with all our particles and have the power to be harmonious or unharmonious to our being. They can alter molecular structure and can change energy patterns within our cells and tissues. A soprano voice, when reaching a certain note, can shatter glass. Light waves, which are more powerful than sound waves, can even change atomic structures.

The seven rainbow rays or colour vibrations which come to earth in natural sunlight play a fundamental part in the function and well-being of our body, mind and spirit. Natural sunlight is the primary nutrient in the universe, for without light there would be no life on earth.

Absorbing Light Energy

The whole basis of colour healing consists of certain molecular reactions that take place in the organs through the medium of coloured rays. Light is *not* just a force outside us – it enters into the centre of every cell, nerve and tissue of the body.

The vibrations of light energy can be converted into the images which we use for sight, but seeing is not their only function for us. When entering the human eye, colour vibrations travel along the optic nerve to the hypothalamus, which in turn controls the pineal and pituitary glands. These two master glands control nearly every function of the body. They affect our energy levels, growth, sexual behaviour, body temperature, blood pressure, water balance, sleep patterns and motor and muscular activity, as well as affecting our mental and emotional bodies. Coloured light travels to the pituitary gland, the master gland of the endocrine system, which governs the production and release of hormones affecting our entire metabolism. Our feelings and emotions are directly affected by the balance or imbalance of hormones in our body.

However, many of our problems start in the mind and soul long before they manifest as physical ailments. The psychosomatic causes of disease have been understood by many ancient systems of medicine, and slowly we are coming to recognize the significance of this wisdom. We *must* nourish the soul as well as the body and mind in order to obtain perfect health and happiness. It is only when all these aspects – mind, body, soul – are in harmony that we can feel at peace and contented with life.

Most of our time is taken up with attending to our physical needs, and this results in our neglecting the needs of our subtle bodies. Rather than placing the emphasis on our physical nature we should begin to look upon ourselves as embodied spirits. Central to our well-being is the nourishment of our soul, or 'sol' – the name of the Roman sun god. This internal soul/sun radiates from our centre, in an array of energy which connects our physical body to our spiritual body.

We must remember that there are five ways in which we take in the colour energy of light into our being: through our eyes, our skin, our breath, the water and food we consume, and our aura and energetic system.

Our Subtle Bodies and the Aura

The seven colour vibrations of light can enter us through the aura that surrounds every one of us. The existence of the aura and the subtle bodies has been known for thousands of years, but has only begun to be accepted by Western cultures in recent times. It is one of the main functions of our aura to absorb bio-energy – light energy – to nourish our subtle bodies. According to ancient Indian and Eastern wisdom, each human being has seven bodies, starting with the physical form which is surrounded by the subtle bodies that radiate outwards from it. The physical body is the most dense and is the one we can see, while the etheric and remaining five auric ones are all invisible to us, except to people with psychic vision.

The aura itself is made up of many beautiful colour vibrations, invisible to the naked eye, which form an egg shape around the physical body. The aura's array of pulsating colours reflects our inner state of health, as these colour vibrations are continuously changing depending on our moods, feelings, thoughts and well-being. Problems in any of these areas show up as bulges or patterns in the shape of the aura, and energy blockages show up there immediately too. The nature of the aura is therefore very important to colour therapists.

The aura is made up of three main layers. First is the physical layer, which is made up of the dense physical body and etheric body. The etheric body is an exact duplicate of the physical body, but vibrates at a higher rate, thus making it invisible. Like the earth's own energy field – the ozone layer – our etheric body can develop holes that allow harmful vibrations through.

Blockages and imbalances show up in the etheric body long before they manifest in the physical body, but colour vibrations can be used to redress these problems before they can be passed on to the copy-cat physical one. The main aim, therefore, of colour therapists is to introduce the colours necessary to correct any imbalances that the aura's etheric body might reveal. (We will see how, by ingesting food of the right colours and following the Colours for Life Diet, we can strengthen and revitalize the etheric body, thus protecting the physical body from onslaught.)

The second layer of the aura is made up of the emotional and mental bodies. The emotional body is often known as the astral body, and as the name implies is related to feelings. We all know how colour affects our moods. We find some colours uplifting and inspiring and others depressing; we often use terms like 'feeling blue', 'seeing red', and 'yellow-bellied', without really thinking of the meaning behind the words.

The emotional body's counterpart, the mental body, can itself be divided into the lower and higher bodies. The lower mind is concerned with learned responses and patterns taught to us in childhood, while the higher mind is linked to the soul and gives us creative and intuitive abilities.

The aura's third layer is made up of three spiritual bodies which connect us to the universe and the spiritual planes. We are linked to the divine energy embodied in the cosmic rays of white light through a system of body energy centres, known in ancient Indian wisdom as *chakras*. The individual colour vibrations are attracted to different energy centres which vibrate on the same frequency as the colour. The energized energy centre or chakra will set up a positive vibration in the sympathetic body systems, organs and glands.

Pure white light energy enters the aura through the crown chakra and travels to the pineal gland, which acts as a prism, splitting up the light into its seven colour components and sending the rays to the etheric energy centres, the chakras, to revitalize them. As each of the seven rays has its own wavelength and frequency, so each has a special energy and vibration which has its own specific qualities and action upon us. The slower wavelengths of red and yellow are warming and stimulating, while the faster and shorter wavelengths of turquoise and blue-violet are cooling and sedating. Green is neither warm nor cool and maintains balance and harmony between all the other elements. For this reason green promotes healing and the healthy growth of our cells and tissues.

Each part of the physical body and body function is sensitive to a different colour, because each organ vibrates at a frequency corresponding to that colour. When an organ or gland is malfunctioning, the organ will lose its correct vibration, in much the same way as losing the tuning of a radio signal. By strengthening the signal or vibration of the colour the organ will be energized, and clear reception and balance in the body restored. Wearing and surrounding yourself with certain colours will also reinforce the action of the colour.

This correspondence of the colours to certain organs of the body has been known by various Eastern and Indian philosophies and religions for centuries. Even in the West, the correspondence

Body Power Centres and their Related Colours	
etheric body, spirit	magenta
pineal, crown	violet
pituitary, third eye	indigo
thyroid, throat	blue
cardiac plexus, heart	green or gold
solar plexus, stomach	yellow
sacral, spleen	orange
base, base of spine	red

has given rise to various sayings. Remember 'yellow-bellied', meaning cowardly: the belly or stomach contains the solar plexus and the solar plexus energy centre is linked to yellow, the colour which rules the nervous system. The connection between the solar plexus energy centre and the nervous system is the reason why we have 'butterflies in our tummy' when we are nervous. Similarly, green corresponds to the heart area, so when we are 'green with envy' we are acknowledging that envy arises from the heart, the centre of our emotion. 'Seeing red' derives from the base energy centre. It is the colour of anger, which also raises our temperatures and pulse and makes us literally turn red. Showing a red cloak to a bull does affect the bull even though he does not see colour (bulls are **colour-blind**). He feels the red vibration, which raises his aggressive energy. We draw up the **life-force** into our physical bodies through the base centre or chakra, from where it travels through us to every cell, filling it with life-giving energy.

The chakras and the body

Chakra name	Related gland	Related body systems	Sympathetic organs and body part
crown	pineal	central nervous system venous blood	head, right eye, spine
third eye	pituitary	skeletal system	left eye, ears, face, sinus
throat	thyroid, parathyroid	respiratory system	throat, upper respiratory tract, neck, upper lung
heart	thymus	heart	digestive system
solar plexus	pancreas	nervous system	liver, gall bladder, diaphragm
sacral	spleen	reproductive system	sex organs
base	adrenals	muscular system, blood	kidneys

Feeding our Subtle and Physical Bodies

When white light flows unobstructed and harmoniously into the chakras our condition is healthy and harmonious. When we are completely balanced and in perfect health, our aura is a beautiful rainbow, for each cosmic ray is able to flow through all of our being, our subtle body and our physical form, connecting us to the spiritual forces of the universe, without obstruction. In a perfect world – one based on understanding, compassion, respect and love – this flow of cosmic energy would happen automatically because our body energy centres would be open, drawing into us all the light we need to sustain us. Unfortunately we do not all live in a perfect world.

Where have we gone wrong?

When humankind first inhabited the earth people lived outdoors, resting only in rough shelters at night. As a result they were exposed to natural sunlight for most of their lives, and as we have seen natural sunlight has a profound effect upon the human metabolism, influencing the body's internal cycles. Therefore, their outdoor existence and exposure to the elements, including sunlight, meant that our ancestors were more in tune with natural rhythms. Their metabolisms and hormones were kept in harmony, attuned to the cycle of day and night. They lived in harmony with the environment, hunting and gathering only what they needed to survive. They revered the earth, the animals and plants which gave them sustenance. Although they suffered great hardships because of extremes of weather and their harsh physical existence, many diseases we know today appear to have been almost non-existent.

When humans originally lived entirely out of doors, people received energy directly from the sun, so receiving light vibrations from all the coloured rays. As soon as they evolved to indoor living, they no longer absorbed direct light energy, and so lost the balance provided by the cycles of night and day. The more time humans spent indoors and out of natural light, the more their ailments and illnesses increased. Their inner and outer colour energies became unharmonious. Some of their energy centres became over-energized while others became under-energized.

Gradually, humankind began to settle on the land, to cultivate the soil and to domesticate animals. With this major change in lifestyle came diseases and illnesses associated with pests which attacked crops and lived on the animals. As the settlements grew and people became increasingly crowded together in towns and cities, other illnesses started to appear, related to the conditions that came from communities living in close proximity and unhygienic conditions.

No longer do we get up at dawn and go to bed at sunset, and we are losing touch with the seasonal changes. Today we live primarily behind our tinted glass windows; when we do go out we often wear tinted sunglasses or sit in cars with coloured windscreens. As we come to spend progressively less time outside in natural sunlight, and as we retreat steadily indoors, we absorb an increasingly inadequate level of light energy into our bodies, and these changes have a profound effect upon our metabolism, resulting in many of us not being able to get a good night's sleep or work to our optimum energy levels. Our life expectancy may have been lengthened, but drugs and chemicals do not improve the quality of life.

As a result of the changes in our lifestyle our metabolism has changed from that of our ancestors and this means that, as a species, we are no longer as able to extract the goodness from our food in the way that our ancestors could. Wrong diet has also contributed towards a host of diseases such as cancers and many of the illnesses related to a worn-out or malfunctioning immune system, preventing the body from absorbing and extracting the nutrients from food.

In the West our diet is still based on meat and cooked vegetables, with the greater part of it consisting of animal products such as meat, poultry, fish, eggs and cheese. It has been found that a diet consisting of a lot of meat protein can build up toxins known as free radicals, which clog up the bloodstream and poison us. These free radicals have also been found in irradiated foods. Westerners also eat too many milk products and sweet puddings, with the result that we are more likely to die from heart disease than any other cause. The modern use of pesticides, hormones and additives also means the good old traditional dinner of meat and two veg is unable to provide us with all the goodness our body needs and has been instrumental in our decline in health.

The toxic waste that we find today in our cells and tissues is a direct reflection of the toxic waste with which we are polluting the earth. During the 1980s there was a general awakening to many environmental issues which remain important today, and facing up to ecological problems and taking responsibility for them is the only way to control and reverse the destructive process. Our body is made up of the same elements as the earth and we need food grown in the earth and vitalized by the sun to nourish us. We are irrevocably connected to the earth, which supports all life, and as our own health depends upon it we should care for the planet so that all life can flourish. The most important thing we can do is to take responsibility for the earth and the plant and animal life which she sustains. This involves looking first at our own lives, and learning to take care of ourselves lovingly and to tend to our own needs. Only then can we really understand the needs of others and our ailing planet.

What Can We Do? The First Step Towards Healing

It is important to remember that it remains within the capabilities of all of us to draw vital energy from sunlight into ourselves and then project it into the darkness of ignorance on this earth. We can exist for some time without food, as we can draw in bio-energy from water and the air we breathe. We cannot, however, exist without cosmic energy. If the flow of cosmic energy is cut off we collapse. This is what happens when we faint, black out, or have an epileptic fit. If our source of cosmic energy is cut off for a longer period we become unconscious and if this state continues we go into a coma from which we may not recover.

We each have the power to influence our ability to absorb vital energy into our system at an emotional and spiritual level as well as a physical level. When our heart and mind are filled with thoughts of love and kindness we draw the light to us and radiate it forth. How often have we described a bride as 'radiant' or 'beaming' with happiness when our hearts were full of goodness and love? These are expressions of our acknowledgement of the power of light. Love is light and light is life.

As a vital first step towards well-being, we can purify our own physical atoms by right thinking if we train ourselves to concentrate on beauty not ugliness, light instead of darkness, success instead of failure. This positive, loving attitude to life can bring about the most wonderful healing. Anger, resentment, stress and fear can all dissolve away. If we train our minds not to concentrate on disease or darkness, turning our attention instead to harmony and light, the light that will flood into us will bring health and harmony to both body and mind.

My teacher of colour therapy, Marie Louise Lacy, puts it like this: 'The power which comes from the heart can reverse negative into positive, can release the blockages in the aura which prevent the light flowing uninterrupted into and out of the body's energy centres, and can restore us to health.'

Light as a Spiritual Bridge between the Visible and Invisible

The cosmic coloured rays of light are a spiritual force that act as a bridge between the visible and invisible worlds, and through them we can work on the both the physical and psychospiritual realm. As we have seen, our primary source of nourishment is not the food we eat but the life-force or cosmic energy.

Many ancient civilizations recognized the importance of cosmic energy in the form of radiant energy from the sun, and used its power in their healing systems. The ancient Egyptians and later the Greeks had sophisticated systems of sun therapy or helio-therapy, drawing upon bio-energetic resources. In ancient Indian philosophy cosmic energy is known as *prana*, which is extracted from the air we breathe.

As explained in the Introduction, a similar concept of energy, the universal life-force energy called *chi*, is found in ancient (and modern) Chinese traditional medicine. According to the ancient Chinese beliefs, man is the connecting bridge between heaven and earth. He is made up of the union of matter and spirit and this link is maintained by *chi*. *Chi* nourishes the physical body and is the essence which also affects our mind and spirit. Without *chi* we would consist of a sack of bones, tissues and blood. White light energy from the sun – *chi* – empowers us with life energy and connects this force to our own internal sun or soul. Each organ and gland has a sympathetic resonance with a particular colour, although every colour will have a different therapeutic effect on any organ. So the heart links to the colour green on an energetic level, but red can stimulate the heart while blue has a relaxing effect.

According to traditional Chinese medicine, light energy cannot be observed with the naked eye or by any scientific equipment as it is carried around the body through a system of invisible energy lines known as meridians. Knowledge of these meridians forms the basis of well-established complementary health practices such as acupuncture and reflexology. Meridians are closely linked to the body's nervous system and energy is transferred based on the idea that every cell in our organism communicates with all others. Each cell is a carrier of the overall programme of the organism. (This was demonstrated scientifically by Dr James Gordon, an eminent American holistic practitioner, who removed an egg cell from a frog and replaced it with an intestinal cell. The latter was fertilized and the result was a frog capable of procreation.) Like light, which only becomes visible when reflected back as colour by matter, bio-energy can only be seen from its effects.

The concept of bio-energy embraces both the biological and the energy-giving elements of nutrition, and once we become aware how important bio-energy is, we can learn how to extract the maximum *chi* from natural foods. A small bowl of primary energy food chewed carefully and slowly will yield as much *chi* energy as a huge meal eaten hastily.

Even today there are spiritual masters, saints and yogis who live on minute amounts of physical food. These and others like them have been showing us for centuries how to live more or less nourished and healed by light alone. These masters often appear to use breathing exercises and meditation techniques to draw sustenance in the form of *prana* (or life-force energy) from the air itself. By raising the vibrations of the physical body through meditation and deep breathing, they clear a channel for the passage of cosmic energy to pass through their system. The fact that they can do this is a lesson to us all, for it shows us how little of the cosmic nutritional content of food and water we usually absorb.

As we have seen, there are five ways colour waves are taken into the body. Light enters our body not only through our eyes and our aura but through our skin and the air we breathe. However, one of the best ways we can introduce a balance of colour energy into our system is through food and drink. Once we become fully aware of how important light energy is, we can learn how to extract the maximum *chi* from natural foods.

Enjoying the Colours for Life Diet

Now that we are aware of the action and qualities of the physical and cosmic nutrients, we are better equipped to know the best way to extract the maximum benefit from our food to feed our physical bodies and our subtle energy centres.

As the majority of us are totally dependent on the energies we absorb from food, we should eat foods that will stimulate rather than obstruct the free flow of energy in the body and will lead to creative harmony. Of course the quality of the food we eat goes hand in hand with the ultimate quality of life we enjoy: if the fuel is faulty, the functions of the organs will be faulty and disease will be the ultimate result. By eating food of the right type and colour we can revitalize our system with cosmic energy.

Food contains not only nourishing chemical nutrients that provide the body with fuel, but also nourishing colour vibrations that the body extracts in much the same way as it does other nutrients. We have seen that the colours of natural foods are closely related to the chemical and vibrational energies contained within them, and that using the wonderful key nature has provided so that we can feed both the body and the spirit their natural colours will help us select the foods that will hold the body's energy levels in balance. Just as we need to eat a varied and balanced diet if we are to be healthy, so too do we need a balance of energy from the seven spectrum colours that form natural sunlight. In chapter 3 we will discover the staple foods of the Colours for Life Diet. The colour vibrations of these foods not only nourish the physical cells and organs but have a powerful influence on our emotional, mental and nervous activity, as well as our spiritual well-being.

In order to balance all the elements necessary for health we must have the correct nutrition from the plant kingdom. Plants, which absorb goodness from the earth and flourish in the sunlight, are imbued with vital *chi* energy, providing foods which are easy to digest and distribute to the appropriate parts.

It is worth noting that many famous people throughout history have been dedicated vegetarians. These include the Buddha and Mahatma Gandhi. There is also a school of thought that believes that Jesus Christ belonged to a religious group known as the Essenes, who were strict vegetarians. Founders of many other non-religious aspects of Western society were also exponents of vegetarianism. These include figures such as the Greek sage and philosopher Pythagoras, and later the philosophers Socrates and Plato. The philosopher and biographer Plutarch was the first known writer on the benefits of vegetarianism; his essay 'On the eating of flesh' describes meat-eating as being only one step away from cannibalism. Other notable vegetarians include the artist and scientist Leonardo da Vinci, the revolutionary Leo Tolstoy and the poet Percy Shelley.

We should also take the natural rhythms heeded by our ancestors into account. Nourishing ourselves is an essential and wonderful part of life, and we each have our own requirements; using colour as a cue, we can learn to eat food that assists our own biorhythms. This means that by eating different coloured food at different times of day, the energy will harmonize with our natural body rhythms and the functioning of the organs and glands. In order to do this we need to gently listen to the messages our body gives us. By using colour and aroma in the selection of seasonal food and eating these at certain times when their energies are most potent, we can create wonderful harmonies of positive vibrations which will attract good health and ensure a long life.

Remember as you read this book that colours are not separated into distinct bands, but run into each other, so some fruit and vegetables span two or more colours. For example, some apples are very green, some are yellow-green and some are yellow. Also, different products made from different parts of a plant may have different colourings.

The Colours for Life Diet introduced in this book is based on seasonal foods and natural rhythms and offers a complete diet based on variety and moderation rather than elimination and restriction. It provides a complete form of nourishment that allows us freedom to improve our own quality of life. Together with colour breathing (*see* chapter 10, pages 204–8) it creates a true mode of living that focuses on the importance of cosmic nutrition and makes provision for our personal and joint needs in the twenty-first century.

The seven basic principles of the Colours for Life Diet

1 Eat in moderation, exercising free eating to suit your individual needs. Free eating is the consumption of wholesome food whenever and in whatever quantities you like, using your discretion and sensitivity to meet your individual needs (*see* chapter 2, page 22).
2 Eat a variety of coloured food, providing the full spectrum of colour energy.
3 Eat natural, organic 'live' foods, rich in both physical and vibrational nutrients.

4 Favour locally grown seasonal food mainly from the vegetable kingdom.
5 Eat a balanced diet using colour as a cue by eating various types of food in proportion to one another.
6 Select certain coloured foods at appropriate times during the twenty-four-hour cycle when their nutritional energy is the most potent and to enhance your biorhythms.
7 Use certain coloured foods to correct energy imbalances in your system.

The Colours for Life Diet encourages you to start using colour intuitively and naturally to create delicious and nutritious meals from which you will extract the maximum energy at all levels. You will start experiencing the joy of free eating and rediscover the pleasure of caring for yourself and others.

2 | The Influence of Colour on Who We Are and How We Eat

Human consumption of food is not merely an animal instinct, but requires our attention and discrimination. Our thoughts and emotions are greatly influenced by what we eat, and a discerning attitude to nutrition will lead to a mature, spiritual outlook on life. Our diet should be joyful and bountiful – not a punishment for wrongdoing. We must again understand the true meaning of the word 'diet' so that its connotations of narrowness and restrictions are replaced by those of expansiveness and freedom.

Finding a healthy diet should be a simple and happy task, and yet we continue to select foods that ruin our health. Very few of us choose to eat food for the reasons we should. We would rather eat food that tastes good and is easily prepared than food that will satisfy our nutritional needs. We steadily continue to replace wholesome foods with more 'pleasurable' but nutrient-deficient foods, resulting in an inadequate intake of many of the essential nutrients and an excess of calories.

During the last few decades many of us, through lack of self-control, have lost contact with our bodies' needs, thereby losing touch with our souls as well. We have been taught that we must assert our egos in order to become happy and free but in doing so have become slaves to our senses. Unfortunately our modern life-style has encouraged laziness and a lack of interest in the *joy* of eating. We watch TV and eat, read the paper or magazine and eat, talk on the phone and eat. We give our concentration to anything but the act of eating itself.

Having lost touch with our bodies in this way, we are unable to distinguish between appetite and hunger. We pay little attention to signals from our bodies and we have forgotten what hunger feels like. We spend hours at the hairdresser, buying clothes, making our homes attractive and clean, or washing and servicing the car – and yet we care so little for our true homes, our bodies.

Like neglected children, our bodies will shout and scream in order to draw attention to themselves. They become overweight and flabby, and if we continue to ignore them illness becomes a last resort. 'Please listen to *me* and *my* needs!' the body is trying to say.

Panicking, feeling guilty, and immediately going on a diet is not going to solve the long-term problem. Fluctuations in weight are the last thing our system needs, for this only encourages illness and obsessive behaviour. Maintaining a steady weight is much healthier, and this is what we should be aiming for. Restrictive diets only malnourish our bodies in a different way, increasing the possibility of serious long-term illness.

There are always occasions when we eat too much, and times when we can't resist something fattening or rich. But there are many ways we can correct a temporary imbalance without becoming guilt-ridden and hating ourselves. We can eat less for the rest of the day or the day after, or we can eat some fruit, which will help clean out our system. Whatever action we take, we need to behave as a caring adult. We must tell our inner child that it has been indulgent, and that it should try not to do this too often. But we do not need to punish ourselves.

We need to learn to eat in response to genuine hunger, and have a bountiful and varied diet, rather than a punitive and restrictive one. True dieting means consuming a colourful diet that provides us with the energy we need.

It is impossible suddenly to change eating habits formed over many years, so a good place to start is by adding healthy foods to your present diet. You will start to feel better in your whole being, and soon you will replace unhealthy foods with nutritious ones.

The Seven Modes of Eating

Let's look at the seven states that influence our selection of food and see how each one aids or hinders our ability to become whole and healthy. Each type of eating corresponds to the psychological quality of a rainbow colour and to a chakra.

Automatic eating – red

Red is the colour of the basic life-force and is the colour of blood. Red stimulates our muscular activity and our 'fight or flight' survival response. We first learn automatic eating in our mother's womb, where we are nourished without any conscious effort on our part. We continue this form of eating to some degree while a baby, taking food in response to autonomic stimuli from our body. We should leave this type of eating in early childhood, but many people continue with automatic eating into their adult life. Some people automatically have a cup of tea when they come home after work, or go to the fridge for a snack even though they are not hungry.

Sensory eating – orange

Orange relates to our sexual energy and our digestive system. When it comes to food, we are quick to learn to respond to positive sensory stimulation. Certain colours, aromas, flavours and textures make us feel good, so we start choosing foods which recreate these pleasurable responses, eating cakes, chocolates, ice-creams and cool drinks for the sensual pleasure they provide. Just thinking of our favourite foods can make us salivate with anticipation. For years the food industry has been making huge profits by exploiting those who indulge in sensory eating, and the majority of people eat on this level.

Emotional eating – yellow

'Emotional eating' can be likened to 'comfort eating', as it's related to emotional needs rather than physical requirements. Emotional eating means that when we are fearful, anxious or upset, we try to comfort ourselves by eating. When our self-esteem is low and we find it difficult to express our true feelings, many of us start filling our mouths, literally to stop them from speaking.

The connection between food and the emotions begins early and may last a lifetime. This is because many of us when children were rewarded with food for good behaviour, so we learned to equate food with approval, pleasure and ultimately love. Even as adults we nearly always associate a good holiday with excessive food consumption. This association of food and pleasure is so ingrained that we have to learn to rise above our emotions and call on our responsible and discriminating 'inner adult' to help us learn that there are other ways of being emotionally comforted than by consuming food.

Emotional eating is linked to the solar plexus, where we hold our nervous energy. The inability to nourish oneself properly is a symptom of other deep-seated mental and psychological problems. Nourishing oneself is closely connected with developing one's self-esteem and self-love, both essential ingredients of a contented healthy person. So often we hear people say that they can't be bothered cooking for themselves. Those who live alone often fall victim to this type of thinking, for they treat themselves with disrespect and undervalue their own needs. The ability to care for ourselves is essential if we are to develop stable loving relationships with others.

One group of people who often deny their own needs is couples in which both partners work all day. Often they say they have no time to shop and are too tired to cook. If you recognize yourself in this statement, you will find good time management helpful, to ensure that you shop weekly for staples such as rice and potatoes. It is not difficult to find a delicatessen or greengrocer who opens late and shop for fresh produce every day or two. To provide variety, working people need to find places to shop which are interesting, fun and attractive.

Shopping for food can be a rewarding activity in itself. Visit a street market, fresh bakery or garden centre, all of which can become part of an enjoyable and weekend outing. Food shopping should be relaxing, not a drain on energy. Delicious meals can be made very quickly, from simple fresh ingredients which are essential for those who lead busy stressful lives.

Automatic, sensory and emotional eating are all detrimental to our health if we preserve them over a long period.

Social eating – green

Green is the colour associated with the heart, through which we are able to give and receive love. It is the colour which connects us to nature and to other people. Through the colour green we are able to reach out and empathize with our fellow man.

Social eating involves the economics of food purchasing,

because many people cannot afford to buy the type of food they would like. Feeding a large family, for instance, can result in cases in which the quantity of food is more important than its quality. Social eating also requires us to eat whether we are hungry or not. This is because it is difficult not to bend to group pressure. If you visit someone who lays on a huge meal with mountains of food, it's very difficult not to eat more than you want. Most of us have eaten to please our parents or grandparents, and families often exert pressure on children to eat up, saying, 'You'll never grow into a big boy, or girl,' or 'Think of all the starving children in the world'. Usually children eat what they need and no more, if left to themselves. In the West children are often pressured into eating much more than they need. This sets up a trend for adult life.

Intellectual eating – blue

Blue is the colour of the intellect, but more importantly it links to the intuitive side of our nature. Intellectual eating is based on ideas about what food is good for us. We may learn the basic principles of nutrition at school and continue to develop these ideas from reading and the media. It is our intellectual capacity which makes us decide to follow nutritional recommendations and adhere to specialized diets. Many diets require expensive and special types of food so the number of people who are able to follow them is small. Restrictive diets are often nutrient-deficient, throwing the body's system out of balance and involving a way of eating which is not appropriate for or available to the majority of us.

Ideological eating – indigo

Indigo relates to power with knowledge and is the colour associated with reform and with philanthropy. Ideological eating is related to the religious and social customs of a group. Most of these rules for eating were originally developed in special circumstances which were appropriate to the environment in which they were originated. Ways of growing, harvesting, preserving and cooking foods, as well as methods of slaughtering animals, make up traditional ways of eating. Except that we are quickly forgetting the benefits of fasting, there is now usually no real benefit to us nutritionally from performing these ancient rites, and some traditions involving eating and serving food can even be detrimental to our health. Ideological eating really serves to keep traditions alive.

Free eating – violet

Violet has the highest vibration of all the colour rays. It embodies all the other colours and is the colour of regeneration and elevation. Violet transforms lower energy to higher energy, connecting us with the cosmic forces. Free eating means eating in harmony with the order of the universe and it satisfies all other levels of eating. Free eating means eating the Rainbow foods in basic proportions, according to the season and your personal needs. It means freely adapting to your surroundings and selecting food according to your freely chosen purpose. By eating freely in harmony with natural rhythms, health and happiness will automatically follow.

Shopping for food, preparing food, eating food, will once more become an essential happy part of your life and not something you do in the quickest possible time and with the minimum amount of thought. Through the choice of colour diet will once more reflect a true mode of living.

Looking at Individual Dietary Needs and the Colours for Life Diet

Types of Food

The seven states of eating, as we have seen, influence what we choose to eat. The flow of vital light energy and the colours we absorb depend largely on the actual types of food we eat.

Indian philosophy acknowledges that food and our mental outlook are closely linked, as our diet affects our emotional and mental condition. According to Indian philosophy, *rajasik* food, or 'sensual' food, makes us crave worldly activity for 'as we eat so our mind becomes'. This food consists of eggs, fish, pastries, white flour, salt and pepper, tea, coffee and hot milk, or any food in large quantities. This type of food gives rise both to bad thoughts related to the lower emotions, such as sexual excess, and to problems related to power and control. *Tamasik* food produces sluggishness, sloth and emotions such as anger and greed. Food of this type includes meat, tobacco and all alcohol, as well as all heavy, oily or fatty foods. It also includes stale food and food with no life-force energy, such as frozen or dehydrated foods.

We need to eat pure food which will encourage pure thoughts and aspirations. Foods which help one develop one's self-consciousness and spiritual growth are known as *satvik* food and consist mainly of gold, white and violet colours. *Satvik* food makes angels while *tamasik* and *rajasik* food makes beasts.

Satvik foods include wholegrains, nuts and seeds, legumes and herbs and white foods such as pacifying milk products, curd cheese and yogurt, rice, tofu and soya milk. Violet foods consist of many nourishing but light dishes of organic fruit, vegetables and herbs. Although this type of diet would never sustain most of us in our present lifestyle and living conditions, we can use it as a model to work towards as we try to find a diet which is appropriate to our present needs. (If you feel your lifestyle can accommodate it and you are very interested in *satvik* foods, *see* chapter 8, page 170 for details of a White/Pink/Gold/Violet consciousness-raising diet.)

Before we will can exist on pure *satvik* food we need to cleanse our own physical atoms by eating foods that nourish the spirit and belong to the Colours for Life Diet. The Colours for Life Diet requires us to eat a variety of natural fresh foods from the vegetable kingdom and all simple light food in small quantities, particularly fruits, vegetables, milk, butter, yogurt, white cheeses and dairy products, honey, almonds, oats, wheat, pulses, rice, legumes, nuts, seeds and wholegrains.

By eating Rainbow foods we will find it easier to train our minds not to concentrate on disease or darkness, turning our attention instead to harmony and light – the light which will flood into us will bring health and harmony to both body and mind.

By adopting the ideas of free eating, becoming flexible and in tune with your own needs, and eating a variety of foods containing all the physical and vibrational nutrients, you will improve the quality of your life and find a diet truly fit for the next century.

Food Cravings and Colour Imbalances

Before you start the Colours for Life Diet it's a good idea to check whether you have any inherited colour energy imbalances, so that you can modify the diet to suit your personal needs.

Colour imbalances usually occur in pairs. If you have one colour energy centre that is overstimulated, another will be depleted of energy. The colour vibrations also work in complementary pairs: red with green, blue with orange, and yellow with violet.

A complementary colour is the colour energy that is the opposite but balancing force to another colour. This means, for example, that if you have too much yellow energy you will naturally become attracted to violet, its opposite and complementary colour. This may happen unconsciously through the food you eat, or consciously through the colours you wear or like to have around you. And so a colour attracts its complementary vibration until a harmonious balance of colour energy is restored.

You can demonstrate this law of attraction by cutting out a square of coloured paper or felt and placing it on a piece of white paper. Stare at the coloured paper for a minute and then immediately look at the white paper to the side. You will see the complementary colour. So each colour energy automatically draws in its complementary force.

Red is complementary to and attracts Green energy.
Blue is complementary to and attracts Orange energy.
Yellow is complementary to and attracts Violet energy.

The rhythms of various glands and body organs work in sympathy with each of these colours, and it has been found that if one gland is malfunctioning it will affect the operation of its partners. So if there is a problem connected with the heart (green), the large intestine and spleen (both orange) will also be affected. If the lungs (green) are causing trouble, the bladder and the kidneys (both red) will also need attention.

An example: you have too much red energy. It's likely that you have too little green energy, so you need to eat more green foods to correct this imbalance. You will also have to look at your diet to see whether you're eating too much red food from an animal source, for this too can produce negative red energy. In order to regain energetic balance, it's necessary to eat foods of both the complementary colours, so if you have too much green in your energy system, you can correct the imbalance by eating both green and red energy foods. We will look in closer detail at colour imbalances and colour-corrective diets in chapters 7 and 8.

For the purposes of introducing the basic principles of the Colours for Life Diet, it is important to understand that we can promote good health by striking the right relationship between the pairs of complementary colours. These proportions will be different for every individual, and it is up to each of us to learn to listen and understand the messages our own body is sending us. Once we can do this we can follow the guidelines to recreate a balanced system. Although no one else will be able to tell any of us exactly when this harmony has been achieved, our family and friends will notice a difference in our looks and behaviour. We will feel good about ourselves and exude love and happiness, as well as brim with good health and energy.

Inherited Colour Bias

There are two main reasons why colour energy imbalances occur in our system. The first relates to the array of colour energy with which we come into this world at birth (our inherited colour bias); the second is the colour energy we extract through our diet. We will concentrate on the first reason now and look at the second in chapter 7.

It may be that we were born with a certain colour bias in our system. This is known as 'original *chi*', which is derived before birth and usually shows up in our natural colouring.

If you have a ruddy complexion, freckles or red hair, you can assume you already have a good deal of red and orange energy in your system. This means you have to watch your intake of red foods, especially those related to the infra-red ray, like coffee, tea, alcohol and red meat.

If on the other hand you have a bluish tinge to our skin, sallow complexion and blue eyes, you are more likely to have a good deal of blue energy. You have to take care that you are eating foods containing red and orange energy in order to build your strength and stamina and keep your spirits up.

If you have a yellow or brown skin, gold hair or brown eyes you will have a good deal of yellow energy, which means you have to pay attention to getting enough exercise and eating foods that aid digestion.

Most people have an original colour bias. Inherited imbalances occur when the mixture of yin and yang energy from both parents favours one part of the colour spectrum.

It is very useful to be aware of your colour bias, as this will indicate the array of your inner colours. Once you know what these inner colours are, you will be able to select the colours for your dress and your home and work environment which will be in harmony with your personal colour vibrations. Your colour bias will also reveal your personality traits and mode of living. It will help you recognize your strengths and weaknesses and any potential danger areas in your system, thus aiding in preventative health care.

If you have an original colour bias you will be susceptible to certain physical problems and illness related to that colour. The body always cracks at its weakest point, and by identifying these points you can make sure you build up your resistance in that area by the colour energies you ingest through food and drink. It does not mean that because you have a predisposition to a certain disease you will contract the illness. As long as you keep harmony within your being, you will remain in good health.

To discover whether you have a colour bias, just answer the simple questions below. Answer yes or no. If the question asks whether you have one of three conditions and you have any of these, answer yes. If you answer yes, score 1 point. If you answer no, score 0. Keep a record of your score for each colour.

Red

1   Do you have red hair or red in your hair, or are you a strawberry blonde?
2   Is your complexion ruddy, or pinky toned, or do you get flushed easily?
3   Are you impatient, with a quick temper?
4   Have you or your parents suffered from high blood pressure or heart disease?
5   Do you like to get things done quickly?
Score _____

Orange

1   Do you have auburn or copper-coloured hair?
2   Do you have a fair skin or freckles?
3   Do you have hazel or brown eyes?

4 Do you tend to have many projects on the go at once?
5 Are you generally outgoing and sociable?
Score _____

Yellow

1 Do you have golden brown or fair hair?
2 Does your skin have a yellow or brown tone to it?
3 Do you need a lot of sleep or have a sluggish system?
4 Have you or your parents suffered from liver, gall bladder or pancreas problems?
5 Do you grasp new ideas and concepts quickly?
Score _____

Green

1 Do you have green or hazel eyes?
2 Do you suffer or your have parents suffered from circulation problems, cysts or cancer?
3 Do you usually find it hard to make decisions?
4 Do you love the natural world?
5 Do you feel that you are able to give and receive love?
Score _____

Blue

1 Do you have pale blue or blue-grey eyes?
2 Does your skin have a 'cool' undertone (as opposed to a pink or yellow/brown tone)?
3 Do you find you often get depressed?
4 Do you suffer from anaemia, lung problems or cold hands and feet?
5 Are you generally quiet and introverted?
Score _____

Indigo

1 Do you have blue-black or grey hair?
2 Do you have deep blue eyes?
3 Have you or your parents suffered from problems related to individual bones or the skeleton as a whole, or the eyes, ears or throat?
4 Do you have a good imagination but frightening dreams?
5 Do you have a dry skin?
Score _____

Violet

1 Do you have deep blue or violet-coloured eyes?
2 Are you an artist, musician, writer, medium or clairvoyant?
3 Would you describe yourself as a spiritual person?
4 Do you suffer from headaches, mood swings or migraines?
5 Do you often change your mind?
Score _____

Key to the Scores for each colour

Score 0–1

If you scored 0–1 for any of these colours, that particular energy centre was probably under-energized at birth. It may be that you have corrected this through your intake of colour energy in your food and drink. Do the colour imbalance test for *chi* derived after birth in chapter 7 (pages 139–146). This will show whether you have corrected this imbalance.

Score 2–3

If you scored 2–3 points for a colour, you received a balance of this colour energy from your parents. This means you have no colour bias for this colour. Check whether this colour energy centre is still in balance by comparing your score with the Colour Energy Imbalance test in chapter 7 (pages 139–146).

Score 4–5

The most important colour for you is one for which you score 4 or 5 points. This colour or colours are your colour bias which you carry with you for life. This colour will indicate both your strengths and your weaknesses, so pay heed to what this colour represents.

Interpreting Your Colour Bias

This section is for scores 4–5 only. For full details of the foods appropriate for your colour bias and how to use them in your Colours for Life Diet, see pages 147–80.

Red

A red colour bias is the most important bias of all the colours, for red is a very powerful vibration and can easily take on negative qualities if over-activated.

Red energy gives us physical strength and stamina, and people with plenty of red are energetic and action-oriented. Red also gives us courage in adversity and the determination to succeed. An abundance of red energy, however, means we can be hot-headed and quick to anger, because red energy stimulates our adrenals and causes us to act quickly, often without much thought. Red-biased people need to try to think more before making hasty decisions.

The potentially weak physical spots are the arteries and heart. Red-biased people often suffer from high blood pressure from heat trapped within their system. This is why they perspire pro-fusely, tend to have hot sweaty palms and skins and flush easily in their faces.

We all need red energy to motivate us and give us strength, but we must make sure that our diet keeps this energy in balance so that we don't develop illness in the weak points of the red system. Red energy must be kept in balance by eating red foods from the vegetable kingdom, because it is usually red foods from the animal kingdom that cause imbalance of this ray.

Orange

If you have an orange bias, you are probably an extrovert. Your physical colouring will be based on shades of coppers, greens, peaches, and browns. You are very practical and straightforward; you are outgoing and fun-loving. Orange is a very sensual colour, and those with an orange bias can often be identified, as they walk with great poise and are good dancers. This link with sexual energy brings orange-biased people the potential for great joy and creativity. They must, however, make sure this creative expression finds an outlet, for if orange energy is blocked it can turn into many physical problems related to the sexual organs, and diges-tive and immune systems. Orange-biased people have lots of energy, but often take on too many projects at once. This can result in fatigue and puts a strain on the immune system. Orange energy must be kept in balance by eating fresh natural orange foods. These include apricots, carrots, papayas (pawpaws), peaches and squashes.

Orange is made up of red and yellow, so if you have a high

orange score but a low red or yellow score, you will also have some red or yellow energy in your system.

Yellow

Yellow is the nearest colour to sunshine. Those people who are born with a yellow bias are bright and cheerful. They have lively minds and are interested in everything around them. People with a yellow bias often hold the yellow energy in their solar plexus. This yellow centre should radiate outwards, sending shining light into the aura. Often we block this yellow energy by fear, and this fear turns inwards causing problems in the liver, gall bladder, pancreas and intestine. If emotions such as envy, greed, bitterness or resentment are suppressed they can manifest themselves as physical matter – gallstones are formed in this way, for instance.

Yellow-biased people often pay more attention to mental activities than they do to caring for their body. They must make sure they get regular exercise, for a sedentary life will cause them problems with assimilating and eliminating food.

Yellow is also linked to the nervous system, which must be maintained and strengthened by eating golden yellow foods, rich in proteins, vitamins and minerals. Wholegrains, nuts and seeds as well as yellow fruit such as bananas are all excellent for maintaining a balance.

Green

If you are born with a green bias, you will be very tuned in to the natural world. You will also have compassion and sympathy for your fellow man, and should be working in a caring role. Green is the colour of harmony in nature, and having plenty of green in your system will give you the capacity to create a loving and harmonious environment. Green-biased people have difficulty in making decisions, because green is found in the middle of the colour spectrum and is neither warm nor cold, active nor passive.

Green links to the heart centre and to harmony within the cells. This is why people develop problems related to cell growth when their green energy is out of balance. Different forms of cysts and cancers can take hold if there is not harmony within the whole system. Green links to love and the ability to love oneself as well as caring for others. We all have to learn to love ourselves for what we are, good and bad. We have to accept ourselves before we can become whole and contented.

A balance of green energy can be maintained by eating plenty of fresh green fruits and vegetables.

Blue

Blue is the colour of peace, loyalty and trust. It is the colour of care, and this is why it is the colour chosen (albeit unconsciously) to represent the medical profession. People with a blue bias are the peacemakers and carers of this world. They are introverts who are searching for peace and quiet in their lives.

Blue is a cold colour and blue-biased people often suffer from low blood pressure and cold hands and feet. They can also be susceptible to lung and throat problems. The blue and the orange energy centres are very closely linked, so if problems relating to relationships (associated with the orange centre) are not expressed, they often cause blockages in the blue throat centre. Blue-biased people, therefore, must make sure they express their feelings. They must talk about how they really feel, for if they don't the blocked blue energy will find other ways to come out. Deep breathing, speaking, singing and other forms of creative expression can all help the blue-biased person.

To keep the blue bias in balance, eat both a variety of blue foods such as fresh blueberries and blackberries and any orange-coloured fruits or vegetables.

Indigo

Indigo is a midnight blue, and is similar to the blue ray, although a much stronger vibration. Indigo-biased people are quiet and studious, with excellent minds, and make great teachers and reformers, but may become very introverted and reclusive. If Indigo people fail to accept acknowledgement for their hard and wonderful work, they run the risk of their very core being eaten away, so they must learn to express their needs and must be careful not to become martyrs – healthy bones can be at risk as well as the production of white blood cells originating within the bone marrow. People with this bias also need to bring more joy into their lives. Mineral-rich foods that nourish the thyroid gland such as kelp are of benefit to indigo-biased people.

If you have a high indigo score but low blue or violet, the indigo, which has both red and blue in it, will provide some energy of these colours although it will be in a much weaker form.

Violet

People with a violet bias are very sensitive and are closely connected with the spiritual side of existence. They are able to plug in to the vibrations filling the ether around them. This is why they are often creative people, and make good mediums. Violet-biased people have very open crown chakras, letting the flow of *chi* rush into their being. They do need to protect themselves from harmful and negative vibrations, which are picked up easily. Violet people are often very sensitive to sound and air pollution and are apt to suffer from different allergic reactions.

People who have violet in their aura are often searching for spiritual development and self-knowledge. They also often have their heads in the clouds and find it difficult to handle everyday responsibilities. Nervous and mental disorders, for example neurosis, phobias and epilepsy, can be the problems related to imbalance with this colour. Violet is a very powerful colour, and people who are empowered with this ray must make sure they are working for the good of others and not merely from egotistical motives.

Violet is a mixture of blue and red, and foods of these colours together with purple vegetables and fruit are excellent for keeping this colour energy balanced within your system.

Other Types of 'Inherited' Bias

The authority on Ayurvedic medicine, Deepak Chopra, MD, identifies three natural body blueprints in his book *Perfect Health*. The three types or *doshas* correspond to the three ranges of colour energies: red/orange, yellow/green and blue/violet. These in turn relate to human body colouring, build and personality.

Pitta dosha corresponds to the red/orange rays and has qualities that reveal themselves as hot, sharp, moist, slightly oily, fluid and sour. *Pitta* people are joyous, confident and enterprising.

Kapha dosha corresponds to the yellow/green rays. The qualities of this *dosha* are heavy, cold, oily sweet, slow, soft, sticky and sluggish. These people are sympathetic, loving, forgiving and calm.

Vata dosha is blue/violet by nature and is typified as dry, cold, changeable, quick and rough. Vata people are imaginative, sensitive and spontaneous, all qualities imbued by the blue and violet rays.

Colour Bias and the Colours For Life Diet

A harmonious diet will help to correct an original colour bias, while an unharmonious diet will add to an imbalance. Whatever your inherited colour bias, the Colours for Life Diet will help you maintain a balance of all the energy required by your body and should be adopted as a way of life. Now you have an idea of your personal colour imbalance, let's take a closer look at the Colours for Life Diet and ways in which it provides a balanced, colourful and delicious approach to nutrition.

3 | The Colour Spectrum and Food

Colour therapy is based on the premise that it is no accident that foods are the colours they are, and that they contain colour-corresponding groups of chemicals and other substances that are essential for health.

All vegetable matter has its characteristic colour, as does all inorganic matter. In the Introduction we looked at the three main colour food groups. A quick reminder: chlorophyll is the pigment that gives green fruits and vegetables their colour; carotenoids give red, yellow and orange foods theirs, and anthocyanidins pink to purple. Red, orange and yellow foods are rich in beta-carotene and are more acidic than the calming blue, indigo foods which are more alkaline. Violet contains both red and blue, so although energizing does not overheat the body. Green foods are neutral, helping maintain the acid–alkaline balance.

Fresh food from the vegetable kingdom is imbued with light energy from the sun as well as magnetic earth energy. Plants absorb certain colour rays, depending on the colours of their leaves, stem, flowers and fruits, and these colour vibrations are transferred into a form that can be easily absorbed by us. Once the food has been eaten, the body breaks it down, converting it into both physical and energetic nutrients. The energy released by the various colour vibrations will be attracted to the sympathetic energy centres, which will be revitalized. All foods have a vibrational harmonic to the seven main chakras, and to the glands, organs and nerve centres associated with their colour-related chakra. Each food energizes, cleanses and heals the particular chakra with which it harmonizes.

In order to be healthy we need a balance of each colour energy as reflected in sunlight, so that we are receiving energy from each cosmic ray in similar proportions. When this is the case, our living system can be called stable and coherent. Once there is a colour imbalance the living system loses its stability. When this happens one or more of our energy centres will become depleted of energy, while others will be over-energized. If this imbalance is not restored, illness and disease may result. The Colours for Life Diet works on the principle of restoring and maintaining a balance of all the spectrum colours through our food and drink.

Most natural foods vibrate on frequencies corresponding to the seven rays. The outer colour of the foodstuff usually indicates which colour vibration that food contains and the action that the colour will have on our system. Foods that contain more than one colour vibration energize more than one energy centre: a pink grapefruit has a skin which is yellowy-green, while the flesh inside is a beautiful pink, and the grapefruit will reflect both these colours. Some foods are difficult to classify from their outer colour, and here the Oriental principal of yin and yang (the positive and negative energies) is a useful tool to help us create harmonious proportions of the colour energies we need for a balanced diet.

Yin and Yang and the Colour Wavelength of Foods

As we have seen, everything in our universe is polarized, made up of a varying amount of yin and yang energy. There is no absolute yin, nor absolute yang, but some things tend to reflect energy at one or other end of the scale. This scale relates to the rainbow colours, which form part of the electromagnetic spectrum that comes to earth in the form of white sunlight, although we can only see about 40 per cent of these vibrations.

On the following chart I have laid out the rainbow colours from the longest wavelength to the shortest. I have also included two invisible vibrations, infra-red and ultraviolet, in order to remind you that there are many other invisible wavelengths such as radio waves, X-rays and microwaves.

In the diagram below we can see relationship of different types of foods with the spectrum colours and whether they contain more yin or yang energy. Ultraviolet is the most yin colour of the spectrum and corresponds to refined sugar. Infra-red at the other end of the spectrum is the most yang and corresponds to salt.

Between the two extremes we find the visible colours of the spectrum, red, orange, yellow, green, blue, indigo and violet.

Foods, Spectrum Colours, and Yin and Yang Energy

YANG			EQUAL YANG AND YIN					YIN
infra-red	red	orange	yellow	green	blue	indigo	violet	*ultraviolet*
salt	stimulants	meat	animal products	pulses	grains	legumes	fresh fruit and vegetables	berries processed food refined sugar

Red blood flows through all animals' veins, and so it is this colour energy which is primary to our system. On the other hand, chlorophyll gives green plants their colouring; and so green is the principal colour of the plant kingdom.

The animal world is therefore mainly yang in nature; that is, there is a good deal of red energy in the systems of animals. This is why food from the animal kingdom tends towards yang, and includes animal products such as red meat, eggs and hard cheeses which are high in salt content. In the West we eat a great deal of yang foods – red meats, eggs and salt. Red-coloured fruit and vegetables also contain yang energy, but of a much lighter wavelength.

The plant kingdom is represented by the middle colours of the spectrum – orange, yellow and green. These foods contain within them transformed light energy from the sun's rays which nourishes not only our bodies but our minds and spirits. Ground crops tend to be more yang in nature as they receive secondary energy through the earth's magnetic field. This life-giving energy is absorbed by our bodies in the form of essential minerals and vitamins. Foods that grow above ground are influenced by the upward thrust of yin energy, while ground crops are influenced by the predominance of yang energy, which pushes them downwards.

We need to balance our intake of yin and yang foods, just as we need a balanced diet of foods containing the seven coloured rays. We must also make sure that we eat some foods that grow below ground as well as those that grow above ground. For example, when selecting red foods, we should eat strawberries or cherries (above ground), and sweet potatoes and beetroot (below ground). Taking into account the earth's natural rhythms, it is beneficial to eat root crops, which are more yang in nature, during the day, while yin foods, growing above the ground, are better consumed in the evening. Seasonal changes naturally provide more ground crops in winter, thus providing us with a bigger proportion of warming yang foods.

Although our natural physiological tendency runs from red to yellow, we need a lesser amount of red and orange food to provide fuel for our physical strength and energy. Red food should be fresh and unprocessed and preferably from the vegetable kingdom. Nor should we forget our spiritual side, but we should ensure that our spirit takes nourishment from food rich in light energy, particularly from flowers, berries and leaves coloured blue or violet.

Just as the opposite poles of magnets are attracted to each other, so yang is attracted to yin. The yang animal craves yin foods such as sweets and fizzy drinks. If the scale is tipped and we eat too much yin food, we then become attracted to foods of the opposite end of the spectrum. You can prove this to yourself next time you eat something salty like a packet of crisps. It is most likely that you will immediately crave a sweet drink. And so we spend our life in a constantly moving state seeking out balance between the two opposed but attracting forces. Green's balancing force can prevent this see-saw action, and fresh green fruits and vegetables and herbs are thus the foundation of the Colours for Life Diet. We should include these foods in our daily diet.

Yang, Yin and the Balancing Effect of Green

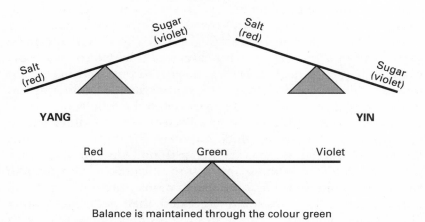

Balance is maintained through the colour green

When using our yin–yang scale we will find that synthetic drugs as well as refined white sugar vibrate on the ultraviolet frequency. When consumed, food falling at this end of the spectrum can cause imbalances typified by obsessional behaviour often relating to eating disorders and also to mood swings. Unfortunately we experience these imbalances all too often as a side effect of taking medicinal drugs. If you have too much ultraviolet-related energy in your system it needs to be balanced by vitamin B, found in pulses, soya beans, nuts, wholegrains, cereals, yeast and especially green vegetables.

Live Food versus Dead Food

Not a year goes by now without huge numbers of people falling ill from various forms of virulent flu and viral diseases. Our resistance levels are becoming progressively lower and our ability to fight these new strains is becoming weak. Many people I know expect to get a cold or flu a few times a year, and this is becoming a frightening norm. Dieticians are also finding that even with a balanced diet few people today absorb all the necessary vitamins and minerals to sustain good health. These days nearly all of us take supplements. It's a sad state of affairs, but it seems to be more and more necessary.

It's not surprising that our resistance levels are low if we continually eat frozen, dehydrated and pre-packaged food. The processed food products' packaging may tell us that they contain added vitamins and minerals, but there is a missing ingredient from all of these products and that is the life-force contained in fresh living food. The life-force of food is lost in ready-made meals, through freezing and reheating, and by microwave cooking (*see* chapter 6, page 127). Whatever nutrients may have been initially added to foodstuffs, many essential vitamins, minerals and enzymes are destroyed by these processes in the long run.

The life-force of objects can now be seen using a kilner screen or Kirlian photography, which captures the light and colour emanations surrounding every living thing. Aura photography, which is rapidly becoming more sophisticated, is also able to reveal the coloured life-force emanations surrounding food. Experiments have consistently revealed that under ultraviolet light bright golden yellow indicates when something is filled with 'light energy', while objects that emit a pale bluish glow contain no life-force. Fresh foods produce bright clear colours whilst frozen or dehydrated foods produce only a dull glow. A dull grey light surrounds meat and synthetically produced foods, showing that they contain little light energy. Considering these factors, it is clear that it is essential that food is as fresh as possible, and eaten raw or lightly cooked if it is to be of any real nutritional value.

Food Irradiation

Now we are also faced with the problem of foods that have been treated by irradiation. Irradiation is essentially the bombardment of food, usually with gamma rays or with ultraviolet light, and although it can facilitate the commercial processing of food it can have damaging results for our health.

Food irradiation makes it possible for food manufacturers to sell low-quality food that lasts longer in commercial storage or on the supermarket shelf, which will still appear fresh and wholesome. Although producers must label wholly irradiated products with a radura symbol, products with one or more components that are not irradiated are not obliged to do so. Manufacturers will thus be able to avoid labelling partly irradiated products unless new legislation is brought into effect.

The radura symbol

Treated with irradiation   **Treated by irradiation**

We are just discovering some of the many bad effects of eating irradiated foods: many of the vitamins are destroyed, and many bad odours and off-tastes are produced, which the manufacturers have to disguise using chemicals. Irradiation also changes the molecular structure of the food, the consequences of which we have little conception of at the present time.

A group of scientists in Christie Hospital, Manchester has detected the presence in irradiated pork, chicken and seafood of free radicals, highly chemically active atoms which can cause genetic damage and even cancer. Free radicals created by food irradiation have also been associated with premature ageing. The effects of free radicals aside, what we do know for sure is the destruction of bacteria by food irradiation also destroys enzymes which are essential to the good quality of the food.

To the naked eye, irradiated food may look appetizing yet contain little nutritional value. To determine its quality we have to find other means of looking at it.

In the nineteenth century a Serbian physicist, Nikola Tesla, showed how high voltages could be used to create an electrical 'aura' to light up around human subjects. In the 1930s research into the human energy field began in earnest when the 'life energy' was captured on film by a Russian husband and wife team, Semyon and Valentina Kirlian. Kirlian imaging has also been used to assess the health and vitality of food. A raw turnip produces a much brighter image than a boiled one, wholemeal bread creates a much bolder image than processed white bread, and organic vegetables show a brighter light than tinned, boiled or microwaved food.

Fluorescence will also give us a clue to the difference between live and dead foods and those exposed to irradiation. Similar to the guiding principles of Kirlian photography, it is the phenomenon in which certain substances are made luminous by the action of ultraviolet light. Butter, for example, glows yellow, while margarine glows blue and fungi in cheese fluoresce a brilliant green. Healthy potatoes show colour, while those affected by ring rot do not. Fresh eggs glow pale red, while older eggs glow a bluish colour. Live teeth glow; dead ones or artificial ones do not. Likewise, naturally and artificially ripened fruits can easily be distinguished. The same test can distinguish real hair from dyed hair or a wig. From this we can deduce that there are special visible qualities of fresh food which are not present in synthetically produced or dead food which is kept too long.

Food Colours, Colourants and Colourings

Nearly everyone is sensitive to the colours of foods. Appetite is quickened or retarded in almost direct relation to the observer's reaction to colour. Red is the colour that has the most appeal in food: a red apple or a red cherry is always seen as mouth-watering. Orange ranks highly too and yellow-green less so. There is a pick-up in appeal in the middle of the spectrum, around green, because we associate green with the freshness of nature. Blue, however, is not always appealing in food, nor is violet or purple. Although blue is not often perceived as suitable for things to eat, it makes an excellent background and will display foods harmoniously. Peach, red, orange, brown, warm yellow and clear green are the true appetite colours. Pinks and tints of blue are 'sweet'. Pale coloured food is connected with subtle tastes and refinement. Mushrooms, asparagus and milk have subtle flavours, as do refined foods such as white rice, white bread and white sugar.

Colour and food are so closely linked in our minds that our expectations are that a red apple will be sweet, a golden-yellow fish have a lovely smoky taste, and red meat be more tender. This is why a meal which has well-balanced colours looks appetizing and gets our mouths watering. We must, however, always be aware that our perceptions of food can be deceived by colour. Eating brightly coloured food may make our mouths water, but the goodness can end there. It is only if food is fresh and is its natural colour that we receive all the necessary energy we need to sustain a healthy state.

Although we can often tell from its colour whether food is fresh or stale, of a good or poor flavour, and whether it contains particular ingredients, these days it is hard to rely purely on food colour for an indication of freshness, especially when buying foods that are already pre-packaged. Whenever we are choosing foods and using colour as a guide, we should remember that the huge variety available is mainly a result of importing food kept in cold storage. It is picked before it is mature and ripened artificially, which means the goodness of the sun's rays are not locked within it, and colour is often added to make it look much fresher and appetizing or to ensure a consistent product by overcoming natural colour variation. Date stamping does help, but this is no indication of the hormones, preservatives and colourants used.

Colour Additives

The addition of colour to food is an emotive issue: colour has been used to deceive us. Colouring in food in earlier times was often toxic, and more recently some of the colours used have been suspected of causing cancer in animals. Today, colouring that is added to food will either come from natural sources or be synthetic. Natural colourants are made from natural plants and foodstuffs, and are entirely safe to consume. An example of a natural colourant is beetroot juice, which is used as a red and pink colouring. Synthetic food colourants are manufactured from chemicals, many of which are known to have side effects that may adversely affect our health. Tartrazine (E102 and FD&C Yellow no. 5) is a widely used synthetic yellow colouring, but it has been associated with some allergic reactions from rashes and swelling to asthma and possibly even behavioural changes.

Even if we try especially to avoid particular colourings we sometimes overlook the fact that drugs can contain colour additives. Many are derived, for example, from plants and natural materials whose colour ranges from bright red to muddy-brown. Red is the colour of fire and anger, and it is the colour of capsicums, cloves, musk and balsam from which many drugs are derived, so we are often prescribed drugs that contain condensed energy from a ray harmful to us. It is therefore very important not to take drugs unnecessarily. It is also advisable to always check drug packaging as well as food packaging for colour additives.

Some Colour Additives and Foods they are Used to Colour

Synthetic colourants			
Name	**Some typical uses**	**European E number**	**US Food and Drug Administration identification**
Reds			
allura red	Azo dye that replaced amaranth.	E129	FD&C red no. 40
amaranth	Burgundy-red coal-tar dye: blackcurrant products, especially soups, jams, jellies and fruit pie fillings.	E123	FD&C red no. 2
carmoisine, azorubine	Red/purple azo dye: sweets, raspberry and chocolate-flavoured desserts, yogurts, jams and preserves, bottled sauces and bread-coated meat products.	E122	—
erythrosine BS	Cherry pink/red coal-tar dye: glacé and other cherries, chocolates, tinned strawberries and rhubarb, packet trifle, biscuits, Danish salami, luncheon meat and stuffed olives.	E 127	FD&C red no. 3

Synthetic colourants (*cont.*)

Name	Some typical uses	European E number	US Food and Drug Administration identification
ponceau 4R or cochineal red A	Red coal-tar and azo dye: tinned red-fruit pie fillings, jams, jellies, ice-cream, dried soup, and cake and cheesecake mixes.	E124	—
Yellows			
quinoline yellow	Yellow to green-yellow coal-tar dye: Scotch eggs and smoked haddock.	E 104	—
sunset yellow FCF, orange yellow S	Coal-tar and azo dye: soup and trifle mixes, marzipan, jams and marmalades, yogurts, sweets and orange squash	E110	FD&C yellow no. 6 (also equals E102)
tartrazine	Yellow azo dye: squashes and fizzy drinks, bottled sauces and salad cream, smoked cod and haddock, biscuits, soups, jams, jellies and sweets.	E102	FD&C yellow no. 6 (also equals E110)
Greens			
green S or acid brilliant green	Coal-tar dye: tinned peas, asparagus soup, lemon and lime drinks, jellies, packet breadcrumbs and mint sauce.	E142	—
Blues			
brilliant blue FCF	Coal-tar dye which when combined with tartrazine can colour foods green: tinned processed peas.	E133	FD&C blue no. 1
indigo carmine, indigotine	Coal-tar dye: gives a blue colour to sweets, biscuits and convenience foods.	E132	FD&C blue no. 2
patent blue V	Dark blue/violet coal-tar dye: deepens shades in such foods as Scotch eggs.	E 131	—
Browns and Blacks			
black PN, brilliant black PN	Coal-tar and azo dye: brown sauce and chocolate mousse.	E151	—
brown HT, chocolate brown HT	Coal-tar and azo dye: cakes with chocolate flavourings.	E155	—

Naturally derived colourants

Name	Some typical uses	European E number	US Food and Drug Administration identification
annatto, bixin, norbixin	Extracted from the fruit of *Bixa orellana*, the annatto tree. Give a yellow or orange-yellow colour to dairy products, such as butter, cheese and margarine, smoked fish and soft drinks. Can replace tartrazine.	E160(b)	73.30
anthocynanins	Extracted from flowers, fruit and leaves, and especially grape skins. Give a red or blue colour to foods with cyanin strawberry and cyanin blackcurrant flavours – jellies, dairy products, cold drinks, sweets, soups.	E163	—
beetroot red, betanin, betanidin	Extracted from beetroot. Jams, jellies, sauces and soups.	E162	73.40
capsanthin, capsorubin, paprika extract	Extracted from the red pepper, *Capsicum annuum*, to give a deep red colour in processed cheese and chicken pie.	E160(c)	73.340
caramel	Manufactured from sugars and starches. Bread and breadcrumbs, meat analogues, sweets and crisps, preserves, beer, wines and spirits. The most widespread colourant.	E150(a-c)	73.85
α-, β-, γ-carotene	Extracted from many plants. Spreads, baked goods, milk and baby products, and cool drinks.	E160(a)	73.95 (β-carotene)
chlorophyll	Extracted from nettles, spinach and lucerne. Fats and oils, chewing gum, ice-cream and soups.	E140	
cochineal	Extracted from pregnant *Dactilopius coccus* insects. Pie fillings and biscuit creams, icings, soup, bakery products and alcohol. Now usually replace by E124.	E120	73.100
curcumin	Extracted from turmeric (Indian saffron), *Curcuma longa*: savoury rice, processed cheese, butter and margarine, fats and oils, fish fingers and curry powders.	E100	73.600

	Naturally derived colourants (*cont.*)		
Name	**Some typical uses**	**European E number**	**US Food and Drug Administration identification**
saffron	Extracted from *Crocus sativus* and used as a natural yellow colour.	N/A	73.500
carbon black, vegetable carbon	Usually made from plant charcoal: jams, jellies and liquorice.	E153	—

The principal sources for this table were Title 21 of the Code of Federal Regulations Part 73, Subpart A: Colour additives exempt from batch certification, with numbers preceded by 73, or Part 74, Subpart A: Colour additives subject to batch certification, and *E for Additives*, by Maurice Hanssen with Jill Marsden (London: Thorsons), to which the interested reader is directed.

Foods to Avoid and their Alternatives

As well as artificially coloured, processed and irradiated foods, the Colours for Life Diet advises against some other foodstuffs, which should be either avoided or consumed in moderation, and as this section shows there are many healthy choices available.

Alcohol

Alcohol in all forms vibrates on the infra-red ray. As we all know, alcohol acts first as a stimulant, then as a depressive. The effect obviously causes an imbalance and an oscillation between the two extremes. Alcohol dulls the brain and our ability to respond effectively to internal and external stimuli. This means that we lose touch with messages coming from inside and outside ourselves. We lose our sensitivity and connection with our body, mind and soul. For those who are on a path of self-development and growth and who wish to connect to that spiritual essence within themselves, alcohol or any drugs will hamper their way forward. In order to connect with the soul and spirit we need to have a clean house in which harmony and peace can reign.

If, however, you are a meat eater, it has been found that a glass of red wine with your meal will aid your digestion of the protein and fats as long as your diet is varied and nutritious, and research into the Mediterranean diet has found that red wine and red grape juice have a beneficial effect in reducing the risk of cardio-vascular disease without overloading the liver. Red grape juice or red berry juice (diluted for the high sugar content) are non-alcoholic alternatives that produce the same results. If you want a glass of wine, drink it at lunch, while consuming only non-alcoholic drinks with the evening meal. Apple juice, elderflower pressé and lemon-flavoured mineral water are good alternatives to wine with supper.

Cooking Oils and Fats

A healthy body needs fat for vital functions in the structure of the body cells, and it is the main insulating material under the skin and around organs such as the kidneys. Fats are also essential for the absorption of the fat-soluble vitamins A, D, E and K into the body from the gut. The human body is normally able to obtain from plant sources all the fats it needs for energy.

There are many types of fats, all made up of fatty acids. Nutritionally, one of the most useful ways of looking at edible fats is by distinguishing saturated from unsaturated fats.

Edible fats have a chain made of an even number of carbon atoms, to which hydrogen atoms bond themselves. Mono-saturated fatty acids have one unused bonding site for a hydrogen atom, polyunsaturated fatty acids have several, and saturated fatty acids have all the possible bonds used up, and so are also known as hydrogenated fatty acids. They are found mainly in animal products such as meat, eggs, milk, cream, butter and cheese, but also in vegetable products such as peanuts, coconut and palm oil, and hard margarines.

Although we need fats, they are very concentrated forms of food, which give twice as much energy for their weight as proteins or carbohydrates, and we only draw on 1–2 per cent of our energy needs from them so we should only consume them in small amounts. Saturated fatty acids make the body form too much cholesterol, which is used to make hormones such as cortisol and to make bile acids. Saturated fat is needed for a healthy brain and nervous system, but is not an essential nutrient because the body can make its own. If you are physically active your metabolism can break down saturated fat and use the energy, so a small amount of food containing it can be eaten, but if you lead a sedentary lifestyle or have a high proportion of fat in your diet it can make you overweight, and unfortunately cholesterol can accumulate in the inner parts of the arteries, leading to a progressive reduction in the diameter of the blood vessels and in blood flow, which can in turn lead to heart attacks, angina, abnormal heart rhythms and heart failure.

To ensure that this does not happen it is better to eat mainly unsaturated fat. While monounsaturated fat does not change the blood cholesterol level, polyunsaturated fat decreases it. Polyunsaturates are essential to humans because they cannot be made in the body: sources include almonds, Brazil nuts and coconut, oily fish such as trout, salmon and mackerel, and oils such as corn or maize, sunflower, sesame seed, safflower and olive; sardines and tuna fish contain both saturated and polyunsaturated fats. Cultures which traditionally use olive or peanut oil for cooking have historically had little coronary heart disease, and an intake of up to 10 per cent of our energy needs from polyunsaturates may help prevent it.

The Colours for Life Diet suggests you use polyunsaturated oils for cooking and salad dressing. Cold-pressed oils are generally the healthiest option: heat destroys essential vitamins and the life-force energy contained in the natural product, and can convert unsaturates into saturates; it also makes fats harder to digest. (If you want to taste the benefits of cold-pressed products, try honey that has been extracted by cold pressing: it's much more nutritious than honey which has been prepared by boiling, and much tastier.) Polyunsaturated oils also contain omega-6 and omega-3, which are structural components of the brain and retina during early development. They also reduce inflammation and the tendency of the blood to clot, which is helpful for heart disease and arthritis. Most oils are in the yellow–green colour range. Olive oil, a good source of omega-6, is essentially green while sunflower, a source of omega-3, sesame, corn and other vegetable oils have mainly yellow energy. (Other good sources of omega-3 include soya bean, rapeseed and walnut oil, and oily fish.)

When deciding whether to use butter or margarine you need to look at your diet as a whole. Since the unsaturate to saturate conversion can happen in soft margarines as they are processed by heat, and since these margarines also contain chemicals and preservatives that are not conducive to good health, butter is a more natural food than margarine and has more life energy. If you have a diet which is rich in fruit and vegetables, butter is unlikely to cause problems with cholesterol levels. If you eat a lot of red meat and dairy products the high saturated fat content in butter could increase cholesterol levels and margarine would be a better choice.

Dairy Products

Many of us were taught that milk is a complete food and because of this it is extremely rich in nutrition. In fact all mammals except humans feed on milk only while they are young, as milk is already transmuted into a form which needs little digestion. Too much milk will impair the body's capacity to process other foods, as milk does not make use of the whole digestive system. It is wise, there-fore, to always have cow's milk separately from the meal. In this way you will be able to prevent and identify a milk allergy much more easily. In an ideal world unpasteurized milk would be the best choice as it is more natural, not having been heat treated; unfortunately, today you do have to be careful about the type of milk you drink as it can become contaminated with micro-organisms, so you should only drink unpasteurized milk from approved and managed herds. Better still, if you love milk and milk products, and don't wish to avoid them, try to find some goat's milk; this is much closer to human milk and more in keeping with our metabolic processes.

For those who wish to avoid dairy produce altogether, nut, oat and soya milks are good substitutes, especially if you wish to avoid animal products or have a lactose intolerance. They are readily available at good health shops and are very nutritious. Coconut milk can also been used in cooking and adds a soothing and aromatic quality to the meal.

As milk is already been processed into an easily absorbed food, it is very soothing and alkaline and is best drunk at night. In fact milk harmonizes with the green ray, as it is from the green grass that it is derived. Do not mix milk products with acid fruits as this causes the milk to curdle in your stomach, and often results in nausea or indigestion.

Other secondary green foods such as natural live yogurt are also soothing and pacifying. Yogurt is a natural antibiotic, containing live bacteria and enzymes which aid proper digestion and elimin-ation as well as replacing the bacteria which protect you against illness. It is best to start the day with yogurt or eat it mid-morning on its own. Again, do not mix yogurt with acid or bitter fruits.

Yogurt can make a good alternative for salad cream or a lovely sauce. Mix it with garlic and herbs and pour over a salad, pasta or vegetables.

The energetic nature of products derived from milk varies according to how these products are made. Hard cheese is very salty and dense, and so belongs to the red end of the spectrum. This applies particularly to cheeses with a dark orange colour or golden colouring. Soft cheese and butter are less yang if unsalted, and contain more orange and yellow rays. Curds, cream and yogurt have a much lighter and expansive quality and so are more yin. This links them more to the colour green. Remember, the more processed the food, the more yin it becomes. This means that although margarine is yellow in colour, it contains the yellow ray if it is cold pressed, but heat processing will move its colour energy towards the blue end of the spectrum.

As hard and salty cheeses are very yang, it is advisable to eat soft light-coloured cheeses, which are less salty and more yin. If you do eat hard cheese, try to do so at lunchtime and not in the evening; hard cheese is difficult to digest and can give you indigestion and nightmares. Low-fat curd, cream, cottage cheese or fromage frais is lovely to eat cold or to cook with, so try it out instead of spicy tomato sauce on pasta or vegetables.

Seafood and Fish

Although fish is acceptable as a good source of protein and minerals, it is not advisable to eat other seafood – especially prawns, shrimps and crawfish (spiny lobsters). These animals are food scavengers, eating the excrement floating in the water around them. Seafood is also prone to be contaminated with mercury and industrial waste materials. The energy provided by seafood is associated with the lower chakras, which are linked to the sex organs and sensual pleasures, which is why seafood is considered to have aphrodisiac qualities.

Should you wish to eat fish occasionally, make sure you purchase it fresh from the fishmonger. Look at the eyes to make sure they are clear and check that the scales are shiny. Richly coloured fish like salmon and tuna are more yang, as are smoked fish and salty fish like herrings and mackerel. The best fish to eat, especially in the evening, are the more yin white-fleshed fish, and freshwater fish, which are not salty.

From a colour perspective, oily fish, such as herring, mackerel, salmon, sardines, trout and tuna, which contain more salt, are violet/red, and white fish, such as cod, haddock, plaice, skate, sole and whiting are blue/violet.

Tea and Coffee

It can be harmful to drink more than two cups of coffee a day, as caffeine retards the absorption of iron and coffee contains infra-red energy that unless kept to a minimum becomes detrimental to our health. If you must drink it, make sure it's caffeine free and do so mid-morning (not at breakfast), then change to green or herb teas for the rest of the day. There are many delicious red and orange teas. Choose, for example, rose-hip tea, blackcurrant tea, peach- or orange-flavoured tea or orange Pekoe tea, or rooibos (redbush) tea, which you can drink with milk. Lovely aromatic and colourful teas include green tea, peppermint tea, fennel tea, camomile tea and lemon tea. Green tea contains good amounts of vitamins C and E and other minerals, as well as flavonoids, which have been linked to the prevention of cancer and have other important antioxidant functions. Research presented at the second International Pyogenol Symposium, in May 1995, indicated that green tea kills viruses and bacteria, and acts as an immunity booster. Common black tea also has flavonoids, and like most fruit and vegetables protects against heart disease. Drinking green, black or red tea also protects against skin cancer caused by ultraviolet light and by hazardous chemicals, and an experiment at Rutgers University's College of Pharmacy found tea greatly inhibited the formation of tumours. Sweeten your tea with honey or brown sugar if you must, but it is obvious that the less sweetener you use, the better.

Foods to Enjoy

There are many delicious fresh foods which can be enjoyed as the flavoursome staples of the Colours for Life Diet. It has been proved that we are healthy and strong when we live on food grown locally and organically; these foods are the best for maintaining constancy of physiological and mental conditions. If you can find 'traditional' or 'heritage' varieties, all the better. Food grown organically and locally in a hothouse is better than food imported and kept in cold storage.

So take as your guide the seasonal colours of fruits and vegetables available at the market or greengrocer and make a high proportion of your diet locally grown produce. This book is intended for people living all over the world, and so I include all types of commonly available fruit and vegetables. For all readers some of these will be imported and available when out of season, so I have identified their colours if you wish to include a small proportion of these in your diet. Colour remains a good guide to freshness when buying food from a market, greengrocer or fishmonger.

The Colours for Life diet is based on improving your diet by including healthy fresh food rather than exclusion and a strict diet regime.

Fruit

There are many different theories about the best time to eat fruit and whether to combine it with other foods or not. Here are some guidelines.

1 Fruit is best when eaten on its own as a snack or after a meal
2 Do not mix acid fruit with milk products or the milk products will curdle in your stomach, making them hard to digest. You may even feel nausea.
3 Use colour as the key for the best times of day to eat particular fruits.

Fruit can be eaten as a dessert, and to aid digestion – for instance, pineapples or strawberries for a fatty meal, papayas (pawpaws) or mangoes for a high-protein meal, and high moisture fruits like pears, apples, grapes and watermelon for a salty or spicy meal. High-carbohydrate meals respond well to figs, prunes or other dried fruit to help keep the digestion unclogged. Wait at least fifteen minutes before serving the fruit.

Eating a fruit breakfast will help to cleanse and purify your system while providing you with some energy. A drink of pure water and lemon juice may also be a refreshing and cleansing morning drink. Lemon juice is alkaline forming. Although it first produces acids, these are expelled by the body within an hour or two, while the remaining nutrients will be alkaline in nature.

If you do eat only fruit for breakfast, you may need to eat a snack mid-morning to boost your energy levels. This is a good time to eat a plate of muesli or natural breakfast cereal. As yogurt or milk is usually eaten with cereal, this will mean that you will not be mixing fruit and milk.

Fruits for breakfast and the morning
Apples, bananas, figs, gooseberries, green grapes, lemons, limes, melons, passionfruit, pineapples, yellow pears.

Fruit for lunch and the afternoon
Apricots, bananas, guavas, mangoes, oranges, papayas (pawpaws), peaches, pink grapefruit, plums, prunes, raisins, raspberries, red apples, red cherries, red and yellow melons, strawberries, tangerines, watermelon, or the juice from any of these.

Fruits for supper and the evening
Blackberries, blackcurrants, blueberries, figs, green apples, green melons, green plums, kiwi fruits, lychees, purple grapes.

Green Food

The colour green has a special place in healing, for it is the colour of nature which holds the health of our planet in balance. The green pigment which forms the basis of most plants is chlorophyll, and like our own blood contains the life-force energy of the plants. It is chlorophyll that turns plants into what the great Swiss nutrition expert Dr Bircher-Benner called 'organized sunshine energy'. Chlorophyll has the unique ability to convert solar energy into chemical energy and then to use this to manufacture carbohydrates. So plants have the capacity to absorb the vital energy from the sun and change it into a form which is easily absorbed into our system.

There are, in fact, extraordinary similarities between the structure of haemoglobin, the red-pigmented molecule which transports oxygen around our bloodstream, and that of chlorophyll, the life-blood of plants. The molecular structure is virtually identical, with the exception that the haemoglobin structure is built around iron whereas chlorophyll is built around magnesium. We are therefore more closely linked to the natural world than we think; chlorophyll-rich green food can actually help to enrich our own blood. Chlorophyll therapy is a fast developing branch of nutrition and can be used to build up our blood count, which strengthens our whole system.

Science is confirming the age-old wisdom of healing an open wound, bite or burn with a handful of green leaves which have been chewed and made into a plaster and applied directly onto the wound. G H Collins, an American doctor who used chlorophyll in the treatment of burns and reported his findings in the *American Journal of Surgery*, thinks that chlorophyll possesses 'the most marked effect of all agents for stimulating cell proliferation and tissue repair'. Chlorophyll is also highly cleansing, alkalizing, and full of minerals, especially magnesium.

Green energy is necessary to keep our metabolism in balance. Green light, directed on the pituitary gland through the point of the third eye chakra or foot reflex, has been found to harmonize the workings of the pituitary gland, which controls our hormonal balance. (Since green light travels to the pituitary gland via the hypothalamus, it is possible to receive the balancing action if we sit near a light with a green bulb or shade.) The pituitary also helps regulate water within the body and other functions central to weight control such as appetite.

Green is a neutral colour, so green food can be combined with food of any other colour; it is essential in keeping our metabolism in balance and in purifying and cleansing our system. It should be included in most meals and can be eaten at any time of day. Fresh green leaves contain the co-enzymes and enzymes that will assist in their own breakdown, and are a primary source of nutrients that are quickly assimilated into the body: vitamins, minerals and other various types of protein, which can be more easily digested than most animal foods, for plants contain high levels of fibre. Enzymes power the immune system, raise our resistance to disease and break down toxins so that they can be eliminated by the body. Green food contains minimal amounts of fattening sugars and carbohydrates, and any fats found in green foods are unsaturated, which are good for us.

Green, leafy vegetables contain a high quantity of organic juice, which consists primarily of pure, natural water, which is cooling to our system. The nutrients in green juice create a highly magnetized reaction while passing through the stomach and intestines. The juice cleanses the body of tissue and cellular wastes, and completely detoxifies the intestines. Scientists at St Bartholomew's Hospital, London, have found that chemicals in green vegetables act as 'disinfectants' against bacteria, including

E. coli, reducing the risks of food poisoning and tumours. This scientific data reinforces the view of colour therapists that the green ray has a detoxifying and cleansing action on our systems.

A well-made green salad is a prescription for health and has a vital role to play in our diet: it picks up and utilizes life-giving enzymes, the mineral and chlorophyll content stimulates the bone marrow to manufacture haemoglobin, thus improving the body's ability to digest and utilize food, it is full of fibre, and it contains important amino acids, which are activated when they are combined with other high-energy foods such as nuts and seeds forming powerhouses of protein rivalling those found in animal products. It builds up the immune system, helping us to resist illness and ageing. To get the maximum benefit, eat it raw and as fresh as possible.

To supplement our green salad we can make use of many more unusual green foods in our diet, especially those rich in chlorophyll such as grasses (especially barley and wheat) and different forms of blue-green algae, literally at the very bottom of the food chain and so the purest form of nutrition you can get.

Spirulina is a blue-green alga which flourishes in the warm-water lakes of Mexico and North Africa. It is made up of 60 per cent protein and is a rich source of essential fatty acids including GLA, vitamins and minerals. It also contains a rich supply of beta-carotene, and so is a worthwhile supplement to any dietary programme. As the quality of spirulina can vary you should always look for the highest quality organic type. Chlorella is another kind of alga, which is also rich in protein, vitamins, minerals and chlorophyll.

A green salad can contain its own supplements and include sparkling spots of colour to feast your eyes. If you are making a green salad it does not have to be entirely green, as long as it includes only a small proportion of other colours. For centuries salads were decorated with bright flowers such as borage, broom, cowslips, elderflowers, lavender, nasturtiums, primroses, rose petals and violets.

Green salads may be made using various beneficial herbs. Many herbs well known for their medicinal properties are listed amongst over seventy ingredients for making a perfect salad in *Acetaria*, a book written as long ago as 1699 by John Evelyn, the English court writer. Of all of the salad herbs, basil is the most calming to the nervous system; spring onions and chives are antibacterial, are good for the heart and help to fight respiratory problems; mint aids digestion and stimulates the brain function; and parsley is rich in iron, calcium, potassium and vitamins A and C.

Foods of other colours

As we saw in chapter 2, red and green are complementary colours, which means they work in harmony with one another. Red and orange foods from the vegetable kingdom contain yang energy; they stimulate the metabolism and aid digestion, controlling uric levels in the blood and helping eliminate toxins and water. The right balance between red and green energy will maintain your optimum weight. The Colours for Life Diet requires that you eat foods from all the spectrum colours, although a colour-corrective diet using both red and green foods can be followed for a short period (from one to two weeks; *see* chapter 8, page 147–8 for the details).

Some modern colour therapy writers suggest that eating red foods will help you slim, while eating a lot of green food will make you fat; this misunderstanding stems from the fact that many large vegetarian animals such as cows or elephants feed almost exclusively on green vegetation, but our digestive system and energy needs are extremely different. It is clear that many overweight people also suffer from high blood pressure and potential heart problems; if they exclude green food from their diet, red energy will build up with a serious risk of damaging the heart. Green foods provide the body with essential nutrients: if you are on a diet which cuts out green foods, you may be doing yourself more damage than good.

Milk and yogurt, curds and other organically produced milk products vibrate on the green ray, having derived their original energy from grass. Other white foods, such as soya milk and tofu, can be also be combined with any other colour food as white contains all other colours and is a balanced food in itself. Naturally white food contains healing qualities for this reason, and helps with the body functions of gathering and storing energy. In Chinese medicine white foods such as white potatoes, rice, soya beans, cauliflowers, celery, garlic, Iceberg lettuce, Chinese water chestnuts and celeriac are thought to contain metal energy. These foods often have a sharp pungent taste, and are very nutritious because many have a high protein content. Soya beans and soya products are especially nutritious and white vegetables also contain vitamin E and phosphorus. Remember, however, that refined white foods such as white sugar and refined salt are not 'live' foods and therefore are harmful to the body's system.

Herbs and Spices and their Colour Energies

Many herbs and spices can be used in cooking, while some make colourful and delicious teas. Like essential oils, some herbs work on two colour frequencies, especially those where more than one different part of the plant is used. These are usually the complementary colours – red/green, blue/orange and yellow/violet. Rosemary is an exception, as it is a top-to-toe herb balancing the bottom and the top chakra, which means it corresponds to both red and violet.

Here are some herbs and spices that come highly recommended for use, with a note of their qualities.

Red
stimulating, warming, tonic
black and white pepper cayenne pepper ginger hibiscus flowers nettles rosemary (red/violet) watercress (red/green)

Orange
warming, releasing, digestive tonic
anise bay (orange/blue) bergamot buchu leaves (*Agathosma betulina*: not suitable for children) coriander cumin mace nutmeg paprika

Yellow
carminative, nervine, stomachic, cleansing for the skin
camomile flowers caraway cinnamon coriander cumin dandelion dill evening primrose golden seal lemon balm lemongrass lemon thyme marigold nutmeg saffron wild mistletoe (yellow dye, poultice on skin good for warts)

Green
cleansing, purifying, balancing, digestive stimulant
alfalfa chives comfrey fennel garlic nettles oregano (wild marjoram) parsley peppermint spearmint tarragon

Blue
sedative, antiseptic, antifungal, bactericidal
caraway (blue and orange) catmint garlic hops Irish sea moss kelp marjoram (sweet marjoram) thyme valerian yarrow

Violet
purifying, sedative, diuretic, protective
bilberry feverfew hollyhock (purple flowers) juniper berries lavender
purple sage sweet violet (this is not suitable for children) vanilla pod wild
passionflower (*Passiflora incarnata*)

Herbal Teas

Red
bergamot flower raspberry rosehip hibiscus flower

Yellow
camomile cinnamon ginger ginseng linden

Green
fennel lemon lime lemon verbena peppermint

Blue
blackberry borage flowers elderflower liquorice root

Violet
lavender (used with care in a small quantity) sage

Herbs can also be made into herbal infusions for medicinal purposes, gargles and compresses. These include apple mint, basil, bay leaves, chervil, chives, coriander, dill, horsetail, hyssop, oregano (wild marjoram), parsley, rosemary, sage, thyme and valerian root.

A herbal infusion is made like a tea, by pouring 450ml/1 pint/2½ cups of boiling water onto 12g/½oz dried herbs or 25g/1oz of fresh herbs, leaving it to infuse for a good 10 minutes, and straining it into a jug. A standard dose is a small teacupful, taken warm or cold, flavoured with honey or lemon, three times a day. You can keep the remainder in the fridge for 24 hours.

The Colours for Life Rainbow Vegetables

Whatever our diet may be there are many families of plants containing an array of colour energy that we should include. Staple foods are traditionally complex carbohydrates such as grains, starches such as potatoes, and legumes and pulses. Before modern farming methods developed these foods were rich in all the basic nutrients we required and were particularly suitable to the climate and lifestyle of the people eating them. The old-fashioned natural varieties were indeed Rainbow foods, for the different varieties reflected many different colour energies, thus containing the full spectrum of physical and subtle energy needed to keep us healthy. Sadly many of these strains have died out because of the commercial pressure for monoculture that responds to perceived consumer demand, so that there is now little genetic diversity and we have lost the benefit of the full range of nutrition they once offered.

Fortunately the renewed interest in nutrition and improving our diet has led to growers reintroducing some of the older varieties, but to experience the colourful and nutritious delights of these lesser known strains we have to cast off our tendency to select only produce with regular shapes and familiar colours.

Remember, organic producers and distributors will usually offer these older varieties in all their seasonal variety, and many seeds can still be sourced from organic cooperatives and societies.

Carrots

Physical nutrients	Beta-carotene, small amount of vitamin E
Vibrational nutrients	Full of magnetic earth energy (yang)
Colour energy	Yellow, orange, purple, violet and white

Most people only know of the carrot as an orange-coloured, regular-shaped root, but it has a long history in which it existed in many different colours and forms. Purple carrots were once cultivated around the Mediterranean, in the Middle East and in Asia and were branched much like the ginseng or mandrake root. It was much later, when they were introduced by the Moors to Spain, that carrots became conical. The Spanish then took them with them to the Americas, where they were a favoured crop for the early settlers. Even as late as the nineteenth century purple, red and scarlet carrots remained popular but gradually the regular-shaped orange varieties became dominant, and although today some carrots are long and tapered while others are cylindrical and stumpy, they are all the same familiar orange colour.

The therapeutic qualities of carrots reflect the qualities of the orange ray, which has a relaxing and opening effect on the muscles of the chest. The tonic effect of orange and yellow and its beneficial effect on the immune system have made carrots useful for helping to fight off infection. The high beta-carotene content also signifies that carrots should be included in our diet to prevent cancerous growths. Carrots have also been thought of as having a beneficial effect on the skin and eyes, so that you literally radiate good health.

Maize

Physical nutrients	Carbohydrates, fibre, some protein and vitamin B
Vibrational nutrients	Full of light energy from the sun (fire element)
Colour energy	Gold, red, white, yellow, purple, blue, orange

Maize has to be one of the oldest cultivated crops in the world, for no wild varieties have ever been found. We know that the ancient Mayan and Inca civilizations cultivated it, and that it was the basic foodstuff of the Aztecs; it became the staple crop of North America after about AD 800. The first types were brought to Europe in the sixteenth century in the form of cobs and corn-meal. It used to be multi-coloured, and cobs of blue, scarlet, brown and almost black seeds predominated in South America, but unfortunately the golden maize varieties such as 'Conquest', 'Honey and Cream' and 'Silver Queen' are now favoured and the beautifully coloured 'Rainbow' maize is only used for its ornamental qualities.

Maize is believed to reduce the risk of certain cancers, heart disease and cavities in the teeth, and corn oil lowers cholesterol levels. In Mexico maize has been used to treat dysentery and as a diuretic and mild stimulant.

Peppers and Chillies

Physical nutrients	Vitamin C and beta-carotene
Vibrational nutrients	Full of light energy from the sun (fire element)
Colour energy	Red, orange, yellow, green, indigo, purple

The capsicum genus includes all sweet peppers, bell peppers, *pimientos* and chilli peppers, and it is a rainbow family, full of solar energy and goodness. All peppers are rich in vitamin C and beta-carotene. They come in an array of colours ranging from red, orange, yellow and green through to a wonderful purple and deep indigo. As they mature, members of the capsicum family change colour through the rainbow from an immature green to a rich red or indigo when ripe.

The great thing about peppers is their versatility, as they can be eaten raw, grilled, fried or added to flavour almost any dish.

Chilli peppers are thought to be the first cultivated capsicum, as seeds have been found in Mexico dating from 7000 BC; their medicinal uses have been known for thousands of years. Sweet peppers were introduced into Spain in the late fifteenth century and by the middle of the sixteenth century had found their way to England.

All peppers which are ripened in the sun contain solar power as reflected in their individual colours. Red chillies warm our entire system by increasing the flow of blood. They also help relax muscles and were used in a muscle liniment. The warm colour energy of red, orange and yellow peppers opens the chest, alleviating bronchitis and emphysema; an old remedy advises drinking 10 to 20 drops of chilli sauce in a glass of water daily to keep the airways free from congestion. The pepper has also been found to stimulate endorphins, which kill pain and give us a sense of well-being, and it may well be that the indigo or 'black' peppers are more likely to produce this effect.

Potatoes

Physical nutrients	Rich in carbohydrates, magnesium, potassium and some vitamin B and C
Vibrational nutrients	Yang and magnetic earth energy (white potato – metal energy)
Colour energy	Red, gold, pink, purple, white, blue

The potato was first cultivated in Chile and Peru around 5000 BC and since then hundreds of different varieties have been developed. The Spaniards introduced the potato to Europe. Potatoes reached a peak of popularity in the UK in 1948, when 988,400 acres were planted, and although they have remained popular there has been a big decline in the number of varieties grown. Unfortunately we have been taught to consider unusual shaped potatoes as unsuitable for eating and difficult to prepare so varieties such as the 'Lumper' (which survived Ireland's potato famine) and 'Pink Fir Apple', which has a lumpy pink sausage shape, have nearly been forgotten. Other colourful varieties which are difficult to find are 'Edzell Blue', which has a beautiful blue skin, and 'Blue Catriona', which is splashed with purple. 'Black Congo' is a small black potato which contains the qualities of indigo colour energy. Varieties which have remained popular are the high yielding 'King Edward' and the 'Golden Wonder', which is used for potato crisps.

Like many plants, potatoes evolved their own chemical means of discouraging pests and green potatoes contain the toxic alkaloid solanine, which can cause vomiting and stomach upsets. The leaves and fruits of the potato also contain this toxin so should not be consumed. Potatoes contain little fat, and are said to be good for rheumatism. Their juice was also used to relieve gout, lumbago, sprains and bruises, and uncooked they could be made into soothing plasters for burns and scalds.

Squashes (pumpkin, marrow, courgette, potiron)
Physical nutrients   Beta-carotene, vitamin C and folic acid
Vibrational nutrients   Earth magnetic energy
Colour energy   Green, yellow gold, orange, blue-grey

Squashes form the *Cucurbita* genus and are native to tropical America. There is evidence they have been eaten in South America for thousands of years, as fragments of pumpkin dating back to 2000 BC have been discovered by archaeologists in Mexico. The word 'pumpkin' comes from the Greek word for melon, which is *pepon* and means literally 'cooked by the sun'. Pumpkins absorb large amounts of light energy as they ripen in the sun and so it is not surprising that they are bursting with orange energy in the form of beta-carotene, which boosts our immune systems.

There are two main groups of squashes: marrows, harvested in summer, and pumpkins, harvested in winter. Marrows or summer squashes are often picked when young and tender and have edible seeds and skin and pale flesh. Varieties include the beautiful red and orange crookneck and the scalloped 'Custard' (patty pan), which is an exotic orange and yellow. Winter squashes are harvested when mature and have hard inedible skins but a much deeper coloured flesh. 'Acorn' is dark green and deep ribbed, and 'Butternut' is pale cream and bell shaped. The sweet-tasting orange-coloured pumpkin, a firm favourite in America for some time, is becoming more popular in Europe. A lesser known variety is 'Banana Pink', which is long, broad, and curved with a pale pink skin, while 'Queensland Blue' is another tasty small variety with a blue-grey skin.

The seeds of squashes have been used as laxatives and purgatives in many parts of the world and this not surprising as orange energy has a releasing action, especially on the bowels.

Vegetables for Breakfast

All the red and orange vegetables contain the fire element, which is warming and energizing and sets us up for the day. They also require the most digestion, so the digestive system must be active at this time in order to process the goodness in the food.

Tomatoes and carrots or their juice can be eaten at breakfast. Also try spinach, which although green in colour contains a high proportion of red energy – if you look carefully at the stems you will see a red hue. Red energy supplies the liver with iron, which is essential for the manufacture of new red blood cells. Red-skinned onions and red-skinned potatoes could be part of a hot breakfast. Rhubarb, which is the stem of the plant, is also good for breakfast.

Vegetables for Lunch

These are mainly fresh green salad vegetables, which should be eaten raw. Root vegetables, which are more yang and have a good deal of earth energy in them, are best consumed during the active part of the day, but you can also include the stems, leaves and tops of plants. Their energy is grounding and aids practical physical activity.

Summer	Winter
avocados	beetroot
beetroot	broccoli
carrots	Brussels sprouts
cauliflower	cabbage
celery	carrots
chillies – red and green	cauliflower
courgettes	dillisk (a deep red Irish vegetable)
cucumbers	Jerusalem artichokes
globe artichokes	kale
lettuces	kohlrabies
maize	onions
mustard and cress	parsnips
new potatoes	potatoes – red skinned
onions – brown skinned	pumpkin
peas	Savoy cabbage
peppers – green, red and yellow	spinach

radishes
runner beans (scarlet runner beans)
spinach
spring onions
summer squashes with orange or yellow flesh
watercress

swedes
turnips

Vegetables for Supper

You need less energy for supper, and the vegetables are much lighter in quality than those for lunch. It is wise to eat more stems, leaves and tops of the plants, while keeping yang vegetables to a minimum; stems, leaves and tops contain water, so balancing the water energy in our own system, and because they are above ground they contain air energy. This air energy connects with our spirit and is found in green, blue and purple foods. The 'light' quality of these foods helps us to sleep.

Summer	**Winter**
asparagus	broccoli
aubergines	cauliflower
beansprouts	Chinese leaves
beans – broad, French (haricots vert, kidney,	endive
snap, string beans)	Jerusalem artichoke
cabbage	Kale
cauliflower	kelp or kombu
celery	laver
chicory	mushrooms
Chinese water chestnuts	parsnips
gem squash	red cabbage
globe artichokes	sea kale
green peas	spring greens
green salad vegetables – any kind	
mangetouts	
mushrooms	
okra	
onions – purple skinned	
peppers – green	
purple-sprouting broccoli	
shallots	
summer squashes with pale yellow	
to green flesh	

Salad Vegetables in Season

Summer	Winter
avocados	beetroot
broad beans	broccoli
carrots	cabbage
celery	celery
cucumber	carrots
lettuce	chicory
mustard and cress	Chinese leaves
olives	endive
parsley	fennel (Florence, sweet)
peppers	leeks
radishes	mushrooms (cultivated)
runner beans	nuts
spinach	onions – red
spring onions	potatoes
tomatoes	
watercress	

The staples of the Colours for Life Diet can be used in many delicious ways, according to the season, the time of day and your own requirements. We will go on to look in more detail at which foods contain which coloured rays, the effects of these rays, and how they can harmonize with your personal needs.

4 | The Colour Keys to Healthy Eating

The Rainbow Steps to Health

Health is a condition of perfect equilibrium, and it can only be maintained as long as there is perfect rhythm and harmony throughout the body, mind and spirit.

Just as we need to eat a varied and balanced diet if we are to be healthy, so too do we need a balance of energy from the seven spectrum colours. These super nutrients not only nourish the physical cells and organs but have a powerful influence on our emotional, mental and nervous activity, and on our spiritual well-being.

But what are the essential foundations upon which to build a healthy and prosperous life? In his book *Perfect Health* Dr Deepak Chopra says, 'Eating is a creative act that selects the raw matter of the world so it can be turned into you.' We should take into our system foods which will activate our full potential. The Colours for Life Diet uses this as a basis upon which to consider the qualities of well-being in relation to colour energies and the foods that contain them. In this chapter I have given you some of the most important foods for each of the Rainbow colours. You can use the principles explained here to choose fresh local, seasonal food for your own needs.

Red-Ray Foods – A Good Appetite

We should all enjoy a good appetite, and have plenty of energy. We should be ready to meet life's challenges and have a healthy sex drive. We need to be able to assimilate the goodness from the food we eat, and eliminate waste material and toxins efficiently. Red-ray energy gives us the ability to understand that we all have a special purpose here on earth that only we can fulfil; this ability to get in touch with the basic life-force energy will give us the motivation and strength to achieve our life's goals. As this energy provides our body with energy and vitality, stimulating the production of adrenalin, it gives us our ability to survive.

Red-Ray Foods

Fruits	cranberries, damsons, raspberries, red apples, red cherries, redcurrants, red plums, rhubarb, rose-hips, strawberries, watermelon
Herbs	cayenne, hibiscus flowers, mint, mustard, peppermint, pineapple sage, red and black pepper, rosemary, thyme
Legumes	aduki beans, black-eyed beans, red kidney beans, red lentils
Vegetables	aubergines, beetroot, Jerusalem artichokes, mustard and cress, radishes, red cabbage, red chillies, red peppers, red-skinned onions and potatoes, red peppers, sea vegetables (red and black varieties), spinach (green with red stems), tomatoes, watercress and any vegetable containing iron such as horseradish, parsley or spinach

Orange-Ray Foods – Plenty of Energy

A healthy body means we also have an alert mind and are interested in everything around us. Our body functions will be tuned and we will have stamina and drive. Our strong immune system will ward off disease and our skin will glow with good health. Our blood circulation will also be good and our digestion strong.

Imagine sitting in front of a roaring log fire, receiving the joy and warmth of orange energy. Orange energy makes us sociable, outgoing and optimistic. It is a very creative colour as it is made up of red energy, which is active and expanding, and of yellow energy, which is linked to the mind and ideas. Orange links to our sexuality, so that we can enjoy and express love of our physical body. Orange energy helps us express our emotions, so we can form strong, healthy relationships. Orange is the colour of health and links to both the digestive and sexual organs and the spleen: orange food is an appetite stimulant and acts as a powerful tonic, giving us physical energy and mental stimulation.

Orange-Ray Foods

Fruits	apricots, orange melons, mangoes, nectarines, oranges, papayas (pawpaws), peaches, tangerines
Herbs	cardamom, coriander, cumin, garlic, ginger, ginseng, mace, nutmeg, paprika, saffron
Legumes	orange lentils
Seeds	all seeds
Vegetables	butternut squash, carrots, brown-skinned onions, pumpkins, swedes, wholegrains
Others	apple cider vinegar, blackstrap molasses, dark honey, egg yolks, white cheeses

Yellow Ray Foods – A Happy and Cheerful Disposition

We all need to have a positive and cheerful outlook on life: positive thoughts help radiate a protective force around us. Yellow symbolizes this radiant life-force. Golden-yellow is the colour of the sun, and of strength and intelligence. This colour energy helps us broaden our horizons with new ideas and possibilities. Gold foods feed the brain which enhances our mind power, improving logical thought and memory.

As golden-yellow is the colour we associate with the sun and daylight it raises our spirits to happy, joyous thoughts and brings a harmonious and optimistic attitude to life. We all need humour and to see the funny side of life, and this can be enhanced by eating orange, gold, golden-brown, golden-yellow and yellow foods.

Yellow-Ray Foods

Fruits	apricots, bananas, golden apples, grapefruit, hazel pears, limes, pineapples, yellow gooseberries, yellow melons
Grains	barley, buckwheat, bulgar wheat, cornmeal, millet, oats, rye, wheat, wild rice
Herbs	caraway, cinnamon, coriander, cumin, nutmeg, pineapple weed, turmeric
Legumes	chickpeas, brown and yellow lentils, mung beans
Nuts/Seeds	all

Vegetables   gem squash, maize, marrow, parsnips, pumpkin, yams, yellow peppers, yellow-fleshed turnips, yellow-skinned potatoes, white radishes

Others   apple cider vinegar, butter, cassava, evening primrose oil, light honey, some unsaturated vegetable oils – corn, safflower, sunflower, sesame, yellow primrose

Green-Ray Foods – A Loving and Understanding Nature

We all need to be able to give and receive love. We need to maintain balance and harmony in our lives, giving us the ability to trust to the process of life. In this way we will attract natural abundance and prosperity to ourselves. Green is the colour of balanced strength, the colour of progress in the mind and body and the colour of nature, which brings peace, balance and harmony and which strongly influences the heart and blood pressure, soothing the nerves. Everyone knows how we need to escape the city to the green of the countryside when we are under stress. There we can breathe more slowly and deeply, and feel the weight of our problems and tensions lift off our shoulders. Green is a refreshing and restorative colour.

People with open hearts will not suffer from high or low blood pressure, and will have strong nervous systems. Their hearts and lungs will be strong and they will have the ability to breathe deeply, receiving nourishment from the air as well as from food.

Green-Ray Foods

Fruits   avocados, figs, greengages, green grapes, kiwi fruits, lemons, limes

Herbs   apple mint, basil, capers, comfrey, garlic, parsley, rosemary

Legumes   green lentils

Vegetables   artichokes, avocados, broccoli, Brussels sprouts, cabbage, celery, courgettes, cucumbers, endives, green beans, green peppers, kale, kelp and other green sea vegetables, leeks, lettuce, okra, peas, spinach

Other   buttermilk, curds, olive oil, skimmed milk, soya milk, tofu, yogurt

Blue-Ray Foods – The Ability to Relax

Our ability to rest and relax is directly related to our energy levels. The blue ray links to the respiratory system, encouraging transportation of oxygen to the tissues, and to our ability to draw in *chi* from the air. If we breathe deeply and strongly we will find that we have lots of vitality, whereas someone who breathes shallowly will be constantly tired. If blue is deficient we will suffer from fatigue due to lack of oxygen in the system and the brain cells.

If you have an abundance of energy that is creatively expressed during the day, you will sleep soundly at night. Unfortunately very few of us get a good night's sleep; we are too often plagued by disturbing dreams and nightmares because our minds are over-stimulated during the day. Eating a large, heavy meal in the evening also puts a strain on the whole body system, and we feel tired and sluggish the next morning. It is very important that we only eat a light meal in the evening, one containing foods of the blue and green rays (*see* chapter 4, pages 68–70). These pacifying foods are soothing and relaxing. Too many people eat foods containing the red or infra-red ray late at night; a bedtime drink of tea or coffee, for example, will not help: both are red foods and stimulants. A cup of milk or cocoa would aid sleep, because milk falls under the green of the grass whence it originated.

We all have to learn how to enjoy proper relaxation of the body, mind and spirit. We are so busy during the day that we allow ourselves little time to process and reflect on the day's events. No wonder we find it hard to make decisions. The old saying of 'go to sleep on it' is really not such a silly idea after all, for we use a different part of our brain when we sleep. We need to connect much more to this intuitive part of our inner self, and we can do this by taking time relaxing on our own. Listening to music, reading a good book, gardening, painting, or another creative activity puts us in touch with this softer, quieter side to our nature. Blue foods will help us to achieve this by uplifting our consciousness away from our bodily processes to the finer things in life.

Blue-Ray Foods

Fruits	bilberries, blueberries, blue plums, cabernet grapes
Grain	blue maize
Herbs	borage flowers, camomile, chicory flowers, clary sage, cloves, hyssop, marjoram, pansies

Vegetables   asparagus, kelp, mushrooms, blue-skinned potatoes, spirulina
Other   brewer's yeast, polyunsaturated vegetable oils, some blue-scaled white fish

Indigo-Ray Foods – Knowledge and Insight

In many Eastern philosophies, the indigo ray is linked to the brow chakra or third eye centre between our eyebrows. This area helps bring focus to our lives, so we can stand back and see things more clearly. Indigo light has a very sedating effect on our lower mind, inducing a state similar to anaesthesia. This detachment promotes connection with our finer qualities, bringing out our ability as human beings to act with compassion, discretion and integrity.

Together with blue and purple, indigo foods have a psychologically calming and soothing effect on us.

Indigo-Ray Foods
Fruits   avocados (the variety 'Hass'), black, red and Texas mulberries, blackberries, black cherries, black figs, blackcurrants, plums, prunes, raisins
Herbs   liquorice root, vanilla pod
Vegetables   aubergines, black Spanish radishes, olives, oyster mushrooms, sweet peppers (black), truffles, French beans (the variety 'Royalty')
Other   soy sauce, tamari sauce, some seaweed (sea vegetables)

Violet-Ray Foods – Creativity and Intuition

We are all creative beings, although many of us suppress or do not acknowledge our creative abilities. Humans alone are able to receive inspiration from music, art, poetry and dance, and develop a spirit of idealism and understanding of our spiritual nature, yet most of us deny this unique side to our being. Violet foods will help to overcome this tendency and will help to stimulate our creativity by heightening our perceptions.

We need to learn to reconnect with our intuition and higher self. This will release our true creativity. Violet provides nourishment for all those cells in the upper brain and links to intuition and spiritual perception. For these reasons purple foods are essential for those who meditate, who are on a spiritual path, or who are working with subtle energies. Healers, therapists, clairvoyants and mediums are all people who should concentrate on these violet-ray energies.

The violet ray links to the brain and central nervous system, which it strengthens and nourishes. Eating purple foods is therefore very important for our mental health.

Violet-ray foods contain the energies of both the blue and the red rays, and the synergy of the two colours produces a colour with its own qualities. On the one hand they are energizing, but on the other they are cooling and refreshing, true mind foods. Violet foods provide energy without overheating our system.

Violet-ray foods

Fruits	dewberries, elderberries, huckleberries, passion fruit, purple prunes, purple plums, purple grapes
Grains	purple maize
Herbs	lavender flowers, pansy, mallow flowers, common sage, sweet violet, thyme, wild passion flower, violet flowers
Legumes	purple kidney beans, runner beans (scarlet runner beans)
Vegetables	aubergines, beetroot tops, Chinese water chestnuts, endives, globe and Jerusalem artichokes, King Edward potatoes, kohlrabies, light purple bamboo shoots, mushrooms, purple cabbage, purple mushrooms, purple onions, purple sea vegetables, purple-sprouting broccoli, sweet potatoes, truffles, turnips, winter radishes

Seasonal Cycles

In addition to the properties of certain foods, the Colours for Life Diet is based on re-establishing our connection with nature and the energies from the earth and sun, so we must also look at the cycles of coloured light energy falling on us every day.

In order to stay healthy we need a balance of all the colour energies, and there are certain times of the day when these energies are at their most potent. By understanding the therapeutic qualities of the various colour vibrations and the times when it is most beneficial to ingest them we can eat food of a particular colour in order to restore harmony when our system becomes imbalanced.

As mentioned in chapter 1, our ancestors were exposed to more sunlight and were consequently healthy when they lived out of doors in close harmony with nature. Humans learned to live by and accept the laws of nature, of which they were a part. From watching the cycle of seasonal changes, humans learnt that life energy is continuously moving and transforming. In fact the whole of life is a continuous cycle of transformation. Things degenerate and die only to give rise to new growth during spring, so that a bountiful summer can follow.

Each season has its own colour energies, too. These are reflected by the quality of the light and colours. During summer the colours are clear and bright. This is the time of active energy. All nature is busy. As the end of summer approaches the colours change to deeper and richer autumnal tones. This signals a time for harvesting and storing energy for the cooler winter months. At the onset of winter the colours change to deep tones and strong contrasts, rich warming red berries and dark green of hollies and fir trees. White and black show up in strong relief. Nature dies back and energy is low. This is why we also lack energy during the winter months. This is a time to turn inward and a time for reflection, whereas spring marks the time of regeneration.

As we have grown away from nature and the natural cycles we have lost the rhythm of life. Modern society demands that we work flat out all year round, and our sleep patterns often have little to do with the rising and setting of the sun. No wonder we have lost our natural balance. We have to remind ourselves that it is natural to have less energy during winter and more during summer.

In spring we often feel like giving ourselves a new fresh start, and this is why we spring-clean our homes. We also need to spring-clean our minds and identify our goals for the coming year. In summer, when our physical energy is strong, we often take up sporting activities or go away on an active holiday. In the autumn we start consolidating our energy and turn it towards the mind. Our mind power is still strong, and autumn is the perfect time to start a new study course.

The quality of the energy of each season is related to the different organs and glands of the body. The seasons' energies affect our eating patterns just as the actual types of food we select stimulate the organs related to providing the right type of energy.

Seasonal Change and the Body

Season	Organ or gland	Seasonal energy
Spring	liver and gall bladder	yellow-green, light green
High summer	heart, small intestine	yellow, dark green
Late summer	stomach, spleen, pancreas	golden-yellow, orange, golden brown, blue
Winter	bladder, kidneys	red, purple, nut-brown

These seasonal cycles are most important as they give our lives rhythm and continuity. The colours in our dress and in our foods can reinforce these natural rhythms, helping keeping our body, mind and soul connected to each other and the natural order of the universe.

The Daily Colour Cycle

Although we have changed our work, sleep and eating patterns, and our metabolisms have been profoundly affected as a result, our bodies still follow the same natural biorhythms and laws as they have for thousands of years. These laws of changing energy levels follow the colour energy changes throughout the twenty-four-hour cycle.

The colour cycle remains the same throughout the year, but the strength of the light increases or decreases. Energy flows through the body, energizing different organs at the same time throughout the year, and although the quality of the light will change from summer to winter we can help keep energetic balance by taking in light energy from the food we eat.

The daily colour cycle

Time of day	Colour
dawn	green
morning	yellow
noon	gold
afternoon	orange
sunset	red
early evening	violet
late evening	indigo
midnight	blue
early hours	turquoise

Seasonal Affective Disorder is a condition brought on by the lack of sunlight in the winter months which is now treated with bright lights. In the Colours for Life model we are taking in light energy through the food, to boost the vital energy from sunlight which is reduced with the shorter days.

In the early hours of the morning around dawn, the quality of natural light is green. This is the time of rising bio-energy. During this time there is a positive flow of vital energy through our kidneys and bladder. As dawn approaches the large intestine is activated and so a healthily functioning body will require us to open our bowels every morning around this time.

The stomach and spleen leap into action during the morning. As the sun continues to rise the sunlight takes on a yellow quality which deepens towards the gold of the noon sun.

From noon to 2pm is the most active part of the day, when our heart beat needs to be strong, and when the heart and small intestine become energized. A light meal is required so as not to tax them. If you have a weak heart or your heart is overstimulated at this time, it is more likely that you will suffer from a heart attack at the time when energy peaks in this organ, in the morning: the study of our internal rhythms, known as chronobiology, has revealed that more people experience heart attacks just before noon than at any other time – a time when the heart is becoming energized.

During the afternoon light takes on an orange bias. The rays are now at their strongest and our skin may need protection. As the afternoon wears on the orange light changes towards the beautiful peaches and reds of sunset. Bio-energy levels are now turning downwards. This is the time that the bladder and kidneys receive a flow of energy. After the sun sets the violet and indigo of evening and then the blue of the night sky bring with them calming, soothing, inward-flowing energy. This is why we need to use this time to sleep. Blue and indigo energy connect us to our intuition and subtle bodies, which we can explore in our dreams.

Many doctors and nutritionists advise us to start off sleeping on our right side, the side of the body where the liver is located: this way the body fluids are drained towards the liver, helping its action while we sleep. The liver receives its vital supply of energy from midnight to around 4am.

The lungs are the next body organs to be revitalized by energy. This happens during the early hours of the morning. We all know that if we suffer from a lung infection, it's in the early hours of the morning that it causes the most problems and our lungs feel the most congested.

The cycle is completed with the pale green light of dawn.

Harmonizing Our Diet with Our Biorhythms

As we have seen, natural sunlight provides us with all the coloured light energy needed to maintain our body in perfect health. Throughout the day, the quality of the sunlight changes, and each colour is amplified one by one, until we have received a balance of each colour energy. At night too, the moon reflects the light from the sun and gives it a special colour quality.

It is obvious, therefore, that we must balance these colours energies within us. We should get as much fresh air and natural light as possible, but as we no longer spend many hours out of doors we have to supplement the coloured energy by paying attention to the colours in our food so that the colour energy contained in it will boost our colour energies. Remember that we need energy from all the colours. Just as we need a nutritionally balanced diet, we need a balance of colour energy.

Today a growing number of doctors are turning to ancient medical treatments, such as the Chinese principle of *chi*, for inspiration about ways to improve the effectiveness of their medications and treatments. The modern practice of chronobiology places an importance on the daily flow of energy through our systems that is particularly reminiscent of the principle of *chi*, as it examines how the human body's biological functions are regulated by an internal body clock. Dr Ronald Portman, a US chronobiologist and a medical director at the University of Texas Medical School, observed in 1997: 'The medical community is slowly awakening to the fact that it's not just important how you treat a condition, but when you treat it.'

This knowledge can also help us to achieve maximum benefit from our food, for if we eat food of a particular colour at a time of day that is in harmony with our natural biorhythms, we can best absorb its nutritious components.

Using the daily flow of biorhythmic energy as a model, we can divide the twenty-four-hour day into four distinct periods, morning, day, evening, and night. These are related to the cyclical movement of energy through the body, so the morning energy moves upwards until early afternoon when our energy descends and continues to do so until dark. During the night energy moves horizontally while we rest.

The Four Energy Periods of the Twenty-four-hour Day

morning	dawn to late morning
day	noon to sunset
evening	dusk and evening
night	midnight to dawn

Morning – dawn to late morning

The first energy period begins just before sunrise, when pale green energy enters the lungs and colon. This transmutes to pale yellow during the early morning and deeper yellow as the morning progresses. As the yellow energy becomes stronger, our stomach becomes more active.

When we wake in the morning our body is still sluggish, as our bodily functions have slowed down during the night. It makes no sense suddenly to fill the stomach with a large heavy breakfast. This is the reason we should not overload the stomach if we take an early breakfast as we need to allow it to eliminate the toxic residue left from the evening meal. Early morning is therefore a good time to drink a glass of pure water into which is squeezed some lemon or lime juice. This purifies the stomach and colon and ultimately clears the skin. Eating a grapefruit or a green or pale yellow melon is good at this time of day because of these fruits' cleansing properties.

An early breakfast should be light and nutritious, based on green and yellow fruits, and a later breakfast should include energizing yellow carbohydrates such as bran, corn, wheat or oat cereals, nuts and seeds. Herb tea can provide liquid refreshment that reflects the yellow or green ray. Tea or coffee should not be drunk at breakfast, for these liquids greatly retard the absorption of iron into the body. Rather, drink these stimulants later in the morning.

Day – noon to sunset

The second energy period takes us through the day, when we are the most active. During these hours we can draw on the energy provided by gold, orange, and red. A brunch is an ideal time to eat golden-yellow and orange food, as the spleen is nourished then, and the spleen plays an important role in providing us with the energy we need for the most active part of our day. Try fresh carrot or orange juice, a poached or boiled egg and wholegrain bread or cereal.

As the morning progresses to noon the heart takes its nourishment, and so a large heavy meal then would tax it and make you feel tired afterwards. Between 1 and 3 in the afternoon the small intestine takes its energy, so it is best to digest a lunch of complex carbohydrates and fibre, as found in salads and vegetables. I suggest a light meal based mainly on green salads, lightly cooked vegetables and a little fish or white meat, or alternatively a carbohydrate like pasta and cheese, or potato and salad if you are food combining. If you like a glass of wine, drink it at lunch, rather than in the evening; red is better than white. Red berry juice is an excellent alternative.

As the sun's rays lengthen and weaken during the late afternoon, the slower wavelengths of light become visible. These include crimson and deep pink.

Evening – dusk and evening
The third energy period in our biorhythmic cycle is the period from dusk to midnight.

As the red energy of sunset turns downward more blue enters the spectrum. Blue light influences our sleep patterns. It was recently reported that scientists at the University of North Carolina have discovered a new light-sensitive pigment called cryptochrome, which is responsible for regulating the body clock. The pigment is found in the eye, alongside various other pigments which absorb different-colour lights and are linked to different vitamin groups. Cryptochrome is linked to vitamin B_2, which can be used to treat seasonal depression. The pigment absorbs blue light, which then sends a signal to the brain, and appears to control the circadian rhythm which regulates functions such as blood pressure, intellectual performance and sleep cycles.

Since most evening meals coincide with the blue–green period, we can take this research into account. Evening meals should consist of yin food mainly of violet, green and blue colouring, although you can include a little red (pink) food in the early evening if it is from the plant kingdom. We can benefit from the calming and pacifying effects of these colours by eating food from the cooler end of the spectrum – fish, soft white cheese or light vegetable protein, lightly cooked vegetables and salad. An early supper, however, should consist mainly of violet, indigo and a

little blue or red. Evening meals should contain half carbohydrates, one-third salads or raw or lightly cooked vegetables, and
one-sixth lean meat or chicken, pulses or legumes, and the later in
the evening we eat the less food we need. Fruits can be eaten at a
short interval after the evening meal, especially the fruit listed in
chapter 3, page 52.

Avoid tea, coffee and stimulants (they fall under the ultraviolet
or infra-red rays) and meals consisting of red meats, hard cheese,
or fats such as cream. If you eat a heavy meal or brightly coloured
food at night your blood pressure will rise as the triple heater is
overstimulated, and it's likely you will end up feeling bloated
because your liver is overloaded. Avoiding these foods will help
you relax so you can sleep well. People who suffer from insomnia
usually find they have been consuming a red food late at night.

It's possible to change the emphasis of the midday and early
evening meal according to your lifestyle. One meal should contain a protein, like lean white meat or fish, lentils or legumes, and
the other should be a combination of carbohydrates, like potato,
rice, bread or grains and fresh vegetables.

Violet, indigo and blue stimulate the kidneys, sex organs,
circulation (or triple heater as it is known in traditional Chinese
medicine) and gall bladder. It's particularly during the early
evening that our sex organs receive their energy, so really a pre-
dinner romp will be more rewarding than an after-dinner liaison!

Night – midnight to dawn
From midnight turquoise energy balances our circulation
through the body system known in traditional Chinese medicine
as the triple heater. The triple heater does not consist of any
physical organs but nevertheless helps us to maintain a constant
body temperature. If it's imbalanced we experience night sweats
around midnight. The liver and gall bladder take in green energy
during the early hours so it's best to take medications or herbal
remedies related to problems in these organs last thing at night.

Now that we have looked at some of the basic guidelines of the
Colours for Life Diet, chapter 5 will look in closer detail at how
these guidelines can be incorporated in menu plans and recipes.

Summary of Daily Energy Flow through the Body

Time	Organ	Light Energy
6am	large intestine	light green
8am	stomach	pale yellow
10am	spleen	yellow
noon	heart	gold
2pm	small intestine	orange
4pm	bladder	red
6pm	kidneys	magenta
8pm	sex organs	violet
10pm	triple heater	indigo
midnight	gall bladder	blue
2am	liver	turquoise
4am	lungs	green

Note: To show how energy flows through the body in this table I am using the parts of the body viewed as organs in traditional Chinese medicine, not in Western medicine.

5 | The Colours for Life Diet – Menu Plans and Recipes

Colour cooking for a healthy body and mind combines the visual aspects of colour with nutritional value related to the colour of foods. Instead of elaborate methods of counting calories and vitamins, we can use a quick, reliable and appetizing method of eating foods of the right type and colour. The key word is variety: to maintain good health we should eat a selection of natural foods reflecting all the different colours. Each meal should consist of approximately two or three handfuls of food. You should leave the table feeling a quarter of your stomach empty, which will help digest your meal properly.

Seven-Day Seasonal Menus

Now let us combine the principles of biorhythms, vital primary source food and Rainbow foods in some appropriate menus. Here follow examples of Colours for Life meal plans, two each for summer and winter, the first for those who prefer to eat some white meat and fish and the second for vegetarians.

In both the lunch and supper menus I have given you examples of seven different choices. The breakfast and snack menus can be varied as suggested. The earlier your breakfast the more light yellow and green food you can include, but a late breakfast can be centred around the yellow and orange rays. The dishes in the menus form only a small number of delicious recipes you can create using colour as your cue. Remember from chapter 4: eat more yellow and orange food during the morning, base your mid-day meal around yellow, orange and red, and have an evening meal containing lighter food of the green, blue and violet range. Combine green food with all the meals. Lunches can be more heavily spiced while dinner should be flavoured with herbs. Once you get the idea of the colour cycle you will find the guidelines of the Colours for Life diet quick and simple to follow. During spring and autumn remember to replace the foods with seasonal foods of an appropriate colouring.

The Daily Colour Cycle and Daily Meals

Colour	Meal
pale green and yellow	early breakfast
yellow and orange	late breakfast
gold and orange	early lunch
gold, orange and red	late lunch
red (pink), violet, indigo	early evening meal
violet, indigo, blue	late evening meal

Recipes for the dishes in capitals can be found in the recipe section that follows these menu plans.

Summer Menu

Early breakfast

a glass of grapefruit juice
two slices of wholewheat bread or toast with lime marmalade or yellow fruit preserve made with rose water or wild-flower honey

Late breakfast

1 fruit salad
2 a plate of muesli or bran flakes
3 a small piece of haddock and mushrooms
4 an egg and baked beans
5 Apple and Cinnamon Breakfast Pancakes, with honey

Morning snack

gold-coloured tea, or decaffeinated coffee, with
a yellow or orange fruit

or a tub of yogurt
or a slice of fruit tart
or a date and apple muffin or scone with apricot jam

Lunch

1 cheese or egg in a wholewheat roll with salad
2 baked potato with tuna and salad
3 Spaghetti with Fiery Red Pepper Sauce
4 spinach or broccoli quiche and Nasturtium Flower Salad
5 Spinach and Feta Cheese Pie or chicken pie and green salad
6 Grilled Salmon with Black Olive Paste, with new potatoes, salad
   and a glass of red wine

Afternoon snack

a piece of orange or watermelon
or a nut or seed snack bar
or rooibus (redbush) or ginger tea
or Mint Barley Sherbet

Supper

1 chicken and mushroom casserole with new potatoes
2 lean white meat with green beans
3 Fusilli with Two-Mushroom Sauce (or pesto)
4 grilled white fish with salad or green vegetables
5 chicken pilau with purple salad
6 pancake with white fish or chicken, with mushroom or asparagus
7 Stir-fried Summer Vegetables, with fish

green or purple grapes
or green melon and kiwi fruit salad
or lemon sorbet or lemon tart with lemon or lime essential oil

Late-night drink

a glass of milk
or camomile or sleepytime tea

Winter Menu

Breakfast

1 a glass of pineapple juice
2 a plate of oatmeal or cornmeal porridge
3 two slices of wholegrain bread or toast with lemon marmalade, gooseberry preserve or honey
4 two eggs with yellow tomatoes and beans
5 yellow herb tea or cereal coffee

Morning snack

an orange fruit
or a tub of natural live yogurt with honey and sunflower seeds
or a slice of carrot or ginger cake

Lunch

1 cheese, ham or mushroom omelette
2 baked potato with fish, cheese or chicken filling
3 Tomato Soup with Sage, with a wholemeal roll
4 sandwich with cheese, egg, white meat and salad on wholegrain or pitta bread
5 cauliflower or macaroni cheese, with mixed salad with thyme flowers
6 Penne with Chestnut Sauce
7 Winter Mixed Vegetable Curry and Red Lentil Dahl

Afternoon snack

herb tea or coffee with
a piece of orange or red fruit
or Sunshine Orange Pancakes, and honey
or a nut and seed snack bar

Supper

1 pale yellow or green coloured soup
2 white fish pie and green vegetables

3 Honey and Soy Grilled Chicken and wild rice
4 lean white meat stew with carrots, leeks and turnips
5 grilled white fish with broccoli or sprouts
6 Leek and Mushroom Lasagne
7 Turkey with Watercress Sauce, with Creamed Parsnips

baked green apples or pears
or Date Rice Pudding

Vegetarian Summer Menu

Breakfast

a glass of fresh celery and yellow apple juice
two slices of wholewheat bread or toast with lemon marmalade
or a green or yellow apple
or muesli with oats, bran, dried fruits and nuts with yogurt

Morning snack

yellow or orange tea or cereal coffee with
a banana or orange fruit
a slice of carrot cake or a wholemeal muffin

Lunch

1 Couscous with Thyme and Poppy Seed Oatcakes
2 cheese or egg with salad with a variety of greens and wholemeal
   bread
3 corn on the cob and avocado salad
4 baked potato with crumbled goat's cheese and shredded baby
   spinach leaves
5 pitta bread with feta and tomato salad or hummus
6 Tabbouleh with Marigold Flowers
7 fruit lunch with brown bread and butter
8 Red Rice and Mushroom Patties, with green salad

Afternoon snack

hibiscus flower and herb tea with
orange or red fruit, eg strawberries or cherries
or a snack bar with sesame or sunflower seeds
or a tub of yogurt

Supper

1 Tempura with Sweet-Sour Dip, on rice
2 Kedgeree of Summer Vegetables
3 asparagus quiche and Greek salad
4 Stuffed Green Peppers, courgettes or aubergine, with Purple
   Summer Salad
5 Walnut and Mushroom Risotto, with mangetout
6 saffron vegetable stew with couscous
7 stir-fried vegetables on saffron rice

Blueberry Buttermilk Pancakes
or a kiwi-fruit flan
or green grapes or fresh figs

Late-night drink

a glass of milk
or a glass of Milo
or camomile or sleepy time tea mix

Vegetarian Winter Menu

Breakfast

a plate of oatmeal or cornmeal porridge
herb and ginger tea or cereal coffee

Morning snack

a yellow apple or pear
or a piece of fruit cake
or a date and orange slice

Lunch

1 Mexican beans and wild rice
2 pasta with tomato and broccoli sauce
3 Lentil Soup or butternut soup, with corn bread
4 baked potato and baked beans or nori (seaweed) flakes and cheese
5 Mixed Vegetable Curry, and jasmine rice
6 Mexican tacos with beans and avocado
7 warm pitta bread with hummus, or felafel with salad

peppermint or fennel tea

Afternoon snack

hot chocolate
or seed or nut snack bar
or nuts and raisins
or a piece of orange or red fruit

Supper

1 tofu and green pepper bake
2 Aubergine Stew with Capers
3 lentil patties and purple winter salad
4 cauliflower and broccoli in a white herb sauce and winter salad
5 stuffed red cabbage and basmati rice
6 Potato and Bean Stew, with couscous
7 pasta with mushroom and herb sauce

Stewed Apple and Fig Crumble
or sago pudding with tangerine essential oil
or baked apple or pears
or blackberry pie
green tea

Late-night drink

hot milk or Milo
camomile tea

Colours for Life Diet Recipes

Colour cooking adds another dimension to cooking for health and beauty. It provides complementary therapy helping to create a balance in our body and mind. Learning to cook using colour and aroma creatively can connect us to our lost feminine energy and give us the ability to eat freely again.

Use your new colour awareness to be creative and experiment – above all, have fun.

Spring Green Salad

A green salad can be a meal in itself, and can be made from the wide variety of different ingredients that reflect the many different shades of green, from the dark shades of watercress to the pale hue of spring onions.

Serves 4

10 small new potatoes
1 small lettuce
1 bunch of spring onions, cleaned and finely chopped
4 sticks celery, trimmed and chopped
½ cucumber, washed and sliced into rings
1 avocado, peeled and cut into chunks
1 bunch watercress, cleaned and chopped

Dressing
2 tbsp/2½ tbsp natural yogurt
juice of ½ a lemon
1 clove garlic, crushed
2 tbsp/2½ tbsp olive oil

Method
Boil the potatoes for 10–12 minutes until cooked, then drain. Cut them in half as soon as they are cool enough to touch. Place all the other ingredients in a bowl, adding the potatoes, then pour over the dressing and toss well. Serve while the potatoes are still warm.

Summer Green Salad

There is no taste with quite the freshness and delicacy of freshly picked French beans. Use them to make a delicious summer salad or as an ingredient of a summer stir-fry.

Serves 4

2 Little Gem lettuces, washed
1 small radicchio, washed and thinly sliced
285g/10oz French beans, washed and topped and tailed
115g/4oz walnuts, lightly crushed
225g/8oz feta cheese, crumbled

Dressing
sea salt
1 tbsp/1½ tbsp balsamic vinegar
3 tbsp/¼ C olive oil
1 clove garlic, crushed
freshly ground black pepper

Method
Arrange the lettuce and radicchio in a large bowl, then steam the beans until cooked but still crunchy (6–8 minutes). Toss with the beans, walnuts and cheese, and top the salad leaves with this mixture. To make the dressing, dissolve the salt in the balsamic vinegar, then add the other ingredients in turn. Pour over the top of the salad and mix in gently. Serve while the beans are still warm.

Autumn Green Salad

In early autumn the late courgettes are still available and the first tender leeks appear.

Serves 4

350g/12oz small courgettes, sliced thickly
6 thin leeks, trimmed and cut into slices

Dressing
350g/12oz soft cheese
1 tsp/1 tsp wholegrain mustard
1 tbsp/1½ tbsp apple cider vinegar
50ml/2fl oz/¼C olive oil

Method
Steam the vegetables for 4–5 minutes until tender but still firm, drain, and refresh in cold water. Gently mash the cheese and mustard with the vinegar to form a purée, then gradually stir in the oil until the mixture is smooth. Dress the vegetables when cool and serve.

Winter Green Salad

Root vegetables make a perfect salad for winter as they are high in fibre and full of valuable minerals and vitamins. The greens in winter are paler and reflect more white light, which we need to counteract the longer darker days. Here their slightly bitter flavour is enhanced by the sweetness of the apple and dates.

Serves 4

1 green apple, cut into wedges
115g/4oz Chinese leaves, finely chopped
225g/8oz white cabbage, finely chopped
1 rounded tsp pumpkin or sunflower seeds
115g/4oz dried dates, chopped

Dressing
2 tbsp/2½ tbsp tahini
100ml/4 fl oz/½C water
1 tsp/1 tsp wholegrain mustard
½ tsp/½ tsp creamed horseradish
sea salt and freshly ground black pepper

Method
Arrange the apple, Chinese leaves and cabbage in a bowl and sprinkle on the seeds and dates. To make the dressing, mix the tahini with about 30ml/1fl oz (1½ tbsp/2 tbsp) water, beating together until smooth, then adding the remaining water

gradually. Add the mustard and horseradish to the tahini mixture and season to taste. Swirl over the salad and serve.

Summer Menu

Apple and Cinnamon Breakfast Pancakes

These healthy and aromatic pancakes are delicious and perfect for a special breakfast.

Serves 4

Batter
225g/8oz/2C wholewheat flour
3 rounded tsp baking powder
I rounded tsp caster (superfine granulated) sugar
a pinch of salt
2 small eggs, beaten
250ml/8fl oz/1C semi-skimmed milk
I tsp/1 tsp vanilla essence
50g/2oz/¼C butter

Filling
2–3 large oranges, peeled and sliced
clear honey
cinnamon

Method
Mix together all the batter ingredients in a blender and leave to stand for 30 minutes.

Heat the griddle and lightly grease with oil. When hot, pour the batter onto the griddle to form a 15cm/6in pancake. Cook until set and turn to cook on the other side until golden brown. Layer up the pancakes with the orange slices and drizzle with honey to taste as you go. Serve the stack hot, sprinkled with cinnamon.

Spaghetti with Fiery Red Pepper Sauce

This meal is based on the colour red found in the vegetable kingdom, so while it provides you with energy it's not fattening.

This is a good late lunch if you don't want to wilt in the late afternoon. Serve it with a fresh green salad of the season to balance the energy.

Serves 4

450g/1lb brown/wholewheat spaghetti
3 tbsp/¼C olive oil
1 onion, sliced
2 garlic cloves, chopped
2 red peppers, deseeded and chopped
2 red chillies, deseeded and chopped
6 sun-dried tomatoes, soaked in water and a little wine vinegar for
    30 minutes, then chopped
100ml/4fl oz/½C water
a pinch of sugar
sea salt and freshly ground black pepper
3 rounded tbsp chopped fresh parsley
2 rounded tbsp pine nuts, toasted

Method

Bring a large pan of lightly salted water to the boil and cook the spaghetti according to the instructions on the packet until cooked but still firm (*al dente*).

Meanwhile, heat the oil in a large pan, add the onion and fry gently for 5 minutes until golden. Add the garlic, peppers and chillies and fry for a further 5 minutes until softened. Add the sun-dried tomatoes and then the measured water, the sugar and plenty of salt and pepper. Cover and simmer for 10 minutes.

Drain the pasta and return to the pan. Add the sauce and the parsley and toss well to mix. Sprinkle with the pine nuts and serve immediately.

Nasturtium Flower Salad

This striking salad is perfect for summer entertaining or when you need an extra lift. Maize pasta is excellent for people who have a wheat or gluten allergy, while the fresh raw fruit adds crunch and plenty of vitamins and beta-carotene.

Serves 2

115g/4oz maize pasta shapes, cooked, drained and thoroughly rinsed in cold water
2 carrots, coarsely grated
1 large apple, cored and chopped
1 orange, peeled and cut into segments
1 head of chicory, sliced
2 celery stalks, sliced
fresh parsley, chopped
12 nasturtium leaves
salad greens, watercress or spinach
6–8 nasturtium flowers

Dressing

1 tsp/1 tsp smooth mild mustard
1 tbsp/1½ tbsp red wine vinegar
4 tbsp/¼C tomato juice
1–2 tbsp/1½–2½ tbsp nut oil

Method

When the pasta is cold, add the carrot, apple, orange, chicory, celery and parsley. Mix together all the dressing ingredients, pour over the salad and toss it well. On a large serving dish arrange a bed of the nasturtium leaves and the salad greens, watercress or spinach, then pile the pasta on to this. Garnish with the nasturtium flowers and serve to your friends.

Spinach and Feta Cheese Pie

Spinach reflects the healing qualities of both red and green and is an excellent source of vitamin C and beta-carotene, which helps prevent cancer. It is also a good source of potassium and folate. This light but tasty pie is excellent for lunch served with a seasonal salad, or can be served for dinner with boiled new potatoes and a seasonal green salad.

Serves 4

175g/6oz/1½C wholemeal flour
a pinch of sea salt
4fl oz/½C vegetable oil, plus some for greasing

1 ½ tbsp/2 tbsp cold water
3 tbsp/¼C olive oil
800g/1¾lb spinach, washed and roughly drained
1 medium onion, peeled and finely chopped
2 cloves garlic, peeled and crushed
juice of 1 lemon
2 large eggs, beaten
2 tbsp/2½ tbsp milk
freshly ground black pepper
½ rounded tsp freshly ground nutmeg
350g/12oz feta cheese, crumbled

Method

Preheat the oven to 190°C/375°F/gas mark 5.

Sift the flour and with the salt. Stir the vegetable oil into it and mix well. Add the water and knead into a dough. Press it with your knuckles into a well-oiled 20cm/8in flan tin and bake for 10–15 minutes until lightly browned. Cool on a wire rack.

Heat the olive oil in a saucepan and add the spinach, onion and garlic. Cover and cook gently for 5 minutes, then squeeze the lemon juice over and cook for a further 5 minutes. Remove from the heat. Squeeze out any excess liquid with the back of a wooden spoon and drain this off. Mix the eggs with the milk, then season and add the nutmeg. Stir in the cheese, and stir the egg mixture into the spinach. Pour the filling into the pastry case and bake at the same temperature for 25 minutes until well brown. Serve hot, warm or cold.

Grilled Salmon with Black Olive Paste

The beautiful colour of the fresh salmon is not only a feast for the eyes but very healthy too. This dish has a contrast of textures and flavours which combine the red and blue rays to provide a balance of energy.

Serves 4

4 salmon steaks

Black olive paste
10 stoned black olives
1 clove garlic

I rounded tbsp capers
50g/2oz/¼C soft butter

Method
Blend the olives, garlic and capers until smooth, then mix in the butter and chill. Grill the salmon steaks for 6–8 minutes. Place a spoonful of black olive paste on each salmon steak and serve with a seasonal fresh green salad.

Mint Barley Sherbet

The cooling properties of mint with its soothing green energy make this a refreshing drink which also stimulates the appetite and aids digestion.

Serves 4

115g/4oz whole barley, washed in 2–3 changes of water
900ml/32fl oz/4C water
25g/1oz mint leaves, finely chopped, and a few to decorate
a pinch of salt
75g/3oz granulated sugar
juice of 3 lemons
grated rind of 1 lemon

To decorate
a few mint leaves and lemon slices

Method
Soak the barley in the water for a few minutes, add the mint, and bring to the boil, then simmer gently for 10–15 minutes. Remove from the heat and strain, reserving the liquid and discarding the barley grains. Dissolve the salt and sugar in the barley liquid, and add the lemon juice and lemon rind. Mix well and make up to 900ml/32fl oz/4C again with cold water. Pour into glasses and serve with crushed ice, a twist of lemon and mint leaves on top.

Fusilli with Two-Mushroom Sauce

Mushrooms are full of potassium which links to the violet ray. Edible fungi have been found to lower blood cholesterol and stimulate the immune system.

Serves 4

50g/2oz/¼C butter
2 cloves garlic, crushed
2 shallots, chopped
250g/½lb oyster mushrooms, washed and chopped (stalks included)
250g/½lb shiitake mushrooms, washed and chopped (stalks included)
150ml/¼ pint/⅔C thick set yogurt
sea salt and freshly ground black pepper
350g/12oz fusilli (pasta shapes)
4 rounded tbsp grated Parmesan

Method

Melt the butter in a heavy saucepan, add the garlic and shallots and allow to soften over a gentle heat. Add all the mushrooms and stir well. Cook for 3–4 minutes, then add the yogurt and season. Cover with a lid and switch off the heat.

Meanwhile, cook the pasta according to the directions on the packet. Drain well, pour the mushroom sauce over and toss well. Serve with a seasonal green salad and Italian style sun-dried tomato or olive bread; hand the Parmesan separately.

Stir-fried Summer Vegetables

The Chinese method of quickly stir-frying vegetables preserves many valuable vitamins and keeps the vegetables crisp, tasty and brightly coloured.

Serves 4

2 tbsp/2½ tbsp groundnut oil
3 cloves garlic
250g/8oz yellow peppers, deseeded and sliced
250g/8oz courgettes, sliced lengthways

250g/8oz baby carrots, halved lengthways
100ml/4fl oz/½C vegetable stock
1 tbsp/1½ tbsp tarragon or rice vinegar
2 tbsp/2½ tbsp soy sauce
125g/4oz mangetout
1 bunch of spring onions, chopped finely

Method

Heat the oil in a wok or frying pan. Add the garlic, and stir-fry over a medium heat for 30 seconds. Add the peppers, courgettes and carrots and stir-fry for about 5 minutes until they soften. Add the stock, vinegar, soy sauce and mangetout and cover. Steam cook the vegetables for a further 2–3 minutes until tender but still crunchy. Sprinkle over the spring onions and serve at once, either with fish or with rice.

Winter Menu

Tomato Soup with Sage

Rich in carotenoids, red or golden sage helps reduce the risk of cancer and was traditionally used to treat liver and kidney complaints. The red in the tomatoes and sage also stimulates the life-force energy through the kidneys.

Serves 4

900ml/32fl oz/4C vegetable stock
2 cloves garlic, peeled and left whole
350g/12oz tomato purée
1 rounded tsp chopped fresh sage leaves or ½ rounded tsp dried sage
1–2 rounded tsp brown sugar
1 tbsp/1½ tbsp red wine vinegar
1 tbsp/1½ tbsp soy sauce
300ml/½ pint/1¼C milk
sea salt and freshly ground black pepper

To serve
4 tbsp/⅓C pouring yogurt
a few fresh sage leaves or sprigs of parsley

Method

Pour the stock into a large saucepan, add the garlic, bring to the boil and add the tomato purée. Add the sage, sugar, vinegar and soy sauce. Bring to the boil again and simmer for 10 minutes, stirring occasionally. Let the soup cool slightly and add the milk. Season well and reheat, being careful not to boil. Serve hot, garnished with a swirl of yogurt and sage or parsley leaves.

Penne with Chestnut Sauce

An unusual low-calorie golden lunch which will give you an energy boost from the carbohydrates and protein it contains. Serve it with a seasonal green salad.

Serves 4

350g/12oz penne
1 tsp/1 tsp olive oil
1 small red chilli, deseeded and chopped
100g/3½oz unsweetened chestnut purée
100ml/4fl oz/½C vegetable stock
50g/2oz cooked chestnuts, roughly chopped
1 × 375g/12oz can flageolet beans, drained
1 rounded tsp chopped thyme
sea salt and freshly ground black pepper

Garnish
paprika
sprigs of flat-leafed parsley

Method

Bring to the boil a large open pan of salted water and cook the penne according to the instructions on the packet.

Meanwhile, heat the oil in a frying pan and gently fry the chilli for about 2 minutes. Add the chestnut purée and vegetable stock and gently stir to make a sauce. Stir in the chestnuts, flageolet beans and thyme, and season well. Cook for a further 5 minutes.

By now the penne should be cooked; drain it and toss it in the chestnut sauce. Sprinkle with paprika and garnish with sprigs of parsley, and serve immediately.

Winter Mixed Vegetable Curry

This mild and sweet curry is excellent for a winter lunch. It has a dry consistency, so team it up with red lentil dahl to make a filling and energizing meal. For a lighter meal eat it on its own with some nan bread.

Serves 4

½ cauliflower, washed and cut into florets
2 medium potatoes, washed and peeled
a half-pumpkin, washed and peeled
3 long carrots, washed
2 stems broccoli, washed
3 tbsp/¼C vegetable oil
½ rounded tsp cumin seeds
25g/1oz frozen peas
1½ rounded tsp salt
½ rounded tsp sugar
¼ rounded tsp paprika
¼ rounded tsp turmeric
¼ rounded tsp chilli powder
25g/1oz raisins or sultanas

Method
Prepare all the fresh vegetables by cutting them into 2cm/¾in cubes. Heat the oil in a saucepan and add the cumin seeds. Add all the fresh vegetables and the frozen peas, the salt, sugar, paprika, chilli powder and turmeric. Fry for 5 minutes stirring well. Cover the saucepan, add the raisins or sultanas, and simmer for 15 minutes. The curry is ready when the vegetables are cooked through. (Please note that no water is added to this curry.)

Red Lentil Dahl

Although this is made with red lentils, when cooked the dahl takes on a rich golden yellow colouring. Lentils contain 25 per cent protein and are an important meat substitute. They also have the lowest fat content of any protein-rich food.

Serves 4

225g/8oz/1C red lentils, washed in three changes of water
350ml/12fl oz/1½C water
¼ rounded tsp ground turmeric
1 rounded tsp ground coriander
1 green chilli, halved
sea salt
4–6 canned tomatoes, chopped
2 sprigs fresh coriander, leaves only, chopped
50g/2oz/¼C butter
1 small onion, peeled and finely chopped

Method

Put the lentils into a pan with the water, cover, and cook over a low heat for 10–15 minutes. Remove any froth with a spoon. When the lentils are tender and yellow, blend until smooth with an egg whisk, then add the turmeric, ground coriander, chilli, salt and tomatoes. Cover and simmer for 10 minutes, then add the coriander leaves and pour into a dish. Keep warm while you melt the butter in a frying pan and sauté the onion until golden brown.

Pour the onions and buttery juices over the dahl and serve with rice or bread.

Sunshine Orange Pancakes

These orange-layered pancakes are perfect for a special occasion such as a celebration brunch. The bright gold and orange of the honey and oranges make for a mouth-watering start to the day and are guaranteed to leave you feeling uplifted and joyful. As this dish includes some sugar and butter it is better to eat it late morning when your digestion will be stronger.

Serves 4

225g/8oz/2C plain (all-purpose) flour
3 rounded tsp baking powder
1 rounded tsp caster (superfine granulated) sugar
a pinch of salt
2 small eggs, beaten
250ml/8fl oz/1C semi-skimmed milk

1 tsp/1 tsp vanilla essence
50g/2oz/¼C butter

Filling
2–3 large oranges, peeled and cut into round segments
clear honey

Method
Sift the dry ingredients into a bowl. Beat the eggs in gradually, then the milk and vanilla essence. Beat until smooth. Melt half the butter and stir into the batter mixture. Heat the griddle and lightly grease with some of the remaining butter. When hot, pour the batter onto the griddle to form a 15cm/6in pancake. Cook until set and turn to cook on the other side until golden brown.

Layer up the pancakes with orange segments and honey, and garnish with a few more orange segments and a knob of butter.

Honey and Soy Grilled Chicken

Honey is full of iron; the darker the honey, the more iron it contains. It also contains C and B-complex vitamins, and it imparts a beautiful golden sheen to the chicken to make an appetizing dish.

Serves 4

4 free-range chicken pieces

Marinade
2 tbsp/2½ tbsp runny honey
1 tbsp/1 tbsp light soy sauce
1 tbsp/1 tbsp lemon juice
1 clove garlic, peeled and crushed

Method
Mix the marinade ingredients together and brush the chicken pieces with it. Pre-heat a grill to maximum, then lower the heat to medium-hot. Grill the chicken, turning once, and serve with wild rice.

Leek and Mushroom Lasagne

This delicious lasagne is a winter favourite, and because it contains no cheese it is low in saturated fat. Serve it with a crunchy salad.

Serves 4

1 ½tbsp/2 tbsp sunflower oil
450g/1lb leeks, finely chopped
225g/8oz mushrooms, finely sliced
2 × 400g/14oz cans chopped tomatoes, without their juice
1 ½ rounded tbsp finely chopped marjoram (sweet marjoram)
1 tsp/1 tsp tamari sauce (soy sauce)
sea salt and freshly ground black pepper
175g/6oz pre-cooked lasagne sheets
225g/8oz natural yogurt
½ rounded tsp of paprika

Method
Preheat the oven to 200°C/400°F/gas mark 6.

Heat the oil and cook the leeks gently for 10 minutes. Add the mushrooms, tomatoes, marjoram and tamari sauce. Cook for a further 3 minutes and then season. Remove from the heat.

Place a layer of this mixture at the bottom of a baking dish and cover with lasagne sheets. Add some more sauce and then another layer of lasagne.

Finish with a layer of lasagne. Pour the natural yogurt over the top to cover all the lasagne, and sprinkle on the paprika. Bake for 40 minutes until the pasta is cooked. The topping should be slightly browned.

Turkey with Watercress Sauce

Watercress is a wonderful diuretic but also a digestive stimulant. It helps counteract anaemia and lowers the blood-sugar levels in diabetes. This is a bright green sauce, with a delicate flavour which also goes well with chicken breasts. Cook it briefly so it doesn't lose its flavour.

Serves 2

25g/1oz/2 tbsp butter
2 turkey breasts
2 cloves garlic, peeled and crushed
1 shallot, peeled and finely chopped
2 tbsp/2½ tbsp white wine vinegar
150ml/¼ pint/⅔C chicken or vegetable stock
85g/3oz watercress
100ml/4fl oz/½C crème fraiche
1 egg yolk

Method
Melt the butter in a large frying pan and then fry the turkey breasts over a medium heat for about 5 minutes on each side. Remove and keep warm. Transfer all the contents to a saucepan and when hot add the garlic and the shallot to the pan and cook until softened. Add the vinegar, then after a few seconds add the stock and bring to the boil. Add the watercress, cover, and heat very briefly until wilted. Blend in a food processor until just smooth, then return to the pan and stir in the crème fraiche and egg yolk, and any juices from the meat. Boil gently for 1–2 minutes. Return the cooked turkey breasts to the sauce and heat through. Serve immediately with creamed parsnips.

Creamed Parsnips

In Roman times, parsnips were considered an aphrodisiac; certainly this orange-yellow dish stimulates the senses.

Serves 4

225g/8oz parsnips, peeled and diced
225g/8oz potatoes, peeled and diced
sea salt
2 tbsp/2½ tbsp milk
freshly ground black pepper
15g/½oz/1 tbsp butter
2 rounded tsp grated orange rind
2 rounded tsp chopped parsley

Method

Boil the parsnips and potatoes together in plenty of lightly salted water until cooked, allowing a little longer for the potatoes. Drain, and bring the milk to the boil in the pan. Immediately remove from the heat, and in it mash the potatoes, parsnips, pepper and butter together. Add the orange rind and parsley, and serve immediately.

Date Rice Pudding

A warming and soothing winter dessert is wonderfully comforting and has a big feel-good factor. Packed with vitamins and minerals and also protein and carbohydrates, this one is a meal in itself.

Serves 4

170g/6oz/¾C brown rice, cooked
250ml/8fl oz/1C–500ml/16fl oz/2C milk (or soya milk or buttermilk)
50g/2oz chopped nuts
100g/4oz raisins
100g/4oz chopped dates
a pinch of sea salt
a dash of lemon juice
3 drops of Palma Rosa essential oil

To serve
toasted coconut

Method

Combine all the ingredients, place in a greased oven dish, and bake in a preheated oven at 180°C/350°F/gas mark 4 for 45 minutes. Serve warm, topped with toasted coconut.

Vegetarian Summer Menu

Couscous

This hearty dish reflects the nourishing qualities of the golden ray, providing you with slow-burning energy. Chickpeas have a massive 20 per cent protein content and are an important meat substitute. They also are a good source of manganese, iron, folate and vitamin A. Serve the couscous with the thyme and poppy seed oatcakes or granary bread.

Serves 4

350g/12oz couscous
3 tbsp/¼C sunflower oil
1 medium onion, peeled and quartered
2 cloves garlic, peeled and crushed
4 small courgettes
1 yellow pepper, deseeded and sliced
6 small potatoes, scrubbed and chopped
4 medium carrots, peeled and sliced lengthways
1 small turnip, peeled and sliced
4 medium tomatoes, chopped
100g/3½oz chickpeas, cooked and drained
125g/4oz raisins, soaked in warm water for 10 minutes and drained
2 rounded tsp coriander
2 rounded tsp ground cumin
1 rounded tsp ground turmeric
sea salt

Method

Put the couscous in a large bowl and stir in 300ml/½ pint/1¼C water. Drain immediately and stand for 15 minutes, giving it an occasional stir to prevent it going lumpy.

Heat the oil in a large saucepan, add the onion, garlic, courgettes, pepper, potatoes, carrots and turnip and stir over a moderate heat for 10 minutes. Add 575ml/1 pint/2½C water and bring to the boil. Put the couscous in a sieve and place it over the boiling vegetables, covering it with a lid. Simmer for 30 minutes then remove. Stir into the vegetables the tomatoes, chickpeas, raisins and spices, and season with salt. Replace the couscous above the vegetables and simmer for a further 10 minutes, stirring occasionally. Drain off some of the liquid into a jug and serve on the side. Stir the spices and salt into the couscous, and serve it covered with the vegetables.

Thyme and Poppy Seed Oatcakes

These delicious and aromatic oatcakes are a good alternative to bread. They make a perfect partner for salads, cheeses, soups and vegetable dishes. The thyme and poppy seeds reflect the blue ray, so these oatcakes would be also be suitable for an evening meal.

Makes 6

250g/8oz porridge oats
1 rounded tbsp dried thyme
½ rounded tsp bicarbonate of soda
1 rounded tsp salt
25g/1oz/2 tbsp butter or margarine
1 egg yolk
1 rounded tbsp poppy seeds

Method

Preheat the oven to 180°C/350°F/gas mark 4 and grease a 20cm/8in flan tin with vegetable oil. Mix the oats and thyme with the bicarbonate of soda and salt. Rub in the butter or margarine and stir in the egg yolk, then mix to a soft dough with a little hot water and knead until smooth. Press into the flan tin, sprinkle over the poppy seeds and bake for 30 minutes. Mark into 6 triangles with a sharp knife, and allow to cool.

Tabbouleh with Marigold Flowers

A wholesome light lunch with a refreshing taste of mint and lemon. The colours are based on the centre rays of gold, yellow and green.

Serves 4

85g/3oz bulgar wheat or millet
50g/2oz flat-leafed parsley, chopped
25g/1oz mint, chopped
juice of 2 lemons
2 tbsp/2½ tbsp olive oil
sea salt and freshly ground pepper
4 small spring onions, trimmed and chopped

3 peppers (1 green, 1 yellow and 1 red), deseeded and diced
½ cucumber, cubed
12 marigold flowers

Method

Cover the bulgar wheat or millet with cold water and leave for 15 minutes to soak. Meanwhile, place the parsley and mint in a salad bowl with the lemon juice, olive oil, salt and a little pepper. Toss the spring onions, peppers and cucumber into the herbs and dressing. Squeeze the water from the bulgar wheat or millet with your hands, and put the grains into the salad bowl. Mix thoroughly with the vegetables and herbs. Decorate with the marigold flowers around the top and serve.

Red Rice and Mushroom Patties

These patties contain a balance of red and blue energy. Serve with a seasonal mixed green salad or green beans for a slow-burn energy-packed lunch.

Serves 4

140g/5oz/1⅓C red Camargue rice
4 tbsp/6 tbsp olive oil
300g/10oz button mushrooms, sliced
2 onions, finely chopped
115g/4oz plain organic flour
100ml/4fl oz/½C milk
100ml/4fl oz/½C thick-set Greek yogurt
2 large eggs
½ rounded tsp grated nutmeg
sea salt and freshly ground black pepper
2 cloves garlic, crushed
1 × 400g/14oz can plum tomatoes, roughly chopped, with their juice
2 rounded tbsp chopped basil

Method

Cook the rice according to the instructions on the packet and drain. Meanwhile, in a pan heat 1 tbsp/1½ tbsp of the olive oil, add the mushrooms and half the onions, and fry gently for 6 minutes, stirring. In a bowl, whisk together the flour, milk, yogurt, eggs and nutmeg. Season, and stir in the mushroom mixture and rice.

To make the sauce, heat 1 tbsp/1½ tbsp olive oil in a pan, add the remaining onions and the garlic, and cook for 3 minutes. Add the tomatoes and their juice. Bring to the boil and simmer for 10 minutes then add most of the basil and season.

Heat the remaining oil in a frying pan. Form 4 tbsp/⅓C of the patty mixture into a round patty and cook briskly for 2–3 minutes on each side. Repeat to make eight in total. Serve with the tomato sauce, garnished with the rest of the basil.

Tempura with Sweet–Sour Dip

This Japanese-inspired dish is made from light, crispy, fried vegetables, served with a thin dip. The colours it reflects will depend on the vegetables used, but for supper choose pale yellow, white, green and purple food. To serve as a lunch dish include more warm-coloured vegetables.

Serves 4

675g/1½lb mixed fresh vegetables cut into chunks – green peppers, baby
   sweetcorn, asparagus, onion, broccoli
vegetable oil for frying

Dip
85g/3oz caster (superfine granulated) sugar
100ml/4fl oz/½C pure water
3 tbsp/¼C rice wine vinegar
2 red chillies, deseeded and sliced
3 rounded tbsp chopped fresh coriander

Batter
2 medium eggs, separated
140g/5oz plain (all-purpose) flour, sifted
250ml/8fl oz/1C pure water
a pinch of sea salt

Method
To make the dip, put the sugar in a pan with the water and bring to the boil, stirring until the sugar has dissolved, then boil rapidly

for 8 minutes until syrupy. Remove from the heat and stir in the vinegar, chillies and coriander and leave to cool. To make the batter, beat the egg yolks, flour, water and salt until smooth. Whisk the egg whites until stiff and fold into the batter mixture.

Heat the oil until a piece of bread turns golden brown in 30 seconds. Dip the vegetables one at a time into the batter, dropping them in turn in the hot oil. Fry for 2–3 minutes until crisp. Remove, drain on kitchen paper and keep warm. Add more vegetables until they are all cooked.

Serve the vegetables hot with the dip.

Kedgeree of Summer Vegetables

A feast of textures and flavours reflecting the many qualities of the colour green. The green lentils and rice combine to make a perfect light but nutritious protein meal.

Serves 4

3 tbsp/¼C vegetable oil
1 rounded tbsp cumin seeds
4 cloves
4 cardamom seeds
4 black peppercorns
2.5cm/1in cinnamon stick
1 rounded tsp turmeric
5cm/2in piece of root ginger, peeled and grated
2 large onions, peeled and chopped
450ml/¾ pint/14fl oz water
115g/4oz/½C green lentils, soaked for a few hours and drained
115g/4oz/½C basmati rice
170g/6oz each of any 4 summer vegetables (eg peas, new potatoes, French beans, mangetout, courgettes), chopped
sea salt

Method

Heat the oil in a large saucepan and briskly fry all the spices except the turmeric and ginger. Then after 2–3 minutes lower the heat, add the turmeric, ginger and onion and cook for 1–2 minutes, stirring well. Add the water, bring to the boil, and stir in the lentils, rice and vegetables and simmer, covered, for 15–20 minutes or until the rice is cooked. Season to taste and allow the kedgeree to stand for several minutes so that the flavours can develop. Serve hot or cold as a side dish.

Stuffed Green Peppers

This delicious summer dish is striking in shape and colour especially when combined with a purple salad. Green peppers are full of vitamin C, flavonoids and beta-carotene, protecting against cancer.

Serves 4

2 tbsp/2½ tbsp olive oil
2 cloves garlic, peeled and chopped
1 onion, peeled and chopped
2 courgettes, trimmed and finely diced
1 × 400g/14oz can plum tomatoes
sea salt
2 tbsp/2½ tbsp balsamic vinegar
150g/2oz long-grain brown rice, cooked
50g/2oz stoned black olives, halved
1 rounded tbsp chopped wild marjoram
1 rounded tbsp chopped marjoram (sweet marjoram)
4 large green peppers
extra olive oil for drizzling

Method
Preheat the oven to 180°C/350°F/gas mark 4.

Heat the olive oil in a large pan and add the garlic and onion. Gently fry for 3–5 minutes until the onion begins to brown. Add the courgettes and tomatoes and season with salt. Bring to the boil then simmer for 10–15 minutes until the tomato mixture is slightly thickened, then remove from the heat and add the balsamic vinegar. Add the rice, olives and herbs.

Slice the stalk end from each pepper and reserve. Gently ease the seeds and ribs from the peppers and discard. Spoon the rice mixture into the peppers and stand them upright in a roasting tin, securing them in position with some crumbled foil between them, and place the tops back on top.

Bake for 35 minutes (drizzle a little olive oil over the peppers if they begin to dry out during cooking): they should be softened and just beginning to brown. Serve warm or cold with a salad.

Purple Summer Salad

A jewel of a salad – each colour intensifies the healing qualities of the others. It contains ruby lettuce, purple chicory and purple, white and golden pansies.

Serves 4

1 ruby lettuce, washed and dried
1 head of purple chicory, washed and dried
12 radishes, washed and dried
a bunch of chives, washed and dried
6 purple, white and yellow pansies

Dressing
4 tbsp/⅓C rice wine vinegar
4 tbsp/⅓C light olive or sunflower oil
1 tsp/1 tsp runny honey

Method
Arrange the lettuce, chicory, radishes and chives on a plate and decorate with the pansies. Mix together the dressing ingredients, pour over the salad and serve.

Walnut and Mushroom Risotto

A delicate but pungent dish which was considered an aphrodisiac not because it is physically stimulating but because of its euphoric mood-enhancing qualities. It is based on the colours of gold and indigo/violet.

Serves 4

2 tbsp/2½ tbsp olive oil
1 onion, finely chopped
375g/13oz risotto rice (Arborio or Carnaroli), unwashed
900ml/32fl oz/4C vegetable stock

225g/8oz shiitake or oyster mushrooms, chopped
75g/3oz/½C chopped walnuts
6 cloves
¼ rounded tsp grated nutmeg
sea salt
I tbsp/1½ tbsp thick-set natural yogurt
chopped fresh parsley

Method

Heat the olive oil in a large saucepan. Add the onion and fry gently for about 5 minutes until golden. Add the rice and stir well to coat the grains thoroughly, then add about 100ml/4fl oz/½C hot stock. Stir well over a medium-high heat until all the stock has been absorbed or evaporated, then add another 100ml/4fl oz/½C stock and continue to stir well, adding more stock each time it is all absorbed. After about 10 minutes, add the mushrooms, walnuts, and spices and continue cooking, adding more stock, until the rice is creamily tender but still firm. Remove from the heat, leave to stand for 1–2 minutes, then season, stir in the yogurt, remove the cloves and serve garnished with parsley.

Blueberry Buttermilk Pancakes

A delicious dessert to complete an evening meal. The blue and green rays are reflected in the blueberries and buttermilk, making this a soothing and feel-good dessert. You can also use blackberries for an excellent result.

Serves 4

225g/8oz/2C plain (all-purpose) flour
1½ rounded tsp bicarbonate of soda
½ rounded tsp sea salt
2 rounded tbsp brown sugar
2 medium eggs
500ml/16fl oz/2C buttermilk (at room temperature)
2 tbsp/2½ tbsp melted butter
200g fresh ripe blueberries or blackberries

To serve
icing sugar for dusting
maple syrup or fresh lemon juice and sugar

Method

Sift together the flour, bicarbonate of soda, salt and sugar into a bowl, add the eggs, buttermilk and melted butter and beat lightly with a whisk until smooth. Leave to rest for 30 minutes. Just before cooking, toss in the blueberries or blackberries, reserving a few for garnish.

Heat a non-stick frying pan or griddle over a medium heat – you may need to wipe it with butter or oil to prevent sticking. Ladle enough mixture into the pan to form 10cm/4in diameter pancakes and cook for 3–4 minutes, until bubbles appear on the surface and the edges turn golden brown. Turn and cook the other side for 2 minutes. Keep the pancakes warm as you cook the rest, then to serve sprinkle them with icing sugar and the uncooked blueberries or blackberries. Hand round maple syrup or fresh lemon juice and sugar separately.

Winter Vegetarian Menu

Lentil Soup

An easy to prepare warming and nutritious soup, which is given an extra zing by the green chilli. Eat it on its own for lunch or with some wholemeal bread for supper.

Serves 4

350g/12oz/1½C red lentils, washed in three changes of water and drained
900ml/32fl oz/4C water
15g/½oz/1 tbsp butter
1 medium onion, peeled and chopped
4 canned tomatoes, drained, chopped and crushed
1 green chilli, deseeded and sliced
2 tbsp/2½ tbsp natural yogurt
sea salt and freshly ground black pepper
1–2 sprigs coriander, leaves only, chopped

Method

Put the lentils into a pan with the water. Cover, bring to the boil, and simmer for 10 minutes. Melt the butter in a small pan and fry the onion until golden brown. Beat the lentils until smooth with an egg whisk. Add the tomatoes and chilli and simmer gently for 2 minutes. Stir in the yogurt.

Season the hot soup and pour into a serving bowl. Sprinkle the top with the fried onion and its juices and the coriander.

Mixed Vegetable Curry

The flavouring of this curry is subtle and aromatic and based on the spices and the texture of coconut, which adds a creamy texture and cooling effect. Vary the vegetables according to the season and time of day.

Serves 4

25g/1oz creamed coconut or 2 rounded tbsp desiccated coconut
300ml½ pint/1¼C boiling water
675g/1½lb mixed vegetables (cauliflower, potatoes, courgettes, white cabbage, mushrooms, broccoli, carrots, parsnips), chopped
30 ml/2 tbsp sunflower oil
2 onions, peeled and chopped
3 rounded tsp garam masala
575ml/1 pint/2½C lentil purée (drain and purée a 397g/14oz can of brown or green lentils)

Method

Pour the water over the coconut and leave to dissolve. Lightly steam or boil the vegetables, then drain and put to one side.

Heat the oil in a saucepan and cook the onions for a few minutes until soft. Stir in the garam masala, simmer for 1 minute, and then gradually add the coconut milk. Add the vegetables and heat through, then add the lentil purée and mix well. Allow the curry to stand for 5 minutes with the lid on, for the flavours to blend, and serve with jasmine rice or nan bread.

Aubergine Stew with Capers

This is a good dinner for a late summer or autumn evening. Its warming rays of violet, red and yellow are balanced by the indigo ray found in the olives and sultanas and the green ray of the capers.

Serves 4

3–4 small aubergines, cut into large pieces
1 yellow pepper, deseeded and cut into large pieces
5–6 ripe tomatoes, peeled and cut into large pieces
2–3 celery sticks, chopped
1 large onion, peeled and sliced
12 large black olives, stoned
2 rounded tbsp sultanas, soaked
2 rounded tbsp capers, drained
1 tbsp/1½ tbsp clear honey
2 tbsp/2½ tbsp olive oil
1 tbsp/1 tbsp white wine vinegar
sea salt

Method
Put all the ingredients except the vinegar and salt in a large sauce-pan, stir together well, cover, and cook over a high heat for 10 minutes until the vegetables have softened.

Add the vinegar and season with salt. Reduce the heat slightly, cover and simmer gently for another 30 minutes or until all the vegetables are tender. Serve hot with fresh wholegrain bread, or with rice.

Potato and Bean Stew

This hearty meal is full of magnetic earth energy. Although potatoes are high in carbohydrate they contain both protein and fibre, so are not fattening. You can vary this recipe by using different coloured potatoes and beans, which will also influence the energetic quality of this meal. Red and brown colours are warming and strengthening, making them good for a lunch-time stew, whilst purple and blue would be more suitable for a meal on a winter's evening.

Serves 4

1 tbsp/1 tbsp olive oil
1 small onion, peeled and chopped
1 clove garlic, peeled and chopped
675g/1½lb waxy potatoes, peeled and cubed

1.1 litres/2 pints/5C vegetable stock
50g/2oz Savoy cabbage, shredded
2 × 400g/14oz cans borlotti beans, drained
2 rounded tsp chopped parsley
sea salt and freshly ground black pepper

Method
Heat the oil in a large pan and cook the onion and garlic for 5 minutes until softened, then add the potatoes and fry for 2 minutes. Pour in the stock, cover, and simmer for 15 minutes. Add the cabbage and two-thirds of the beans and simmer for 10 minutes, then remove a third of the potatoes and mash well with the reserved beans. Return to the pan, stir in the parsley and season. Ladle the stew into bowls and serve with crusty bread or couscous.

Stewed Apple and Fig Crumble

This spicy crumble is a real after-dinner treat on a cold winter's night, and although it is filling the figs and apples do not overload the liver. Figs are high in potassium and fibre and together with the apples will cleanse the system while you are asleep.

Serves 4

225g/8oz/2C flour
a pinch each of cinnamon, allspice, ginger and nutmeg
115g/4oz/½C butter
50g/2oz/⅓C chopped nuts or seeds
1 kg/2½lb green apples, peeled, sliced and lightly stewed
225g/8oz dried figs, chopped

Method
Mix the flour with the spices, then rub in the butter to form a crumble. Add the chopped nuts or seeds and sprinkle on top of lightly stewed green apples and dried figs. Bake at 180°C/350°F/gas mark 4 for 20 minutes until the crumble is browned.

How to Solarize Food and Water

It is not a new idea to use the sun to energize food and drink. Thousands of years ago, the ancient Egyptians placed beautiful jewel-encrusted bowls containing cooking and aromatic oils, food, water and medicine in sunlight so that the sun would increase their potency. In India to this day there are sophisticated systems of sun-ray therapy whereby people lie in baths of coloured water in the sunlight.

We can all take positive measures towards improving our own health and rectifying colour imbalances by drinking solarized water. Water that has been solarized in glass of a particular colour will contain concentrated, potent quantities of that colour's vibration, which can be used for healing. Therefore, by selecting the colour of the container, you will be able to determine the healing properties of water that has been solarized in it. Solarizing water with the energy of a particular ray could not be simpler, as today coloured glass is gaining popularity, and there is a large selection of beautiful blue, red, yellow and green recycled glass available in the shops suitable for this purpose. Many modern manufacturers also bottle water, drinks, lotions, creams and bath oils in blue or green glass as they know that this makes these items more appealing. However, they may not be aware how these colours will also affect the taste, quality and freshness of their product, whereas if you solarize your own drinking water you can use colour consciously in ways that will benefit you personally. You will notice that animals prefer to drink solarized water, and pets often drink from ponds and streams in preference to tap water. Your pet will benefit if you give it pure filter water, especially if you energize it first.

To energize water you should use only natural spring water (commercial brands should be labelled 'bottled at source' to ensure their purity), as tap water has many chemical additives. You can either use a coloured glass bottle to place the water in, or you can wrap a coloured acetate or plastic filter around a glass or bottle. Place this in the sunlight for 30–60 minutes. You do not have to have full sunshine for the water to absorb the sun's rays, but natural light is a prerequisite. The water can be kept in the fridge for a day or two, but it works best when freshly solarized and should be consumed the same day for maximum effect. Use glass rather than plastic as it is a natural product allowing the sun's rays to penetrate into the contents without interference.

For your daily intake you should first make sure the water is pure before empowering it with light energy. Once you have solarized it according to your needs, drink the desired colour every day for a week or until you feel that you are back to a more balanced harmonious state. If you need more than one colour energy, alternate the glasses of differently 'coloured' solarized water. Drink water that has been solarized with one colour on the first day, the second colour on the second day, and so on.

The magnetic colours (red, orange, yellow, magenta) can be drunk by the tumblerful, but not more than half a glassful at a time of the electrical colours (green, blue, indigo, violet) should be taken – and then only in sips.

You can use the complementary colours if there is any over-reaction to the original colour. These complementary colours are different from the standard model, as I have used a colour wheel with eight colours – the seven rainbow colours and magenta – not six. I blame Isaac Newton, who divided the spectrum into seven instead of six colours, by including indigo. In order to complete the wheel we add a mixture of violet and red, magenta.

RED is complementary to BLUE
ORANGE is complementary to INDIGO
YELLOW is complementary to VIOLET
GREEN is complementary to MAGENTA

Water that has been solarized with the different colours can be used in many different ways.

Red

Use if you're lethargic or lacking in energy, or if your hands and feet are blue. One tumblerful is helpful for anaemia. It will help raise low blood pressure and is also good for sciatica. *Do not use* if you are hyperactive, suffer from heart trouble, high blood pressure or varicose veins, or have violent tempers as the red ray can over-stimulate.

Orange

Use to free phlegm from the system, for asthma and for wet coughs, fever, digestive problems, difficult menstruation, kidney problems and colitis. Bathe boils and abscesses in orange-energized rain water as this has a drawing action. Orange is a good tonic, and builds up the immune system, so drink orange-energized water if you are tired, suffering from stress, or just need an energy boost.

Yellow

Yellow energy promotes the flow of vital fluids and also stimulates the spleen, pancreas liver and kidneys. It has a purifying effect and cleans sluggish conditions, especially constipation. Yellow-energized water stimulates the mind and clear thinking, and reduces memory loss, so it is a good idea to drink yellow water before an exam, interview or talk or lecture.

Turquoise and Green

These colours reflect soothing and healing qualities. Turquoise is sparkling and refreshing and is good for using to revive a tired mind or when you want freshening up. Green is a good nerve sedative and is particularly useful during times of emotional stress or shock. It relieves head colds, hay fever and neuralgia.

Blue

One of the most useful solarized water colours is blue. Blue-solarized water is a great healer. You can find many blue bottles in the shops these days, and it is a good idea to keep a freshly energized one in your household medicine chest. Blue soothes, cools and lowers temperatures: take three times a day before meals for hot flushes, fever, or any problem where there is heat in the body. It is wonderful if dabbed on cuts, stings, bites or burns, or rubbed on the skin to treat rashes or inflammation. Blue water is also good for any problems of the nose, ears or eyes, and gargling with blue water has a dramatic effect on a sore throat, which heals very quickly. Soak two cotton-wool pads in the blue-solarized water and put them over your eyelids for a soothing refreshing relief for tired or sore eyes. Sip half a wineglassful daily before a meal for colitis or biliousness, and for kidney problems and diarrhoea.

Indigo

Bathe sore, tired or inflamed eyes and place a cloth dipped in indigo-energized water on the forehead for a headache or migraine. Drink it to cool the system and after sunstroke. Use indigo-energized water for a sore throat if blue is not strong enough.

Magenta

Sip magenta water for the skin, especially if it is dry, and also take some as a gentle stimulant for lack of energy.

Solarizing Other Types of Food and Drink

If you want to experiment and solarize other types of food and drink, there are many options; for example, milk can be solarized in a jug, with the appropriate filter, on the window sill for half an hour – but don't leave it too long or it will sour! You can solarize cooking oils, especially if you also place herbs in them so that they infuse the flavour and quality of the herb through the oil. Other solid foodstuffs can be solarized as well; sun-dried tomatoes and dried fruit are good example of this and the latter should especially be included in our diet. The colour ray of the food, herb or oil should be the same as or complementary to the colour ray with which you're solarizing it, to reinforce its healing power.

You can also try solarizing vinegar, vitamin supplements, flower essences and carrier oils for essential oils. The Colours for Life Diet is all about experimentation and variation, about finding out what suits *you* best.

6 | Creating a Colours for Life Diet to Suit Your Own Needs

Meeting Your Energy Requirements

In recent years some members of the scientific and medical communities have come to the conclusion that the physiology of the human body is designed so that the natural lifespan should be about 150 years. It would be possible to live this long if only we were able to maintain perfect health. Factors such as our emotions, environment and levels of stress affect longevity, as do the foods and liquids we consume. So creating a harmonious and balanced lifestyle that involves adapting our diet could have a great effect on our ability to live disease-free to a ripe old age.

When planning a colour menu, you should take into consideration your lifestyle, and what you learnt in chapter 4, especially pages 75–9, 'Harmonizing Our Diet with Our Biorhythms'.

You may, for example, want to make a warming meal which stimulates the body's systems: a meal based on orange or red does wonders on cold days, or for those with bad circulation or depression. A meal of soothing green and purple, on the other hand, will cool the body and calm the nerves. To help the mental faculties for work or study, you can make sure you eat a heartening yellow meal. However, in all of these cases be aware that you are only eating food of a particular colour to boost that colour energy in your energy centres in the body. Once you have regenerated that colour centre, you can reduce the proportion of that colour food in the meal, returning to a plate with a variety of colours in it. Balance is the key with colour cooking.

Children's Meals and Cooking for the Elderly

The elderly and the young can benefit greatly from colour cooking: colourful aromatic meals aid alertness and renew interest in life. Is it any wonder that school children, the ill and the elderly, when subjected to watery, pale, overcooked institutional food, lack energy, have poor concentration and show little interest in life? As well as being unappetizing, the loss of natural colour confirms the loss of essential vitamins and minerals.

Older people may find raw food and wholegrains difficult to chew and digest but can enjoy nourishing drinks make of pure fruit and vegetable juices. Stewed fruit and lightly cooked vegetables will give them ample nutrients while nourishing their subtle bodies.

Many children say their vegetables are horrible! Unfortunately, if they're fed processed or dehydrated vegetables, or some frozen types, they're right. If you're cooking for children, introduce them to fresh, organically grown fruit and vegetables early, so that their palates will become educated to the subtle and delicious taste of fresh foods. If they get used to eating salty and heavily spiced foods, these will destroy their tastebuds so that everything else – especially vegetables – seems tasteless by comparison. Steer clear, however, of the old maxim, 'Eat your greens, they are good for you!' Yes, greens are good for you, but if your children don't like particular vegetables, don't force them–try other foods of the same colour or present the food in a different way.

Remember that children respond instinctively to colour. Encourage them from an early age to look for colours on their plate. Does the dinner have any food which is yellow or orange in it? Is there something green on the plate? Colour on the plate should be appetizing and fun, and by using the psychology of colour and the nutritional value of food as revealed by its colour you can produce a meal that is both healthy and appetizing in appearance for all the family. After all, two-thirds of appetite is anticipation, so food should look as good as it tastes. The colour of the food starts a chain reaction, causing saliva in our mouths and our stomach juices to be released aiding digestion and eventually energizing our bodies.

The variety of colours in food can provide all of us with a balanced diet, as long as we eat live energy rich foods. These will give our bodies the best chance of absorbing and obtaining all the nutrition they needs to stay healthy. We will be feeding not only our bodies but our minds and spirits.

Eating Patterns and Weight Loss

If you are constantly eating food of one particular type or colour, your body may be craving something contained in that particular food. You will need to establish whether your need is emotional or sensual, or for something desired by your body. Look at any physical and emotional problems you may have, and this will indicate the reason why you crave it.

Most of our eating patterns are formed from habit. We need to identify our eating habits before we can free ourselves from negative ones (*see* chapter 2, page 18 for the seven modes of eating). We have to learn to respond freely and in harmony with nature, learning to eat in moderation and only when we are hungry.

If you follow the Colours for Life Diet and tailor it to your own needs, your body will receive all the energy needed, without the excess oils and carbohydrates it has to store as fat. Your body will find its optimum weight. If you are overweight your body will slowly but surely redress any imbalance you may have and you will lose weight naturally and permanently. Your weight may fluctuate from time to time depending on the weather, the types of food you eat and your health and hormonal balance, but this is a perfectly natural process.

The Colours for Life Diet is designed to be flexible enough to cater for every individual's needs. We all have different types of metabolisms. Some are quick while others are slow. People with a fast metabolism tend to burn up fat more quickly than people who have a slow system. This will also have an effect on our body shape and weight, and what you eat and how often you eat will vary according to how much exercise you take. You need to discover what is normal for you, and whether you are naturally slim and muscular or if your natural tendency is towards a more curvaceous and broader silhouette.

People are overweight for many different reasons, and a good way to understand the problem is to find out if you have a definite colour imbalance. This will help you discover the cause of your problem, which might be physiological, emotional or mental, and guide you to a diet which will help you regain balance. Combine the results of the inherited colour bias test you did in chapter 2 (page 26) with the colour imbalance test in chapter 7 (page 139). If you need to correct a colour imbalance, follow a single-colour diet along the lines of those listed in chapters 7 and 8 for a week or two before starting on the Colours for Life Diet.

As with our dress and the colours we choose to surround ourselves, the colours and flavours we use in cookery can reflect and harmonize with our personality and metabolism. You should always eat food containing the most physical and energetic nutrition, and that means finding natural alternatives to refined sugar, salt, starches and fatty animal products. Food should be fresh, and eaten raw or lightly cooked.

The Basics of a Truly Hearty Meal

Next time you plan a meal, look through a recipe book, and note down the dominant colours of the dishes you choose. Do you have a balanced spread of colours or is there one colour or group of colours which forms the basis of the recipe? If the dish is based on a particular colour, make sure you serve it with food of the complementary colours. Each day try to create variety and balance in the colours of the food you serve.

If you are used to eating a meal consisting of meat, two vegetables and potato, all you have to do is shift the emphasis and proportions of the food on your plate. Base your dinner around a carbohydrate such as potatoes, rice or pasta, which should account for half of the meal – complex carbohydrates give off energy over a longer period than proteins, providing slow-burning energy throughout the day. Fresh seasonal salads or vegetables should be a third, and a sixth should be protein: legumes, pulses or nuts, or for non-vegetarians fish, lean meat or poultry. Add to this various yin (blue) foods, which include blue fruits and yeast. As a healthy option, for example, you can finish your meal with a dessert of blue fruit or berries.

Yogurt is the most desirable milk product, and sweetening should come from fresh fruit and a little honey. Milk should be drunk separately from a main meal. Acid fruit such as oranges and pineapples should not be mixed with milk products.

Snacks

If you feel hungry between meals, eating a natural snack will keep your energy levels high. Fresh fruit, nuts and seeds, raisins and dried fruit all make excellent snacks. If you need something more substantial then wholegrain bread with yeast extract, peanut butter or baked beans will give you slow-burn energy. Remember to eat when you are hungry and not out of automatic or emotional needs.

If you have succumbed to a piece of pie or chocolate cake, you need not worry; the occasional indulgence is nothing to be guilty about. We are all fallible, and as long as we return to our normal diet we will suffer no ill effects. Drink some herb tea to clear your system if you have eaten too much or had a rich meal, or use the appropriate fruit to aid the digestion (*see* chapter 4, page 67).

The Emotional Quality of Food

Our well-being is affected not only by the vibrations of food itself, but also by the vibrations given off by the person preparing it. If the cook is in a bad temper the energy field around the food will take on a greyish tinge, while food prepared lovingly will retain all its goodness and take on the wholesome energy surrounding it. If we understand this principle it is easy to understand how Christ was said to feed the multitude with very little bread. The life-force contained in it was so great that a mere crumb would have given one man enough energy to sustain him. Most of us can eat far less than we usually do without any bad side effects, as a little whole food prepared with love is worth many times its weight, unlike a large meal thrown together carelessly.

If we eat food which contains vital light energy we should only need approximately two or three handfuls of food at each meal. We should never eat until we feel completely full; leaving the table feeling that you still have room for more allows you to digest your meal well and also extract *prana* from your food.

Eating Tips
- Eat in a settled atmosphere and not when you are upset.
- Make sure you sit down.
- Make sure you eat plenty of fresh raw fruit and vegetables.
- Eat mainly foods of the red/orange, golden-yellow, gold, yellow and green rays, unless you suffer from a colour imbalance (*see* chapter 7, page 139). Red and purple fruit and vegetables will provide you with all the necessary iron contained in the red ray.

Avoid foods that correspond to the infra-red or ultraviolet range, especially salt, red meat and sugar.

- Eat steadily and slowly, chewing your food well.
- Sit for a few minutes quietly before getting up after the meal.

If you observe these simple rules, you will be receiving the maximum benefit from the food you eat. You will enjoy your meal and process it well, thus enhancing your level of *chi* and maintaining your correct body weight.

The Importance of Surroundings

The benefits of the use of colour in cooking extends to the environment in which you prepare and eat the food. It is important to surround yourself with supportive colours in the kitchens and dining area as well as giving thought and care to table settings and crockery.

The cook's mood imparts good or bad vibrations to the meal being prepared, so you need to be in the right frame of mind when you cook. Here again, colour can come to the rescue, for the colours you have around you will influence your emotions and state of mind. Colour has a great effect on our subconscious. I remember reading about a cafeteria chain that wanted to improve its salad sales and did so by simply replacing the usual white crockery with pale green plates. The sales went up 100 per cent!

A kitchen can often be a very vibrant place, with a wonderful mix of aromas and colours from the food itself. If you are preparing a colourful variety of natural food it will naturally get the creativity flowing and will act as a source of inspiration.

If you regularly have to cook a meal after a hard day's work, it might be helpful to have a soothing colour as the main backdrop in the kitchen. Turquoise is refreshing and clears the mind, while a rich blue cools and relaxes you while you cook. Or, to get your tastebuds in gear, use warm orange or apricot. Peach colours arouse hunger and have been proven to be the most appetizing hue for eating places in tests conducted by cafeterias and restaurants. Light coral and light yellowy-cream are also effective.

Yellow or cream are good colours for a dining room or kitchen/ dining room, as cream, yellow and gold aid digestion, and are revitalizing and rejuvenating. Orange is good for the digestion too and is a joyous light colour, helping us to relax our bodies and to let go of serious thoughts.

Too much of any one of these colours can be overpowering, so it's best to combine the wall colour with its complementary colour in the crockery or tableware. Yellow walls in the dining area can be combined with green pot plants and blue crockery. A cream room could have an orange wallpaper border and be teamed with French provincial green and orange tableware.

Kitchens lend themselves to natural earthy colours, the rich browns of wood, cream, yellow, apricots, peaches or green. It is best not to have too much green on the walls as prolonged exposure to large surfaces of green can be depressing and sometimes nauseating. This effect is related to the concept of colour imbalance, which we will be looking at in detail in Chapter 7. Colour, like everything else in the plural universe, has good and bad qualities. When there is balance we experience the good qualities of a colour, but when there is imbalance we experience the negative aspects. Imbalances often show up in discolorations of the body.

The negative aspects of green feature in the greeny-yellowing coating that can discolour the tongue or a greenish tinge to the whites of the eyes, which can reveal liver problems or jaundice respectively. Whilst clear bright colours are harmonious, dark or muddy colours are generally unharmonious, so an attraction to olive or dirty green can reveal emotional imbalance, and this is the reason that we often associate green with envy or jealousy. In the kitchen, limit the greens to plants and kitchen accessories or combine it with plenty of white.

Blue-green has been found to enhance both the appetite and the appearance of food when used as a backdrop, so is a good choice for the dining areas, but is not a good colour for lighting.

Lighting also effects how we perceive our food. I read once that blue fluorescent lighting in one railway company's dining cars was making the coffee look weak and grey. The regular diners complained that the coffee was awful – but they were tasting the coffee with their eyes. As soon as the blue lights were removed, passengers reported that the quality of the coffee was much improved! We can learn from this story that we should stay away from blue light and lampshades in the dining area.

If food has been prepared in unfavourable conditions, as might happen in a careless restaurant for instance, rock crystals can be used to re-energize it. We can also make use of a rock crystal to absorb 'bad energy', for although energy is neither good nor bad in itself, it can have a negative effect if its flow is blocked, as the resulting 'stagnating' energy blocks cause internal imbalances (*see* chapter 7, page 136). We can use a small crystal to circle the plate and pull away the grey negative energy. Also try having a vase of fresh flowers nearby in the kitchen when preparing food, to soothe, relax and inspire you while you work.

Clearly, in addition to the immediate surroundings in which food is prepared and the mood of the person preparing it, cooking methods themselves influence the quality of what we eat. To save time and effort, many of us cook using microwave ovens. Vitamin and mineral loss is less when food is cooked in a microwave oven than in a conventional oven, but microwave ovens heat food by changing the polarity of the food's atoms thousands of times per second, thereby altering the food's electromagnetic field. This means that the essential life-force of vegetables cooked in a microwave oven is destroyed, and so food cooked by this method will have a big strain on the body if it is eaten every day.

Microwave ovens also emit LFV, or low-frequency vibration, as do television sets and most electronic equipment. Research has shown that LFV can have a depressing effect on the emotions, just as fluorescent and artificial lighting has been proved to be physically detrimental. (In fact tests involving children who had learning difficulties or behavioural problems showed that their behaviour improved when put in a room with good natural light.) Try keeping a crystal near your television(s) or microwave oven to counteract the negative effects of LFV.

Osteopaths and applied kinesiologists have revealed by muscle testing that microwaved foods depress the body's systems. In Munich Dr Wolfgang Gerg found that many of his patients suffered from physical ailments that began soon after using microwaves in their homes. He suggests that this may be caused by additional demands on an already stressed system suffering from other forms of electromagnetic stress. Successful cancer therapies such as the Bristol diet make great use of fresh, raw foods to fortify the immune system.

Colour, Climate and Culture

When studying different diets we notice that the healthiest populations are those of cultures whose diet is in harmony with their environment and climate. They suffer from the fewest life-threatening diseases, live the longest, and display the qualities of health listed in Chapter 4.

Many ancient cultures may share common approaches to health but adapt them to their own needs. An example is the complementary drink that invariably accompanies food, balancing the whole meal and aiding digestion by breaking down fats and acids. In many countries it takes the form of a herbal tea: in the Middle East and the Japanese archipelago, a green tea, in China, Bancha tea, and in Australia and southern Africa a bush tea brewed from the twigs of certain plants. The drink is not usually alcoholic, except in countries in which there is high consumption of animal protein: the French and Italians complement their meat and fish dishes with red wine, which helps to digest the fats and protein. When the drink is removed from the diet imbalance results, and there is a marked increase of digestive illness.

The colour of this drink often relates to either red or green. Green tea, peppermint tea and white wine (made from green grapes) aid the digestion and settle the stomach. Yogurt and milk, which are essentially derived from grass, are also found to have harmonizing qualities. Red wine and redbush tea stimulate the metabolism and help to break down heavier meals, particularly those containing animal fats.

Nowadays, we are not restricted to cooking traditional fare from the country in which we live; we can draw inspiration from ingredients and cooking techniques from other cultures, and when applying the Colours for Life Diet we should draw upon the wisdom of other cultures and cook in many styles using ingredients available locally. Using our creativity and originality, we can gain the beneficial effects of many simple and healthy diets, and learn about the benefits of the lifestyles they support.

Eating in Harmony with Our Local Seasons

Colour influences the best seasonal cookery around the world and gives us a strong and easy visual guide for healthier eating. It is interesting that people everywhere who eat plenty of fresh locally grown food (such as a high intake of garlic, onion and olive oil in the Mediterranean countries) have a low incidence of cancer and heart disease. The lifestyle and relaxed way of eating contribute to their well-being.

If we eat locally produced foods seasonally, we will connect with the earth energies, getting the correct vitamins and minerals as the temperature and the seasons change. If we live in an area where the seasons are distinct, the cycles of colour in natural foods provide us with warming, energizing foods in winter and cooling foods in summer.

In tropical and temperate zones we need less salt, fish and grains, and more water, nuts and fruits. If we eat a lot of fish in a warmer climate, we need a lot of raw vegetables or fruit to balance our diet. White fish corresponds to the blue wavelength, and needs to be balanced by green, as it is in the traditional Japanese diet in which green tea, drunk with every meal, counteract the effect of salty fish. They also ate sparingly cooked fresh vegetables, providing a carefully tuned diet. Many serious illnesses were almost unheard of before elements of a Western diet and lifestyle were adopted.

The diets emerging for the turn of the millennium are often either vegetarian or contain some lean meat or fish, but the main emphasis should be on balance, and as we have seen this requires some radical changes in our ingrained ideas about nutrition. Before we look at some of the most balanced diets in the world so we can learn how they relate to the colours and harmony of the peoples with their environment, here's an initial guide to making these changes in your diet.

Try to base your diet on as much fresh organic local produce as possible, bringing an international flavour to your cooking with the addition of some imported products, particularly spices, and flavourings. Sun-dried products do not lose their energetic qualities, so organic rice, poppadoms using organic flour, sun-dried tomatoes and organic dried fruit are good ways of introducing food which does not grow locally or is not in season.

It can often be difficult to follow this advice: when faced with a choice of two varieties of the same product, one local but not organic, the other organic but from halfway round the world, which is better? In order of preference (best first) here is a guide to the different types of food for the Colours for Life Diet.

1 organic local produce
2 organic imported produce
3 sun-dried organic food
3 local inorganic produce
4 imported inorganic produce

5 frozen or bottled produce (check for synthetic colour additives)
6 tinned produce (check for synthetic colour additives)

Northern Europe and cold countries: carbohydrates, starch, sugars and proteins

Many Western countries in the northern hemisphere have built up a diet high in carbohydrates, starch and proteins. Before the introduction of central heating we needed a great deal of warming food to fuel us. The basic needs of life required much more time and energy, and we spent a good deal of time in physical activities that are now automated, which used up most of the extra calories.

Until very recently imported products were restricted to those that could be transported easily without refrigeration, such as tea, spices, dried fruits and grains, and salted and preserved meat and fish, and on the whole people ate locally produced seasonal foods. In summer there was a wealth of many coloured fresh fruits and vegetables. Autumn brought with it golden-orange wheat, barley, rye, deep-shaded plums, lovely red and blue berries and ground crops. Winter continued with orange and golden winter varieties of ground vegetables, turnips, parsnips, carrots, together with winter varieties of red and yellow apples and pears. Warming winter soups were made using warm magnetic colours. Spring arrived bringing with it new shoots of pale greens and yellows.

The good wholesome cooking of our grandmothers was right for the time, but it is a diet ill-adapted to our present needs. First, we are much warmer than we used to be, in the home, at work, and out of doors; we also spend much more time indoors and we take less exercise. The result is that we are unable to utilize all the starches and fats we eat. Second, the food itself has changed. With modern farming methods using pesticides and fertilizers, much of the nourishment is lost before it reaches us, and it embarks on a devious journey before it can reach our table. However, there are many benefits to living in the latter half of the twentieth century. Many delicious varieties of fruit and vegetables are now available and can be grown very successfully in local conditions, especially for use in salads. These grow well in summer, the months when we most need the soothing and cooling greens.

So the principle of fresh home-baked foods still holds true, but with the dramatic changes in our lifestyle we need to make correspondingly dramatic changes in diet if we are to promote good health. A much lighter diet is now needed, changing the focus from starches to complex carbohydrates, and including much more fruit and vegetables. We also need to eat less fat, less sugar and less salt, and to revert to fresh natural foods. 'Health' foods should be everyday foods. Eating complex carbohydrates and complete proteins found in wholegrains and legumes is the surest way to optimum nutrition and stamina. If you do eat meat, make sure it's only lean white meat, and take plenty of exercise. This will eliminate any toxins before they become harmful.

The Mediterranean: fresh fruit and vegetables, garlic, bread, fish, wine

The Mediterranean diet, like its people, is extremely colourful and a perfectly balanced one. It makes use of all the rainbow foods – which really are miracle medicines.

The Mediterranean diet has been recognized as one of the healthiest in the world. This takes into account the numbers of people free from life-threatening disease, and their fitness and longevity. Their diet revolves around a great deal of fresh foods and fruits. Bread is eaten with most meals, and unlike the Northern European diet, in which bread is smothered with butter or vegetable oils, it's eaten dry and used to mop up the sauce or dressing. Olive oil is used instead of butter, and as this a poly-unsaturated fat, it's much more healthy. Little meat is eaten in this diet; the emphasis is on freshly cooked fish. Fish protein is light and nutritious without the inclusion of harmful fats and acids.

Most people living in Mediterranean countries and other lands with similar hot climates still buy fresh food and bread from a local market on a daily basis, because food keeps poorly in the heat, its quality and taste deteriorating rapidly. This inevitably means few preservatives and food rich in energy.

Garlic is an important feature of the Mediterranean diet. Garlic has many curative and health-giving properties, and with onions and scallions (spring onions) is especially good in the prevention of cancer, particularly gastrointestinal cancer. Ajoene, a garlic compound, is toxic to malignant cells. Garlic also boosts immune functions that destroy tumour cells.

Wine is taken with most meals, and its natural acidity helps digest the food. Nutritionists have long suspected that drinking a glass of wine a day as part of this diet has beneficial effects, and it now seems clear that this decreases the risk of cardiovascular

disease without overloading the liver. However, recent studies
have shown that the colour of the grapes is as important as the
wine itself, and red grape juice will provide this benefit.

Citrus fruit, especially oranges, grapefruits, lemons and limes,
grow prolifically in the Mediterranean region. They possess a
natural substance that neutralizes the powerful chemical carcinogens in animals. (Some Eastern European countries also make
great use of citrus and other fruits in their cooking, the neutralizing effect of the fruit working in harmony with the meat dishes.)
Swedish studies found that those who ate citrus fruit daily reduced
the risk of pancreatic cancer by half.

Special dishes, like the Spanish paella, also have a complex
carbohydrate as their base, with the inclusion of beautifully
coloured vegetables and seafood; Italian pastas, too, are carbohydrate based, often covered with sauces of either red or green
vegetables; Greek dishes are renowned for their variety of vegetables, and lavish use of olive oil.

In hot conditions, yellow, orange and red/brown predominate
in our surroundings and the skin can become flushed red or
brown, with the blood hot. If this is the case, use the cooling
colours for your cooking and the more yin foods according to the
yin–yang principle of Oriental philosophy. These foods are vinegar,
wine, ginger, spices, grains, legumes, raw green vegetables, and
fermentations such as marinades.

The Middle East: pulses, legumes, onions, garlic, water-retaining fruit and vegetables, dried fruit, bread, herb teas

People living in hot and arid or desert conditions have for centuries enjoyed a diet based on dried pulses and legumes and
sun-dried fruits, giving adequate protein and minerals imbued
with vital light energy. In the harsh climate few fresh fruits or
vegetables are available, so sun-drying food became the perfect
way of preserving food when it was in season, especially figs, dates,
raisins and desiccated coconut. Fresh vegetables and fruits such as
onions, garlic, cucumbers and melons are all water retaining
and provide the cooling liquid that is much needed in a hot
dry climate.

More yang foods, such as meat, need to be modified to make
them more yin in order to increase their cooling properties. This
is done by marinades and fermentation and the use of vinegar,
wine, ginger and other spices.

Japan: fish, raw fresh food, green tea, vegetables

For centuries the Japanese diet provided a truly balanced and nourishing diet for the people of those islands. The base of their diet was complex carbohydrate, rice or noodles, supplemented by fresh fish, raw and lightly cooked fresh vegetables. Green tea was drunk with every meal, and like the consumption of wine in the Mediterranean countries provided a perfect balance. Like peppermint tea, green tea has a calmative and soothing action providing the perfect complement to a Colours for Life Diet. Recent research in Japan has confirmed the benefits of green tea, and the subjects who drank more than 10 cups a day had lower cholesterol levels than those who drank less.

Not until recently, with the introduction foreign foods, especially American-style fast foods, did the Japanese suffer from many ailments which plague the West. Cancer rates were very low, stomach and bowel function problems rare. Japanese women rarely the experience hot flushes commonly associated with the menopause in the West, and it is now evident that a soya-rich diet is full of plant protein containing phytochemicals, which harmonize with the balancing qualities of the green ray. This is a good example of how importing an inferior diet based on fast foods and food tampering causes untold damage.

India and China: rice, seafood, legumes, light vegetables and spices

Indian and Chinese diets are based on the staple ingredient of rice. The Indians use fresh vegetables and especially chilli peppers, red, yellow and green peppers in their curries. (As we saw in chapter 4, the pepper family is a rainbow family of foods, containing the highest amount of vitamin C of any fruit or vegetable.) Red or yellow lentils provide the protein, supplemented by a little meat or fish. Cooling, soothing yogurt and also coconut feature strongly as balancing agents.

Chinese food often includes fresh vegetables cooked very lightly, often by steaming, which are added to small amounts of meat or fish or soya bean products. Soya curd, soya sauce and soya milk together make up the binding green force which balances this diet.

Using Your Diet to Heal

Special Diets

The Colours for Life Diet does not restrict you to any style of cooking. Its principles can also be used in combination with other special diets, such as a food-combining diet (Hay diet), Fit for Life (for arthritis), the Bristol diet (for cancer), or a Mediterranean diet (to prevent heart disease). All of these diets are highly recommended for our modern style of living and the large variety of food available to us, although you should always make sure whatever style of cookery you follow is appropriate to your particular needs, climate and culture. More importantly, if you follow the colour code you will reinforce the benefits of all these diets by complementing physical nutrition with energetic nutrition.

Food combining is particularly appropriate for people who have a problem with food absorption through poor digestion or food allergies. Traditional meals containing both protein and carbohydrates, like meat and potatoes, can leave one feeling bloated, sluggish and without energy. Combining food correctly will result in an effective metabolism which will supply tons of energy. Learn to listen to your body and it will tell you which foods suit you, and which combinations it does not like.

If you are following the Hay food-combining diet, do not mix protein with carbohydrates at the same meal; make sure one meal a day is protein based, one is carbohydrate based and the third is neutral, and remember the principles in chapter 4, 'Harmonizing Our Diet with Our Biorhythms', especially pages 75–9. Using the colour cycle code for choice of food appropriate to the time of day to be eaten reinforces a food-combined meal. For example, if you are a vegetarian you could select a fruit breakfast (neutral), a baked potato and salad for lunch (carbohydrate) and a tofu and vegetable supper (protein). Alternatively you could elect to have a muesli breakfast (carbohydrate), a lentil and vegetable lunch (protein) and a vegetable and rice supper (neutral). Using colour as your guide, make sure the meals earlier in the day contain more red, orange and yellow energy, while the evening meals are based on green, blue and violet food.

The Healing Properties of Colour

Colour energy can itself be an effective way to minimize or even prevent disease; indeed, harmonious cosmic vibrations may even add years to the average lifespan of a human being. Lord Clifford of Chudleigh, who has studied the action of light shades on vegetable growth for years, believes that every disease can be cured by a certain colour. His research shows, for example, that a particular shade of yellow light is the restorer of nerves while some wave-lengths of green light increases vitality.

By using colour to heal at a very deep level, we are giving support to other medical practices in a holistic way. It is only by clearing deep blockages which may be inside our cells and muscle tissue that we can hope to really cure ourselves, and colour has a vital role to play in this.

7 | Healing Colour Imbalances

Energy Imbalances and Blockages

Most of us have persistently created barriers between ourselves, nature and the healing power of light. These energy blocks come both from within and from outside our bodies. The way we live, the food we eat, our thought patterns and desires, all create vibrations in our physical and subtle bodies affecting our health and that of others who come into contact with us. The amount of natural sunlight we absorb is also a vital consideration.

The receptor cells of the hypothalamus in the brain need the full range of colour vibrations in sunlight to stimulate all the glands of the endocrine system and keep the metabolism functioning in harmony. If certain colours predominate the proper functioning of the pituitary and pineal glands will be adversely affected.

In order to be healthy we require a balance of all the colours in the rainbow, which are present in natural sunlight and manifested in food. Remember that when food is digested the energy is transformed by the spleen and pancreas into light vibrations which are distributed to the chakras around the body. The coloured vibrations flow through our energy system, filling us with vitality and light energy. Most of our physical ailments arise when this light becomes blocked within us, preventing the perfect connection with the cosmic forces.

It is most important therefore that we all get plenty of natural sunlight. Not only does sunlight provide us with the primary cosmic nutrient to sustain us in perfect health, but it also causes the skin to produce one of the most important vitamins required by our body, vitamin D. This essential sunshine vitamin controls the assimilation of calcium, phosphorus and other minerals from the digestive tract into the bloodstream. Direct sunshine is not necessary; the colour vibrations penetrate cloud and other atmospheric conditions. Looking at our lifestyle is essential: few people realize how little full-spectrum light they get entering their eyes. Great numbers of people spend most of their day indoors under artificial lights. When they go out, they might wear tinted sunglasses, and if not they get into cars or vehicles which have tinted windscreens. Obviously only certain colour vibrations will constantly enter their eyes, while others will be deficient.

Energy blocks can also occur for other reasons. They are often a result of internal forces such as bad diet, lack of exercise, repressed emotions and negative thoughts and attitudes, for our attitudes and thought vibrations also affect our bodies right down to the cellular level. For example, fatigue manifests itself mentally. If you are generally negative about life, prone to saying *Everything is too difficult, too tiring and impossible,* these negative thought vibrations also hamper your ability to become healthy.

When we are healthy we experience no fatigue, and our immune system successfully fights off attacks from bacterial and viral invaders. When we are overworked, stressed or continuously in a poor environment our immune system is under constant strain. The human body's defence system can deteriorate so much that catching a cold or flu can make you tired for years!

The body that's under stress, tired or in any weak condition always gives at the weakest point, and we have to learn to identify the warning signs long before we become physically ill. If, for example, you are prone to backache or asthma, that's where your body will crack in times of stress. Whenever and wherever they appear, pain and illness are our cells' cries for help, drawing attention to an inner imbalance and telling us that we have to change some aspect of our mode of living. If we do not change, the illness will persevere and recur until we finally get the message.

It is, however, rare that illness starts in the physical body. More often it arises as the result of an imbalance of energy in the emotional and mental body. These unharmonious vibrations are passed through the etheric body to the physical body, which translates the energy blocks into physical symptoms, often causing pain. It is only when these energy blocks are decongested that harmony can be restored and the coloured energy rays can flow once more.

To understand this, imagine the etheric body as a large radio set. Each energy centre or chakra in the body is a radio station connected to a certain colour frequency (*see* chapter 1, page 7). When any station loses the signal, the other stations receive discordant signals. So if one colour energy centre is over-stimulated – that is, if its volume is too loud – another centre becomes under-energized: it's drowned out by the stronger one and the result is an energy imbalance or blockage.

We can easily tell those suffering from energy imbalances. For example, most of us will have met someone who has too much red energy. They are easily recognizable by their ruddy complexions and hot, sweaty skins. These people are quick to temper. Their blood pressure can be high and they tend to eat foods from the warm end of the spectrum – red meat and fats, salty or sweet foods – and maybe even consume a great deal of red wine. On the other hand, people who have too much blue in their system are often dark-haired and have a sallow complexion. They have low blood pressure and may suffer from anaemia. They will be lethargic and find it difficult to motivate themselves. If you have too much blue in your system depression often develops. In cases of all energy imbalances and blockages, we need to retune that particular colour station so that the colour signal is once again received loud and clear. Harmony has to be restored by introducing the colours needed to redress the balance.

It is important to remember that colour vibrations are neither good nor bad in themselves, and their effect upon us depends upon whether they are working in harmony with each other. When working in harmony, they are able to set up a protective force field around us which can protect our whole being against the onslaught of pollution and a hostile environment, and the pressures of our society and modern lifestyles. Their qualities and actions can benefit us greatly. The right amount of each vibration in our system will help us achieve balance, good health and peace. If, on the other hand, they are unharmonious, they can do us considerable harm. When we have too much of one colour in our system or are exposed to colours which are not in harmony with our own inner vibrations we feel 'off colour' or 'washed out', and if this persists illness may occur.

All of us must therefore identify our weak points and work towards building up these areas with light energy. We can then introduce certain colour vibrations into our system to redress any energy imbalances and by so doing treat any specific ailments and weaknesses we may have.

By reintroducing the colours that we individually lack, we can regenerate our depleted energy centres, build up our immune system and clean out the toxins and bad vibrations we have retained.

Chi Derived After Birth

In chapter 2 we looked at the idea of inherited colour bias, or original *chi*. Original *chi* is the first possible cause of a colour imbalance in our systems. The second is *chi* derived after birth: the type of food and drink we consume, and any temporary imbalances caused by illness, exhaustion, stress or an operation. Our emotional and mental states may play a great part in depleting a particular colour energy centre, which results in another becoming over-energized, creating further imbalance.

To find out if you suffer from an energy imbalance, complete the following quick test.

Test for Colour Energy Imbalance

Look at your original score for the Inherited Colour Bias test in chapter 2. Now complete the following test, scoring 2 points for often, 0 points for rarely and 1 point for sometimes. Once you have finished, add your scores from your colour bias test to these points for a total colour energy count on each colour. (For example: if you scored 3 points on yellow in the colour bias test and 12 points on this colour energy imbalance test, your total energy score for yellow will be 15.)

Red

1 Do you respond to stress with anger, resentment or frustration?
2 Do you have more than three cups of coffee or tea (excluding green or herbal tea) a day?
3 Do you get hot easily or perspire a lot?
4 Do you have lots of energy?
5 Are you a perfectionist?
6 Do you eat a lot of salty or sugary foods?
7 Do you drink an alcoholic drink more than three times a week?
8 Do you suffer from rashes, boils or an itchy skin?
9 Do you like hot or spicy foods?
10 Do you eat red meat more than three times a week?
Score:_____

Key to Total Red Score

Score 0–11

You are in need of red energy in your system. We all need red energy to give us strength, stamina and energy. On the emotional and mental level, red energy motivates us and helps us to find our purpose in life. It also helps us take action and get things done by connecting us with magnetic earth energy. If your blue energy score is high, you may be suffering from depression, low blood pressure or anaemia and should follow the red colour balancing diet for one or two weeks. You will also need to eat more natural vegetable red-ray foods rather than red meat and dairy products.

Score 12–17

This score indicates that you have plenty of red energy in your system, but make sure you are displaying the positive attributes of red. You should have plenty of energy and enthusiasm for life, take regular exercise and have the ability to make decisions easily. You will have natural strength and stamina and are a good survivor. A good supply of red energy can promote leadership qualities.

Score 18–25

A score of 18 points or more indicates a very high presence of red energy in your system. It is important that you take a close look at your intake of red-energy foods as these can cause excessive heat in the body. If you do not change your diet you run the risk of developing an illness connected with fiery red. This can result in rashes, boils, itches, heart troubles and high blood pressure as well as irritability and anger. The best thing to do is to choose red foods that are not animal in origin; these will not congest your system. Remember every colour has its positive and negative aspects. You need to encourage the positive side of red to you. It is also important that you seek advice on an exercise programme that will suit your capability and lifestyle. It is also a good idea to go on a green/blue corrective diet for a few weeks before changing to the full-spectrum diet.

Orange

1 Do you think about past times?
2 Do you have a healthy sex drive?
3 Do you eat fruit more than three times a week?
4 Do you suffer from any allergies (hay-fever, sinus, food)?

5 Do you catch colds and flu?
6 Do you suffer from depression?
7 Do you drink more than three glasses of pure water a day?
8 Do you find it hard to show affection to your friends, partner or family?
9 Are you a pessimist?
10 Would you describe yourself as a practical person?
Score _____

Key to Total Orange Score

Score 0–11

You have a good balance of orange energy in your system. This means that you are joyful, loving, caring and emotionally stable. You enjoy a normal amount of good deep sleep and have a steady flow of energy. Orange energy is very practical energy as it is made up of both red and yellow energy: red promotes physical activity while the yellow stimulates the mind. The Colours for Life Diet will help you to maintain your orange energy levels.

Score 12–25

Your sacral centre, where orange energy is focused, is blocked. This means that there are emotions which you are repressing. This probably has to do with a past relationship and you are harbouring feelings of bitterness and resentment. You could be living in the past and finding it difficult to move forward in life. Unless you learn to express your feelings, they will have bad effects on your health. A cleansing diet will do you a lot of good, after which the Colours for Life Diet will help you to unblock some of these hidden feelings and desires.

Yellow

1 Do you suffer from diabetes, allergies or asthma, or problems from being overweight?
2 Would you describe yourself as a nervous person?
3 Do you like to sleep in late or feel drowsy during the day?
4 Do you suffer from skin problems?
5 Are you affectionate and forgiving?
6 Are you fond of collecting, storing or saving things?
7 Do you avoid physical exercise?
8 Do you find it easy to remember things?

9 Are you partial to sugar, salt or fatty or oily food?
10 Do you suffer from fluid retention?
Score _____

Key to Total Yellow Score

Score 0–11
You have a flow of yellow energy through your system, making you a bright, sociable and interesting person. Yellow energy stimulates the mind and nervous system, as well as cleansing and stimulating the liver, spleen, gall bladder and pancreas People with a good flow of yellow energy have a clear skin and strong nervous system.

Score 12–16
Your score reveals that you have good deal of yellow energy in your system, which is not necessarily a bad thing. We all need yellow energy to stimulate our mind and mental processes. This helps us open ourselves to new ideas and possibilities. We also need yellow energy to aid our digestive processes and our ability to assimilate and eliminate food adequately. It may be that you place a great deal of emphasis on the mind and are neglecting the body through a sedentary lifestyle. If this is the case, eating yellow fruit and vegetables will help balance the yellow ray and have a cleansing action on your entire system.

Score 17–25
This is a high score and indicates that you have an energy block of the yellow ray which will be reflected by a sluggish, congested system. You might also be bogged down in some area of your life, for instance your work or relationships. Ailments related to an imbalance of yellow energy include water retention, a poor digestion, cysts and growths, mucus, asthma, allergies and hepatitis, and problems with the liver, spleen and gall bladder. On an emotional level the negative qualities of yellow appear as jealousy, possessiveness, insecurity and feeling unwanted. A cleansing diet of green and yellow food is required and a reduction of fatty foods of animal origin – eggs, salty cheese, butter, full-cream milk and red meat. Eat more yellow and green vegetables and unsaturated vegetable oils and margarines.

Green

1 Do you suffer from lung problems (asthma, bronchitis)?
2 Do you believe everything always turns out right?
3 Do you find it difficult to get motivated?
4 Do you feel unsupported or unloved?
5 Do you find it hard to make decisions?
6 Do you feel you are in a rut or trapped?
7 Are you self-critical?
8 Do you get jealous?
9 Do you eat green salad more than three times a week?
10 Do you prefer to sit in the shade than the sun?
Score ____

Key to Total Green Score

Score 0–11

Green energy brings balance and harmony to your whole being. Your green levels are low, and this may show in a number of ways. It could be that you are indecisive and feel unloved or unsupported. You will have to learn that in order to be loved by others or to love anyone else you first have to love yourself – with your good and bad points. It is likely that you suffer from low self-esteem and this will show by a high score in red colour energy. If this is the case you need to take in more green energy to cool and calm your system.

Score 12–20

You have a balance of green energy, which will help maintain harmony in your physical, mental and emotional bodies. Enjoy and express your green energy. Connect with nature, with the plants, animals, children and humankind. You have a great deal to give and the healing arts or environmental studies may interest you. Make sure you maintain fresh green foods in your diet.

Score 20–25

We all need plenty of green energy, but when the green energy level is too high it takes on the negative aspects of this colour. Too much green can make us feel insecure and threatened. It does not help us with decision-making and often a green imbalance makes people sit on the fence, withdrawing from the action and behaving as a voyeur, rather than a participant. Instead of rejecting green food in the diet, you need to find the right balance between red and green foods. Follow the red/green balance diet for a week, and see how much more positive and free you feel.

Blue
1 Do you have recurring problems with your throat or thyroid?
2 Are you sensitive to loud noise?
3 Do you find it easy to express your real feelings?
4 Do you suffer from cold hands and feet?
5 Do you feel depressed?
6 Are you intuitive?
7 Do the healing arts or music interest you?
8 Are you a vegetarian?
9 Do you find it hard to trust people?
10 Do you lack energy during the afternoon?
Score ____

Key to Total Blue Score

Score 0–11
This is a low score for blue energy, and so it is important to look at your orange energy levels too. You need to introduce more orange energy into your system to bring more joy and happiness into your life. Blue energy is related to your softer, caring and intuitive side. Perhaps you are denying this part of yourself, relying on your left-hand brain, expressed by logic and reason. Try to trust in the process of life and your feelings rather than always requiring exact answers to everything.

Score 12–17
You have a balance of blue energy in your system. You are a quiet and peace-loving individual. You still have to learn to trust others and put your faith in your own intuition. Make sure you have a balance of orange foods in your diet.

Score 18–25
You are an extremely blue person. This means you are very sensitive and easily hurt. You are susceptible to depression and have to be careful that you do not withdraw into yourself. Make sure that your home and work surroundings are peaceful and that the people you mix with are loving and supportive. You definitely need more joy and laughter in your life, so boost yourself with red and orange foods and solarized red water.

Violet

1 Do you use your creativity?
2 Do you enjoy listening to music?
3 Do you do charity work, or work for others?
4 Do you daydream?
5 Do you find your dreams provide answers to your problems?
6 Do you suffer from any phobias?
7 Do you speak very softly?
8 Do you find it difficult to put your ideas into action?
9 Are you on a spiritual quest?
10 Do you enjoy these foods: mushrooms, asparagus, artichokes?
Score ____

Key to Total Violet Score

Score 0–10

You are not in touch with the creative and spiritual side of your nature. Everyone has this part of them, but have to learn to connect with these qualities. Maybe you are too concerned with everyday tasks and centred on the physical senses. Introduce some purple foods into your diet to help raise your consciousness and heighten your aspirations.

Score 11–17

You show a balance of violet energy, which means you are using the more intuitive side of your nature. We all need to develop and pursue our quest for self-development and self-growth. You can use blue and violet foods to help you on your path.

Score 18–25

You are have a great deal of violet ray energy in your system. This means your crown chakra is very open, connecting you with your spirit and other spiritual forces. Many sensitive people, such as artists, musicians, and painters, and healers, clairvoyants, mediums, and the spiritually advanced, have a great deal of violet energy in their auras. People who have a high violet score must be very careful to protect themselves from negative forces. They must make sure their body is a clean vessel for harmonious vibrations, as this will attract positive and healing forces to them. Many violet people are reluctant souls who have their heads in the clouds and find it difficult to live on the earth. These people need to eat plenty of yang foods – red energy foods and foods containing the other magnetic rays of orange, gold and yellow. Ground crops and root vegetables can boost their earth connection. This will help them achieve their life's work on this earth and put their creative ideas to practical use for the benefit of others as well as themselves.

Red:
Red Dragon Pie, see page 159
Winter Green Salad, see page 89

Orange:
Potato and Bean Stew, see page 114
Carrot Salad, see page 153

Yellow:
Sunshine Sweetcorn Chowder, *see page* 175
Thyme and Poppy Seed Oatcakes, *see page* 105

Green:
Figs, Yoghurt and Honey, see page 173

Blue:
Blueberry Buttermilk Pancakes, see page 111

Indigo:
Trout with Lime Herb Crust,
served with green beans, *see page* 168

Violet:
Purple-Sprouting Broccoli and Pine Nut Stir-fry, served with aromatic saffron rice, see page 167

A Colours for Life meal:
Gazpacho, see page 156
Kedgeree of Summer Vegetables, see page 108
fresh fruit for dessert

8 | Menu Plans and Recipes for Colour-Corrective Diets

Creating Corrective Diets

If we tune in to our bodies, they will usually draw to us the foods we require to correct an energy imbalance. For example, craving yellow or orange fruit probably means we need to boost our vitamin C levels and to energize our immune system. Craving sugar is likely to be the result of having too much red-ray food, and we need to balance this by eating plenty of food containing the green ray. (This is why so much importance is placed by dieticians in eating fresh salads and vegetables. The colour green balances the whole system. Its cleansing and harmonizing effect helps correct the blood circulation and helps the body eliminate toxins which may have built up.) Unfortunately we often do this only when our body forces us to take notice, when we are pregnant or if we are ill.

If there is a pronounced colour imbalance within our system, eating foods of the complementary colour and following a colour-corrective diet can help to restore balance. Colour-corrective diets involve preparing meals consciously, based on foods of one particular colour. These can help with recuperation after an illness, especially for one in which synthetic drugs formed part of the treatment. Whenever we suffer from an energy imbalance a colour-corrective diet can be adopted for one to two weeks until we sense an improvement. Pay attention to your feelings, your mental activity and the messages your body gives you. You should feel a shift in energy after the first week. You may decide you need to keep to the diet for a further week, until you feel a general improvement in your well-being or a particular problem starts to change. At this point take the Colour Energy Imbalance test again to make sure that balance has been fully restored, then revert to the Full-Spectrum Colours for Life Diet.

Menu Plans and Recipes for Colour-Corrective Diets

Here are four recommended diets for various colour imbalances. When creating your colour-corrective diet, bear in mind green food can be combined with all diets. Recipes for the dishes in capitals can be found either in the recipe sections that follow the menu plans or in chapter 5.

Red Energizing Diet

If you have too little red, too much blue or too much green in your system.

1   Eat plenty of fresh dark green leafy vegetables, like spinach, kale and spring greens.
2   Eat plenty of fresh red/orange fruit for both breakfast and lunch, including apricots, guavas, red apples, red cherries, red plums and strawberries.
3   Eat plenty of red-coloured lentils and legumes, including red kidney beans and red-skinned potatoes for both lunch and supper.
4   Spices to use include coriander, ginger and garlic, parsley, rosemary, red or green chillies, and sage.
5   Drink a glass of fresh beetroot, carrot, guava or tomato juice for breakfast or at mid-morning.
6   No oily or fried foods.
7   No processed, refined, tinned or dehydrated foods.
8   Try having a fresh green leafy salad every day. In winter you can use Chinese leaves, spinach leaves, cabbage or kale.
9   For meat eaters, a little grilled fish (salmon or red mullet) or sliced liver with fresh vegetables. Alternate the fish one day and the liver the next day.
10 Take a seaweed or kelp supplement every day before meals or as directed on the bottle.

11 Tea and coffee strip the body of iron and iodine, so drink delicious red, orange or green herbal teas – apricot, orange, peach, redbush, rose-hip.

Red Energizing Menu

Before breakfast

a glass of solarized red water

Breakfast

a glass of orange or guava juice
muesli with strawberries or red apples
yogurt
2 slices wholegrain bread or toast with a red fruit preserve
kelp or spirulina tablet (or as directed)

Lunch

fresh carrot juice
carrot and coriander soup or beetroot soup
Spinach and Feta Cheese Pie
pasta with tomato and green pepper sauce
Tomato and Lentil Soup
ginger and garlic stir-fry vegetables with wild rice
tuna salad
Eggs Florentine

Supper

cauliflower and broccoli with herb sauce
baked potato and mushroom sauce with artichoke salad
almond-stuffed yellow and green peppers
aubergine bake with green beans
broccoli and mushroom lasagne and mixed salad
grilled white fish with parsley and mangetout
Lentil Bake, with mash and peas
spinach pasta with pesto sauce and purple salad

Red/Orange Energizing Recipes

These recipes comprise a soup, a lunch dish, a main course, two salads, a dessert and a cocktail drink.

• Tomato and Lentil Soup
• Eggs Florentine
• Lentil Bake
• Tomato and Orange Salad
• Carrot Salad
• Carotella
• Summer Fruit Cup

Eggs Florentine

This recipe is light but full of goodness and makes an excellent lunch dish. The eggs and cheese are rich in protein, while the spinach provides fibre, vitamins and minerals. The eggs are poached and placed on a bed of spinach then topped with cheese. Serve it on its own or with a chunk of wholemeal bread.

Serves 4

900g/2lb spinach
100ml/4fl oz/½C Greek style yogurt
sea salt and freshly ground black pepper
a pinch of nutmeg
4 free range eggs
30g/1oz/½C grated Cheddar or Parmesan cheese, grated

Method

Preheat the oven to 200°C/400°F/gas mark 6. Wash the spinach thoroughly and shake off the excess water then put it into a heavy-bottomed pan and cover with a lid. Cook it gently in its own liquid for 6–8 minutes until tender, then squeeze out as much moisture as you can and chop it finely. Return the spinach to the cleaned pan and add the yogurt, salt, pepper and nutmeg. Stir this over a gentle heat for 1 minute, then transfer to a greased gratin dish and make four spaces for the eggs in the top of the spinach mixture. Break an eggs into each space, then sprinkle with cheese. Bake in the oven for 10–12 minutes until the eggs have set. Serve immediately.

Tomato and Lentil Soup

This simple nourishing soup is characterized by the deep orange colour given to it by the combination of split red lentils and tomatoes.

Serves 4

3 tbsp/¼C sunflower oil
1 large onion, finely chopped
1 clove garlic, finely chopped
750g/1½lb ripe tomatoes, peeled and diced
115g/4oz/½C split red lentils
2 rounded tbsp chopped parsley
1 rounded tbsp chopped or 1 rounded tsp dried thyme
1 rounded tbsp chopped or 1 rounded tsp dried marjoram (sweet marjoram)
575ml/1 pint/2½C vegetable stock
sea salt and freshly ground black pepper

To serve
4 tbsp/6 tbsp natural yogurt

Method
Heat the oil in a saucepan on a low heat and put in the onion and garlic. Cook for a few minutes until soft, and then add the tomatoes, lentils and herbs, saving some parsley for the garnish. Stir for 2 minutes or until the tomatoes are soft then pour in the stock and bring to the boil. Cover the pan and simmer for 45 minutes or until the lentils are soft. Season with sea salt and freshly ground black pepper, and serve with yogurt swirls on the top and the remaining parsley sprinkled over.

Lentil Bake

This bake resembles a vegetarian shepherd's pie. It's full of earthy goodness – red lentils and pearl barley are packed with protein – and will give you energy for many hours.

Serves 2

115g/4oz/½C split red lentils
50g/2oz/¼C pearl barley

225g/8oz carrots, grated
1 medium onion, finely chopped
1 × 400g/14oz can of tomatoes
300ml/½ pint/1¼C vegetable stock
450g/1lb red-skinned potatoes
6 tbsp/8 tbsp milk
a pinch of nutmeg
85g/3oz Cheddar cheese, grated (you can use a low-fat variety)

Method

Preheat the oven to 200°C/400°F/gas mark 6.

In a large saucepan add the lentils, pearl barley, carrots, onion and tomatoes to the stock. Bring to the boil then cover the pan and simmer for 40 minutes or until the lentils and barley are soft. Meanwhile, boil the potatoes in their skins, drain them and peel them as soon as they are cool. Bring the milk to the boil, remove from the heat, and add the potatoes; mash them with the nutmeg and add the cheese.

Put the lentil mixture into a pie dish, pile the mashed potatoes on top and spread them out evenly. You can make patterns using a fork. Put the pie into the oven for 20 minutes or until the top begins to brown, and serve it with lightly cooked runner beans, or Brussels sprouts in the winter.

Tomato and Orange Salad

In this colourful and filling salad the turnip and broccoli bring yang qualities to vitamin C rich tomatoes and oranges. The salad is also rich in calcium and folic acid (folate). The slightly tangy dressing adds to the pervading orange flavour.

Serves 4

225g/8oz broccoli, washed, trimmed, blanched for 5 minutes, drained and refreshed
4 tomatoes, sliced
2 oranges, peeled and segmented
115g/4oz turnip, scrubbed and chopped

Dressing
sea salt
1 tbsp/1½ tbsp white wine vinegar

1 tbsp/1½ tbsp sunflower oil
juice and rind of ½ an orange
¼ rounded tsp grated nutmeg
freshly ground black pepper

Method
Mix all the salad ingredients together. To make the dressing, dissolve the salt in the vinegar, and add the remaining ingredients in order. Mix well, pour over the salad and toss well. Serve immediately.

Carrot Salad

The carrot salad is made in the style of Gujarat (a region of northwest India), which was favoured by Mahatma Gandhi towards the end of his life. He undoubtedly drew strength from the intense orange colour of the salad.

Serves 4

2 tsp/2 tsp peanut oil
1 rounded tsp black mustard seeds
170g/6oz finely grated carrots
1 rounded tsp salt
4 rounded tbsp chopped coriander or parsley
2 tsp/2 tsp lemon juice

Method
Heat the oil in a skillet and then add the mustard seeds. When they start to splutter, add the other ingredients. Stir over a high heat for 1 minute, and then cook for another minute. The carrots should still be crisp. Serve with mashed potatoes or rice as Mahatma Gandhi did.

Carotella

This is a delicious and fragrant dessert. It is soothing on a cold night and can be served cold in summer.

Serves 4

1.1 litre/2 pints/5C milk
450g/1lb carrots, shredded
200ml/7fl oz/1C canned evaporated milk
115g/4oz granulated sugar or 2 tbsp/2½ tbsp honey
50g/2oz raisins
seeds of 8 small cardamoms, crushed
2 drops of rose water or vanilla essence
50g/2oz pistachio nuts, chopped
50g/2oz chopped blanched almonds

Method

Put the milk into a pan and simmer over a low heat until reduced to 900ml/32fl oz/4C. Add the carrots, cover and cook for 15 minutes. Add the evaporated milk, sugar or honey, and raisins. Cover and simmer gently for another 5 minutes. Remove from the heat. Stir in the cardamom seeds and rose water or vanilla essence and pour into a serving dish. Sprinkle the nuts on top and serve. Chill if you wish to serve cold.

Summer Fruit Cup

Drink in the colour of this a summer fruit cocktail, low in calories and an excellent source of vitamin C.

Serves 2

115g/4oz strawberries
115g/4oz raspberries
250ml/8fl oz/1C red grape juice

Method

Purée the strawberries and raspberries in a blender or food processor until smooth. Sieve the mixture to remove the pips, dilute to taste with the grape juice and serve chilled.

Red/Blue Normalizing Diet

If you have too much red in your system or if you have you have too little blue in your system.

The red/blue balance will help to balance the body temperature and benefits the circulatory system, which it clears and stimulates. Green, balancing tissue congestion, is included in all diets, but is especially helpful here.

1 No red meat, hard cheese, eggs, cream or ice-cream.
2 No processed, refined, tinned, frozen or dehydrated foods.
3 No deep-fried foods. Use only olive oil for shallow-frying and salad dressing.
4 Drink a maximum of two cups of tea, coffee or alcohol, and never after midday.
5 Drink any herb teas, but green or yellow coloured are best.
6 Do not eat cooked tomatoes and only eat fresh raw tomatoes for breakfast or lunch.
7 Helpful herbs are parsley, fennel, garlic and basil.
8 Do not eat chillies. Use green or red peppers instead.
9 Eat only red foods from the fruit and vegetable kingdom; these contain more yin qualities.

A Sample Red/Blue Normalizing Menu

Breakfast

a glass of carrot, guava or grapefruit juice
pink grapefruit, papaya (pawpaw) or strawberries
muesli or bran flakes with yogurt and nuts
two slices of wholegrain bread with honey
scrambled egg or haddock with tomato and mushrooms
red or orange coloured tea

Lunch

melon and rice salad
three-bean salad and baked potato
Gazpacho
pasta with red or green pesto sauce
omelette with mushrooms or ricotta cheese
cauliflower cheese and mixed salad

Supper

trout or sole/hake and green pepper kebab on risotto
butter-bean and leek gratin, using ricotta and yogurt
aubergine and courgette lasagne with green salad
lemon-baked chicken with couscous
stuffed mushrooms with buttered cabbage with rosemary
green fruit
Blueberry Yogurt
baked green apples with cinnamon
green or yellow herb tea

Red/Blue Normalizing Recipes

These recipes comprise a soup, two salads, a starter, two main
courses, a pudding and a fruit drink.

- Gazpacho
- Grape and Radicchio Salad
- Mushroom and Pasta Salad
- Stuffed Mushrooms
- Penne with Red and Green Peppers
- Red Dragon Pie
- Blue Poppy Seed Cake
- Blueberry Yogurt

Gazpacho

This colourful and refreshing soup is served chilled, and is delicious with olive bread. It is high in fibre, rich in vitamins A and C
and low in fat, and the tomatoes are uncooked.

Serves 4

1 red or green pepper, deseeded
6 spring onions
½ cucumber
575ml/1 pint/2½C tomato juice
2 cloves garlic
1 tbsp/1½ tbsp apple cider vinegar
4 tomatoes, deseeded
3 tbsp/¼C olive oil

Method
Roughly chop half the pepper, spring onions and cucumber and finely chop the other half. Pour the tomato juice into the bowl or jug of a blender or food processor and add the garlic, vinegar, the roughly chopped vegetables, tomatoes and olive oil, then blend until smooth. You can add some water if necessary to give the right consistency. Chill, adding the reserved finely chopped vegetables. Allow a couple of hours before serving for the flavours to develop.

Grape and Radicchio Salad

This salad combines the crisp taste of almonds with the aniseed taste of fennel and sweetness of grapes. It is served with a low-calorie dressing.

Serves 4

225g/8oz seedless green grapes
350g/12oz fennel, trimmed and chopped
50g/2oz blanched almonds, halved
115g/4oz radicchio

Dressing
150ml/¼ pint/⅔C natural yogurt
1 rounded tsp grated horseradish
¼ rounded tsp turmeric or saffron infused in a little water

Method
Place the salad ingredients in a serving bowl, combine the dressing ingredients together, pour over the salad and toss well. Serve with a pasta or lightly grilled white fish.

Mushroom and Pasta Salad

This simple neutralizing combination of pasta and mushrooms helps maintain the acid and alkaline balance in the body. It is cooling and easily digested, making it a good dish for either midday or the evening.

Serves 2

225g/8oz pasta bows
225g/8oz button mushrooms, sliced
I large clove garlic, crushed
300ml/½ pint/1¼C natural yogurt
sea salt and freshly ground black pepper

Method

Boil the pasta in plenty of salted water until cooked but still firm. Drain, rinse in cold water and cool, then mix with the mushrooms in a large bowl. Add the garlic to the yogurt, season, toss the pasta salad in the dressing and leave to marinate for at least an hour before serving. Serve on its own or with a sliced tomato and curd cheese.

Stuffed Mushrooms

Mushrooms make a light, low-fat meal and are a good source of potassium and some trace elements. Wild mushrooms have a wonderful texture and an earthy flavour. Their softness and dark-coloured juice show that mushrooms are a yin food with an affinity to the pacifying blue ray.

Serves 2

225g/8oz flat mushrooms
I small red onion, peeled
2 garlic cloves, peeled
I tbsp/1½ tbsp walnut or hazelnut oil
75g/3oz freshly chopped hazelnuts or almonds
50g/2oz fresh brown breadcrumbs
50g/2oz half-fat Cheddar cheese

Method

Preheat the oven to 190°C/375°F/gas mark 5. Remove the stalks from the mushrooms and chop them finely with the onion. Crush the garlic and add to the mixture. Heat the oil in a saucepan and fry the chopped mixture for a few minutes until the onion becomes transparent. Remove from the heat and stir in the hazel-nuts or almonds, breadcrumbs and cheese. Stuff the mushroom cups with the mixture, and bake in the oven for 20 minutes. Serve on a bed of shredded lettuce.

Penne with Red and Green Peppers

This simple but tasty dish is bursting with strong rustic charm. The flavouring given by the coriander and garlic is pungent and aromatic – perfect for an energy packed but healthy meal.

Serves 4

1 red pepper, quartered and deseeded
1 green pepper, quartered and deseeded
100ml/4fl oz/½C olive oil
2 cloves garlic, peeled and sliced
sea salt and freshly ground black pepper
450g/1lb penne (pasta quills)
a small bunch of coriander, finely chopped

Method

Grill or roast the peppers until the skins blister. Seal them in a plastic bag to cool, then peel them and cut them into strips. Heat 2 tbsp/2½ tbsp of the olive oil in a saucepan and cook the garlic until soft. Stir in the peppers and cook for a minute or two more. Season to taste and add the rest of the oil.

Boil the penne for 10–15 minutes until firm but cooked. Drain and toss in the pepper mixture. Stir in the coriander and serve immediately, accompanied by a green salad.

Red Dragon Pie

This pie is made of red aduki beans, which are much prized by the Chinese for their goodness. Serve with a classic seasonal green salad to balance the strong red ray in the pie.

Serves 4

115g/4oz dried aduki beans, soaked overnight in 1.1 litres/2 pints/5C water, and drained
50g/2oz/¼C brown rice
1.1 litres/2 pints/5C water

1 tbsp/1½ tbsp vegetable oil
1 onion, peeled and chopped
225g/8oz carrots, diced and blanched
170g/6oz small button mushrooms, whole
1–2 tbsp/1½–2½ tbsp soy sauce
2 tbsp/2½ tbsp tomato purée
1 rounded tsp mixed herbs
450g/1lb potatoes, peeled
30g/1oz/2 tbsp butter
sea salt and freshly ground black pepper

Method

Preheat the oven to 180°C/350°F/gas mark 4. Cook the aduki beans with the rice in the water for about 45 minutes, until cooked. Drain, reserving 300ml/½ pint/1¼C of the liquid. Heat the oil in a saucepan and fry the onion gently for about 5 minutes. Then, off the heat, add the carrots and mushrooms, and the cooked beans and rice. Mix the soy sauce, tomato purée and herbs with the aduki bean stock, and pour this over the bean and vegetable mixture. Bring to the boil and simmer on a low heat for 20–30 minutes, until the flavours are well blended. Meanwhile, boil the potatoes until soft and mash them with the butter.

Season the rice mixture to taste and add a little more liquid so that it's moist. Transfer to a greased 1.5 litre/2½ pint/6¼C casserole and spread the mashed potato over it. Bake for 35–40 minutes until the potato is crisp and brown.

Blue Poppy Seed Cake

The poppy seeds give this cake a subtle flavour and texture. Eat it for afternoon tea or as a dessert in the evening with a glass of milk or herb tea.

Makes one 20cm/8in cake

110g/4oz blue poppy seeds
250ml/8fl oz/1C milk
225g/8oz/1C butter
225g/8oz/1⅓C light raw cane sugar
3 free range eggs, separated
225g/8oz/2C plain (all-purpose) flour
1¼ rounded tsp baking powder

Method
Preheat the oven to 180°C/350°F/gas mark 4, and line and grease the cake tin.

Put the poppy seeds into the milk and bring to the boil in a small saucepan. Turn off the heat, cover and let them soak for 25 minutes. Meanwhile cream the butter and sugar together. Add the egg yolks, one at a time, and beat them into the butter and sugar mix thoroughly. Sift the flour and baking powder together and fold this into the creamed mixture. Stir in the poppy seeds and milk. Finally, whisk the egg whites until stiff and carefully fold them in. Spoon the mixture into the cake tin and bake for 1 hour or until the centre feels firm. Let the cake stand in the tin for 10 minutes on a rack before turning out.

Blueberry Yogurt

This nutritious smooth drink is delicious fresh from the fridge.

Serves 1

225g/8oz fresh or frozen blueberries
100–250ml/4–8fl oz/½–1C thin natural yogurt

To serve
a sprig of fresh apple mint

Method
Purée the blueberries in a blender or food processor. Add to the yogurt and blend together. Serve chilled with a sprig of fresh apple mint.

Yellow/Purple Cleansing Diet

If you have too much yellow in your system or low violet energy.

This diet cleanses the system, especially the liver, gall bladder, pancreas and spleen. It aids the assimilation of nutrients and elimination of waste material and is beneficial for the skin. The Yellow/Purple diet also aids study, as it nourishes the mind. Try to take regular exercise to suit your capabilities; this will assist your colour diet.

1 Grapefruit, orange or papaya (pawpaw) can be eaten at breakfast.
2 Eat plenty of yellow foods for breakfast and lunch and mid-afternoon.
3 Make use of yellow-skinned fruits and nuts. Banana and nuts with yogurt makes a perfect breakfast or lunch.
4 Make sure you have a good complex-carbohydrate meal. Either have it for breakfast (muesli and wholegrain bread or toast) or for lunch (potato, rice or pasta).
5 Do not have yellow dairy foods (eggs, cheese) for supper or in the evening, as these are difficult to digest and will not help you sleep.
6 Do not eat hard cheeses, which are very salty. Find low-fat cottage, cream or curd cheese instead.
7 After both lunch and supper drink a cup of either fennel or camomile tea.
8 Use olive oil, sunflower or soya oil for cooking or salad dressings.
9 Avoid all oily foods including peanuts and avocados. You may eat all other nuts. Fish must be white fleshed and not oily.
10 This diet is low-sugar, so use honey or fruit for sweetening.

A Sample Yellow/Purple Cleansing Menu

Before breakfast

a glass of water with the juice of half a lemon
a glass of solarized yellow water

Breakfast

banana, yogurt and sunflower seeds
grapefruit, orange or papaya (pawpaw)
2 slices wholegrain bread or toast, margarine, and honey, apricot fruit compote, or low-sugar marmalade
or muesli with nuts and dried fruits

Lunch

Fennel Soup, or any green soup, or carrot, lentil or sweetcorn
  soup
hummus with pitta bread
corn on the cob
mung dahl and vegetable curry and brown rice, cottage cheese
  and salad sandwich
maize or wholewheat pasta and spinach salad
mushroom or cheese omelette with parsley

Supper

stir-fried vegetables (may include chicken strips) and saffron rice
baked white fish with fennel and green vegetables
Lentil and Mushroom Slice, with baked butternut squash
baked potato and purple salad
aubergine bake with celeriac
buttered asparagus with mangetout
purple grapes
lychee and melon fruit salad

Yellow/Purple Cleansing Recipes

These recipes comprise a soup, three salads, three main courses,
two vegetable dishes and a dessert.

- Fennel Soup
- Lentil and Mushroom Slice
- Purple Pasta Salad
- Lemon Rice Salad
- Pasta, Olive and Aubergine Salad
- Purple-Sprouting Broccoli and Pine Nut Stir-Fry
- Trout with Lime Herb Crust
- Baked Onions
- Tropical Cocktail

Fennel Soup

Fennel is renowned for its benefits to the digestion and its effect on alleviating hunger. This delicious creamy coloured soup makes a wonderful lunch served with garlic bread.

Serves 2

2 fennel bulbs
45g/1½oz sunflower margarine
2 rounded tbsp plain (all-purpose) flour
300ml/½ pint/1¼C milk
150ml/5fl oz/⅔C thick set yogurt
sea salt
1 rounded tbsp chopped dill

Method
Simmer the fennel whole, in a pan of boiling water, for 40 minutes. Meanwhile melt the margarine in a pan, stir in the flour and add the milk gradually, stirring as the sauce thickens. Add the yogurt and simmer for 10 minutes. Season to taste with a little salt and then purée with the fennel in a liquidizer. Stir in the dill and serve either hot or chilled.

Lentil and Mushroom Slice

This is a wholesome and simple dish which contains a balance of yellow and purple energy. Serve it with a salad of radicchio and Iceberg lettuce and warm sage bread, which reflects the violet ray.

Serves 2

170g/6oz/¾C green lentils, soaked for 1 hour and drained
1 bay leaf
1 large purple-skinned onion, peeled and chopped
175/6oz button mushrooms, sliced
25g/1oz/2 tbsp butter or margarine
1 rounded tbsp chopped parsley
6 tbsp/½C vegetable stock
1 tbsp/1½ tbsp soya sauce
1 egg, beaten

I rounded tbsp mixed dried herbs
sea salt and freshly ground black pepper

Method

Preheat the oven to 190°C/375°F/gas mark 5 and grease a 1.5 litre/2½ pint/6¼C loaf tin.

Cover the lentils and the bay leaf in cold water and bring to the boil, then simmer for about 25–30 minutes until tender. Drain the lentils, discarding the bay leaf, and mix with the rest of the ingredients. Spread the mixture in the loaf tin and bake for 45–50 minutes until set. Leave the loaf to rest in the tin for 10 minutes before turning out onto a serving dish. Serve hot or cold.

Purple Pasta Salad

This purple salad can be eaten as a main dish or side salad. It is made from the combination of colours and tastes of purple beans and leaves with pale pasta shells.

Serves 4

450g/1lb red kidney beans, cooked, drained, rinsed and cooled
350g/12oz conchiglie (pasta shells) or spirals, cooked, drained, rinsed and
    cooled
1 green pepper, chopped finely
20 black olives, pitted
1 rounded tsp capers
4–5 sprigs of fresh parsley, chopped
2 small purple-leafed lettuces such as rosa pablo, ruby, lollo rosso or oakleaf

Dressing

1 rounded tsp sea salt
1 tbsp/1½ tbsp lemon juice
200ml/7fl oz/1C olive oil
1 rounded tsp sugar
2 rounded tsp finely chopped basil leaves
2 cloves garlic, crushed

Method

Mix together the kidney beans, pasta, green pepper, olives, capers and parsley. Mix well. To make the dressing, dissolve the salt in the lemon juice and add the other ingredients in order. Pour over the pasta, mixing it thoroughly and allowing 10 minutes for the flavours to develop. To serve, arrange the lettuce leaves on a serving dish and top with the salad mixture.

Lemon Rice Salad

This golden salad has the aromatic flavour of basmati rice with the added crunch of pine nuts. The lemon juice bleaches the turmeric so the resulting colour looks like saffron.

Serves 4

225g/8oz/1C basmati rice
1 bay leaf
1 rounded tsp turmeric
2.5cm/1in piece fresh root ginger, peeled and grated
juice of ½ a lemon
50g/2oz pine nuts
6 spring onions, chopped

Method
Boil the rice with the bay leaf, turmeric and ginger for 10–12 minutes until cooked. Cool slightly, then remove and discard the bay leaf and add the lemon juice, pine nuts and spring onions. Serve either slightly warm or chilled.

Pasta, Olive and Aubergine Salad

This yellow and purple salad, rich in vitamins and natural anti-oxidants, makes a filling but light lunch, which can be served on its own or with other dishes. Durum wheat pasta is a good complex carbohydrate that releases its energy slowly. The tangy taste of olives and aubergines give the pasta a variety of textures and flavours.

Serves 4

1 medium aubergine, washed
1 tbsp/1½ tbsp olive oil

350g/12oz conchiglie (pasta shells), cooked, drained, rinsed and cooled
1 large green pepper, deseeded and sliced
20 pitted black olives, halved
1 rounded tbsp capers
4–5 sprigs of fresh parsley, chopped
4 handfuls green or red salad leaves

Dressing
1 rounded tsp herb salt
1 tbsp/1½ tbsp lemon juice
200ml/7fl oz/1C olive oil
2 rounded tsp finely chopped basil leaves
2 cloves garlic, crushed

Method
Cut the aubergine in half lengthways and rub the cut surfaces with a little olive oil. Grill under a high heat for a few minutes on both sides, until the flesh is soft but not mushy, then allow to cool for 10 minutes. In the meantime combine the pasta shells, green pepper, olives, capers and parsley. Dice the aubergine into bite-sized pieces and add to the salad. To make the dressing, dissolve the salt in the lemon juice and add the other ingredients in order. Add to the salad and toss well. Serve on a bed of the salad leaves.

Purple-Sprouting Broccoli and Pine Nut Stir-fry

This quick and tasty dish preserves all the goodness in the vegetables, making it a light and easily digested meal. Serve it with aromatic saffron rice.

Serves 4

2 tsp/2 tsp olive oil
50g/2oz pine nuts
1 rounded tbsp chopped sun-dried tomatoes
350g/12oz purple-sprouting broccoli florets
350g/12oz Chinese leaves, chopped
1 tbsp/1½ tbsp tamari or soya sauce
juice of 1 lemon
1 tbsp/1½ tbsp pure water
sea salt and freshly ground black pepper

Method

Heat a wok or large frying pan. Add the oil and lightly fry the pine nuts, then remove them from the oil and drain on kitchen paper. Add the vegetables and stir-fry for 3–4 minutes, stirring all the time. Add the liquids and stir well. Sprinkle over the toasted pine nuts, season and serve immediately.

Trout with Lime Herb Crust

The violet ray in the trout is balanced by the yellow energy in the limes, to make a light and aromatic supper dish. Serve with green beans for perfect balance.

Serves 4

4 large trout fillets, skin removed
3 limes
4 rounded tbsp mixed chopped parsley, dill and tarragon
2 rounded tbsp fresh brown breadcrumbs
25g/1oz/2 tbsp butter

Method

Preheat the oven to 200°C/400°F/gas mark 6 and check all the bones have been removed from the fish by running your fingers over the flesh.

Grate two of the limes and mix the zest with the herbs and breadcrumbs. Melt the butter in a small pan and add the juice from two of the limes. Put the herb mixture on a flat plate, dip the skinned side of each fillet in the buttery lime juice, then press down firmly on the herb–breadcrumb mix. Put the herbed fillets on a baking sheet and very gently spoon over the remaining butter. Bake for 6–8 minutes and leave to rest in the oven for 2 minutes. Serve with green beans and the remaining lime cut in half.

Baked Onions

Baking small yellow-skinned onions brings out their sweetness and flavour while keeping in all their goodness. Onions are used as decongestants in traditional medicine.

Serves 4

675g/1½lb small onions or shallots
2 rounded tbsp sea salt
2 tbsp/2½ tbsp olive oil
juice of 1 small lemon

Method
Preheat the oven to 220°C/425°F/gas mark 7. Put the onions in a large roasting tin. Sprinkle with the salt and olive oil, and add enough water to cover the bottom of the tin. Bake the onions for 40–50 minutes until they are browned and sticky. Turn them occasionally and add a little more water if they dry out. Remove the onions when cooked and arrange on a plate. Squeeze over the lemon juice. Serve hot or cold, with crusty bread to mop up the juice.

Tropical Cocktail

This is a refreshing drink with all the zing of summer. It is cooling and cleansing. Choose yellowy-green seedless grapes, rather than the green variety, and dilute with sparkling mineral water to make a fizzy drink.

Serves 4

125g/4½oz seedless grapes
225g/8oz pineapple, chopped
225g/8oz watermelon, chopped
1 bottle sparkling mineral water, bottled at source
4 sprigs of apple mint leaves

Method
Purée all the fruit together in a blender or food processor. Sieve to remove the fibrous flesh. Dilute to taste. Decorate with a sprig of apple mint in each glass.

White/Pink/Gold/Violet Consciousness-Raising Diet

If you have a good balance of violet energy in your system or if you have a good balance of blue or green energy in your system.

This diet can help to link us to our intuition and creative energies. It is excellent for anyone who is following a spiritual path requiring meditation. This type of colour diet is known by some Indian spiritual practices as a *satvik* diet, which we looked at briefly in chapter 2 (page 23). It is based on light foods that help us develop our own individualized diet for spiritual life. These white, gold and violet foods have a vibrational harmonic to the heart and crown chakras. Green and pink food also balance the heart chakra and can for this reason accompany any meal but are especially relevant here.

This light energetic diet will nourish the spirit, but it can also leave you vulnerable emotionally, so take care to protect yourself as much as possible from the onslaught of a hostile world.

Every cell in our body is light sensitive, and it is well known that when light enters a cell certain reactions take place that affect the behaviour and growth of the cell. The DNA, which is the blueprint for the cell, can also be altered in structure, causing the vibratory rate of the cell to alter. It is therefore quite logical to suppose that the vibrations of the cells can be increased with the quality of the vital light energy entering our system.

Taking this process to its natural conclusion, it does not seem so incredible that it is within our capability to raise our level of consciousness to a higher vibration. As we raise the level of vibration at cellular level the physical body becomes less dense and we can take on an ethereal quality usually accredited to spiritual masters and angelic beings.

Once we reach the state of elevated consciousness that has been attained by many sages and yogis throughout history, the body needs very little physical sustenance, and vital energy from light, air and water can provide all the energy we need.

This consciousness-raising diet should be a natural progression from the cleansing yellow/green diet through a light vegetarian diet, and should only be undertaken when you are leading a lifestyle which protects you from the harsher elements of everyday life. Only continue with this diet if you feel comfortable doing so, otherwise revert to the Full-Spectrum Colours for Life Diet to make sure you are receiving a balance of all the rays.

1 Eat fruits, vegetables, nuts, seeds, grains and dairy products produced organically.
2 Exclude eggs: these are stimulating in vibration because they provide a vehicle for life.
3 Exclude meat and fish: vibrations of fear are held within the flesh and pollute the body.
4 Exclude tea, coffee, alcohol and other stimulants.
5 Four or five smaller meals a day are recommended. Eat only when hungry.
6 The meals eaten during the day should be made up of predominantly gold foods. Honey and blackstrap molasses are excellent nourishing gold foods.
7 The greater proportion of the evening meal should be white or pink or violet food.
8 Green foods can be eaten with any meal.
9 Herbs of the gold, green and purple vibrations should be used.
10 Exercise and deep breathing are essential accompaniments to this diet.

A Sample White/Pink/Gold/Violet Consciousness-Raising Menu

Early Morning

deep breathing with white light (*see* page 205)
glass of gold-solarized water

Breakfast

fruit such as apricots, bananas, golden apples, gold grapefruit, papaya (pawpaw) and peaches
herb tea – camomile or ginseng

Midmorning

live yogurt with nuts, seeds and honey
1 tbsp/1½ tbsp blackstrap molasses

Lunch

coconut and sweetcorn curry or risotto
corn on the cob and wholegrain bread
golden millet with orange, yellow or green peppers
butternut squash or pumpkin soup and wholegrain bread
maize, butterbean and purple kidney bean salad with marigold
   flowers
Bulgar Wheat and Chickpea Salad, with herb yogurt
pasta with olives, spring onions, walnuts and basil

Afternoon

dried fruit
fresh green fruit
nuts and raisins

Supper

tofu and green vegetable stew with scarlet runner beans
lentils and cauliflower in herb sauce with purple salad
globe artichoke hearts in garlic butter
Butterbean and Leek Pie, with sweet potatoes
toasted poppy seed and egg noodles
stuffed cabbage leaves with curd cheese and juniper berries
stir-fried mangetout, purple mushrooms and baby sweetcorn
purple grapes, watermelon, passionfruit, blackberries, blueberries
or bilberries

Evening

colour breathing and meditation (*see* page 206) with gold, violet
   and white light
camomile tea

White/Pink/Gold/Violet Consciousness-Raising Recipes

This diet is nourishing but pacifying, with no strong yang foods or strong flavourings, which resonate with the base chakras and sensual stimulation. Energy is obtained from the golden and pink rays, while the soothing qualities of yin are reflected in the white and green foods.

The recipes comprise one breakfast, two salads, one starter, three main courses, a rice dish and a dessert.

- Figs, Yogurt and Honey
- Green and White Salad with Tofu
- Bulgar Wheat and Chickpea Salad
- Sunshine Sweetcorn Chowder
- Asparagus with Tahini
- Saffron Risotto
- Sweet Lentil Curry
- Butterbean and Leek Pie
- Fragrant Rice Pudding

Going on this colour diet is a very personal decision, and you should not expect your partner (or anyone else) to go on it unless their lifestyle and expectations are similar to yours. For this reason the recipes below serve two people only, so you can share your food or make some recipes last for two meals.

Figs, Yogurt and Honey

The beautiful colouring of fresh figs reveals green and pink energy and these fruits are packed with nutrients. Fresh figs contain calcium and iron, potassium and B vitamins. Dried figs have a concentration of nutrients, so you get more vitamins and minerals. They also contain pectin, which is a soluble fibre believed to lower blood cholesterol.

Serves 2

2 fresh figs, halved, or 4 dried figs, quartered
6fl oz/¾C Greek set yogurt
1 tsp/1 tsp runny honey
1 rounded tbsp sunflower seeds

Method

Place the figs in a bowl and cover them with the yogurt. Drizzle the honey over the yogurt and top with the sunflower seeds.

Green and White Salad with Tofu

This is a crunchy salad which is high in protein and a good source of calcium, copper and vitamins C and E. The smooth aniseed dressing makes it easier to digest.

Serves 2

115g/4oz mild onion, peeled and chopped
50g/2oz mung bean sprouts, rinsed
50g/2oz shelled fresh peas
½ cucumber, diced
50g/2oz pumpkin seeds

Dressing
½ × 300g/10oz packet of tofu
1 tbsp/1½ tbsp cider vinegar
1 tbsp/1½ tbsp sesame oil
½ rounded tsp aniseed

Method

In a large bowl, mix all the salad ingredients together. To make the dressing, mix the ingredients, mashing or blending the tofu into the cider vinegar and sesame oil. Toss into the salad and serve immediately.

Bulgar Wheat and Chickpea Salad

This makes a tasty and nourishing snack, which requires no cooking. The golden earth energy contained in the bulgar wheat and chickpeas is fortifying for the mind and body, while the green herbs and yogurt bring freshness and uplifting quality to the meal.

Serves 2

225g/8oz bulgar wheat
1 × 432g/15¼oz can chickpeas, drained

½ cucumber, chopped
4 rounded tbsp chopped parsley
2 rounded tbsp chopped chives

Dressing
2 tbsp/2½ tbsp natural yogurt
2 tbsp/2½ tbsp olive oil
juice of ½ a lemon
1 rounded tsp curry powder
1 clove garlic, crushed

Method
Soak the bulgar wheat in warm water for 30 minutes. Drain, squeezing out the excess moisture with the back of a spoon. Put it in a bowl with the chickpeas, cucumber and herbs. Whisk together the dressing ingredients and fold them into the salad.

Sunshine Sweetcorn Chowder

This beautiful creamy soup is packed with light energy and is nourishing too. Serve it with warm granary bread and enjoy its radiant colouring.

Serves 2

2 medium sweetcorn cobs (or 1 × 285g/10oz can sweetcorn)
300ml/½ pint/1¼C water
25g/1oz sunflower margarine
6 spring onions, chopped
2 rounded tbsp plain (all-purpose) flour
300ml/½ pint/1¼C milk
a pinch of cayenne pepper
sea salt and freshly ground black pepper
a handful of chopped parsley

Method
If you're using fresh corn, cook the sweetcorn in boiling water for 15 minutes until cooked. Cut the corn off the cob. Add the water and then purée with a blender or liquidizer. If you're using

canned corn, add the water and then purée with a blender or liquidizer.

Heat the margarine in a pan and cook the spring onions for a few minutes. Stir in the flour and then add the milk gradually, stirring all the time until the mixture thickens. Season with the cayenne, salt and black pepper. Simmer for 5 minutes and add the sweetcorn purée. Garnish with chopped parsley and serve with warm bread.

Asparagus with Tahini

In the tradition of Buddha and of Pythagoras, the ancient Greek philosopher Plutarch taught the benefits of vegetarianism. This recipe, which is made from tender pinky-coloured asparagus tips, reflects the popularity of asparagus at the time. The sesame tahini reflects the golden ray and imbues the recipe with a nutty flavour. Eat it on its own or with warm wholegrain bread which you can dip into the sauce.

Serves 2

a large bunch of fresh asparagus
3 tbsp/¼C golden olive oil
3 cloves garlic, crushed
1 medium brown-skinned onion, finely chopped
4 tbsp/⅓C sesame tahini
550ml/18fl oz/2¼C water
sea salt
2 tbsp/2½ tbsp miso paste

Method

Preheat the oven to 190°C/375°F/gas mark 5. Cut off and discard the tough woody ends of the asparagus and scrub the stalks and tips, then divide the stalks into small bunches and tie with string. Stand the bunches upright in a tall fireproof pot with 2.5cm/1in of water at the bottom, cover and steam gently for about 8–10 minutes or until the spears are tender. Remove and set aside.

In a large skillet, heat the olive oil then add the garlic and onion. Cook for a few minutes until the onion turns golden-brown. Add the sesame tahini and about a third of the water. Stir until the tahini and water are well blended. Cook for 5 minutes then add the remaining water and simmer until the sauce thickens. Add the miso paste and mix this in well.

Place the asparagus spears in a casserole or ovenproof serving dish and pour over the sesame sauce. Bake for about 20 minutes, until the sauce is brown and bubbly. Serve immediately.

Saffron Risotto

Saffron is the most highly prized spice in the word. It gives this rice dish a fragrant and radiant gold colour.

Serves 2

½ rounded tsp saffron filaments
2 tbsp/2½ tbsp hot milk
2 tbsp/2½ tbsp vegetable oil
115g/4oz/½C basmati rice
85g/3oz cashew nuts
2 whole cardamom seeds, crushed
350ml/12fl oz/1½C pure water
225g/8oz peas (shelled weight)
sea salt

Method

Soak the saffron in the milk and leave it while you heat the oil in a pan and pour in the rice. Stir the rice in for a few minutes so that the rice becomes coated with oil. Add the cashew nuts and cardamom seeds, and pour in the water and add the peas with salt to taste. Give this a stir and then cover and cook slowly until the liquid is absorbed – about 20 minutes. Add the saffron in its milk and stir until it is mixed in with the rice grains and they are well cooked. Remove from the heat for a minute or two and serve.

Sweet Lentil Curry

This recipe is the dish prepared for George Bernard Shaw by his cook, and according to Alice Laden was one of his most loved recipes. It comes from *The George Bernard Shaw Vegetarian Cookbook* by Alice Laden and R J Minney.

Serves 2

225g/8oz/1C lentils, washed, soaked overnight, and drained
225g/8oz/1C rice
2 medium onions, chopped
2 large cooking apples, chopped
2 bananas, sliced
1 rounded tsp brown sugar
1 rounded tsp curry powder
1 tsp/1 tsp lemon juice
85g/3oz/⅓C raisins
1 tbsp/1½ tbsp chutney, finely chopped
30g/1oz/¼C shredded coconut

Method
Put the lentils in a saucepan, cover with boiling water and simmer until soft. Meanwhile boil the rice in lightly salted water until done. Add the cooked lentils, onions, apples, bananas, brown sugar, curry powder, lemon juice and raisins and simmer for 15 minutes, then strain off excess liquid and turn into a hot serving dish. To serve, mix the rice with the chutney, form it into a ring and sprinkle with the coconut.

Butterbean and Leek Pie

This filling pie, white, gold and green, is full of nutritional and energetic goodness. It is gently flavoured with honey, mustard and onion, and has a pacifying creamy texture.

Serves 2

3 medium leeks, chopped
½ cauliflower, cut into florets
25g/1oz/2 tbsp butter
1 small onion, chopped
2 cloves garlic, chopped
1 rounded tbsp plain (all-purpose) flour
1 rounded tsp ground coriander
sea salt and freshly ground black pepper
250ml/8fl oz/1C vegetable stock
1–2 tbsp/1½–2½ tbsp coarse-grain mustard

1 tsp/1 tsp clear honey
400g/14oz butterbeans, soaked overnight and drained
50g/2oz ricotta, crumbled
115g/4oz fresh wholemeal breadcrumbs

Method

Preheat the oven to 180°C/350°F/gas mark 4. Cook the leeks and cauliflower in boiling water for about 15 minutes until tender. Drain and set aside.

Melt the butter, add the onion and garlic, and fry gently for 5–8 minutes until soft. Sprinkle over the flour and stir for a further 5 minutes. Add the coriander, season, then add the stock, stirring constantly until smooth. Stir in the mustard and honey and cook over a low heat for 2–3 minutes.

Add the butterbeans to the leek and cauliflower mixture, stir in the sauce and pour into an ovenproof dish. Mix the ricotta and breadcrumbs together, sprinkle over the top and bake for 30 minutes.

Serve with a mixed salad and crusty bread.

Fragrant Rice Pudding

A creamy rice pudding is soothing and settling, especially on a cold night. For the healing energy of the indigo ray add raisins, and spice it with a vanilla pod.

Serves 2

8 rounded tbsp pudding rice
300ml/½ pint/1¼C milk
300ml/½ pint thick-set low-fat yogurt
1 vanilla pod split in half lengthways or 1 tsp/1 tsp vanilla extract
a large knob of butter
100ml/4fl oz/½C water
4 rounded tbsp caster (superfine granulated) sugar
50g/2oz raisins
50g/2oz chopped blanched almonds

Method

Put the rice in a heavy-based pan, then pour in the milk, yogurt, vanilla pod or extract, butter and water. Bring to the boil over a medium heat, then turn down the heat until the milk is simmering gently. Cook for 15–20 minutes until the rice is soft. Remove the vanilla pod. Add the sugar, raisins and almonds and simmer for a further 5 minutes until the pudding is really thick. Serve hot or cold.

9 | Healing Specific Ailments

As we have seen, when we're healthy vital light energy flows freely around the body, but if it becomes blocked illness and disease are quick to follow. Each food contains colour energy which energizes and heals a particular chakra and also the related body system, organs, and glands controlled by that centre.

Our internal organs vibrate at different rates corresponding to the vibratory rate of specific colour wavelengths. Should a gland be malfunctioning or diseased, we can consciously introduce the colour needed to correct the unharmonious vibrations of the organ. The colour vibration sets up a positive blueprint, which is transferred to the organs and glands through sympathetic resonance. The colour vibrations act as a catalyst triggering the body's own healing mechanisms.

Remember the radio signal image that we used in chapter 7. When the tuner moves slightly off the station, instead of receiving the signal loud and clear we hear all sorts of unharmonious crackling and squelching sounds. A chakra centre can also lose its harmonious vibration and the unharmonious vibrations will transfer to its related organs and glands.

For example, a block in the flow of blue energy will result in the throat chakra losing its frequency, and this may result in the lungs becoming congested. By introducing blue energy by way of breathing, eating blue-coloured food or drinking blue-solarized water, we can retune the chakra and the blocked energy held in the lungs will be released. When colour harmony has been achieved it will allow the natural free flow of energies around the body once more which will also promote a healthy mental and emotional state.

We do have to keep in mind that we need a balance of all colour energies in the body, so while we should eat some food with a specific colour healing energy for a specific illness we must look for foods from all the other rays as well to aid the healing process. As an example, consider jaundice, which entails an energy block created in the liver. Yellow and green foods and drink will cleanse the liver, while anti-inflammatory, soothing alkaline foods of the blue ray will also be useful.

Once the colour imbalance has been corrected, you will feel an improvement not only in the area where your discomfort originally lay but in your whole being. You will also feel better mentally and emotionally and be more at peace with yourself.

You need to use your intuition in order to decide how much colour corrective food is required and when to revert to the Full-Spectrum Colours for Life Diet. The messages your body gives you will let you know when the healing process has been completed. Returning to the Colours for Life Diet will maintain an inner balance and keep all parts of your being strong and protected.

Here are some recommendations for colour treatments of specific ailments that may relate to physical, emotional or mental problems.

Red

Chakra: base of spine
Glands/body organs: adrenals, kidneys, bladder, liver, legs
Action on: muscular system, blood

This ray provides our body with energy and vitality. It vibrates in harmony with the area at the base of the spine. Treatment with the red ray stimulates this centre and promotes heat – raising the body temperature, stimulating the circulation of the blood and getting the adrenaline going. It disperses feelings of tiredness and inertia, as well as chronic chills and colds. Red's psychological effects include feeling confident, stimulated, uplifted and full of initiative; red energy helps us overcome depression, and gives us will-power and courage.

Red meat, poultry and animal products also fall into the red and infra-red part of the spectrum, but as these are dead foods – devoid of light energy – they should be avoided. Foods derived from the animal kingdom are physically high in cholesterol and also retard spiritual development. If you must eat meat, however, poultry is less yang than red meat and lower in saturated fat, so it is the better choice. Animal products contain the four elements (earth, air, fire and water) whereas plants only contain one active element, water. This also means according to ancient Eastern wisdom that by eating plant materials alone we accumulate less negative karma. Karma is an Indian term which encompasses one of the fundamental laws of the universe – that of cause and effect. It is based on the principle of reincarnation and the notion that we accumulate the consequences of our actions for every life we experience. Negative karma refers to the effects of our bad thoughts and actions in this and previous lives; it will ultimately hold us back from escaping from the endless cycle of rebirth.

Salt is one of the most yang foods vibrating on the red ray. Too many salty or heavily spiced foods will almost certainly result in imbalances, leading also to a sugar craving. If, however, you crave salt, it may be that you need more sodium and chlorides in your diet. These are needed for the absorption of nutrients into the cells. Foods that help such cravings include apples, asparagus, beetroot, celery, cucumber, figs, oatmeal, olives and peaches.

Lycopene is the pigment that gives tomatoes their red colouring, and in fact tomatoes contain higher levels of it than any other fruit or vegetable. It is a powerful antioxidant, which fights certain toxins that can trigger cancer cells. As tomatoes are consumed in large quantities in some Mediterranean countries it may account for the low incidence of prostate cancer in those regions. (It is also interesting to note that the hue of tomatoes – red – is the colour of physical love, and that older men from Mediterranean countries are known for their interest in lovemaking!)

Another pigment which gives food its natural red colouring is porphyrin, a red compound that forms the active nucleus of haemoglobin. Related to this structure is the polypyrrole molecule of vitamin B_{12}, which is essential to the formation of healthy red blood cells.

Cell salts are essential elements for good health, and when one or more salts becomes deficient, normal cell function is disturbed and disease will result. Strawberries contain six biochemic cell salts and are probably the richest fruit in these salts.

Red foods can be an excellent help if you suffer from anaemia, paralysis, poor circulation or blood disorders, or are chilled and cold. Extreme tiredness or being generally run down can best be helped by eating food that has a stimulating and energizing effect; tired people need red energy to balance their body's energy system and should eat fruit and vegetables rich in the red ray, which can regenerate depleted energy centres, build up the immune system and clean out the retained toxins and bad vibrations.

Ailments Related to the Red Ray

High Blood Pressure
If you suffer from high blood pressure, avoid strong spices, especially those on the red and orange ray such as mustard, black pepper, ginger and nutmeg. Use instead green-ray herbs to flavour food (*see* chapter 3, page 54–5), and eat plenty of green leafy vegetables. Cooked tomatoes become very acidic, and people with high blood pressure and many heart conditions are recommended by nutritionists not to eat cooked tomatoes as they may aggravate the condition. Avoid all citrus juices and acidic forming berries such as blackcurrants, grapes and cranberries. You still require red-ray energy, and pink watermelon is excellent for providing this energy; watermelon also has green energy, so it will not aggravate the condition.

Gout
Gout means the bloodstream needs to be cleansed and stimulated. All animal products of the red ray should be cut out, as gout is usually the product of over-indulgence of yang foods. Violet is a good colour to help gout sufferers as the blue within it cools and heals while the red stimulates blood flow. Juniper berries can be used as food flavouring, also red sour cherries. Parsley and ginger are red-ray foods that can be used without ill effect. Green juices are highly recommended, especially celery juice. Carrot and pineapple juice will also act as blood cleansers.

Kidney Disease
Avoid spinach and rhubarb; these red-ray foods contain oxalic acid, which will inflame the kidneys. Eat instead plenty of foods from the green and blue energy rays, including asparagus, garlic, mushrooms and potatoes. Red-ray energy can be obtained from horseradish, parsley, watermelon and watercress. Neutral foods like cottage cheese and honey are both soothing, as are bananas and papaya (pawpaw).

Muscle Spasms

Muscle spasms are usually caused by mineral deficiency. Manganese and silica supplements should accompany a diet rich in foods containing minerals and cell salts. Strawberries and red cherries are particularly rich in these. Honey also soothes and relaxes the muscles. The darker the honey is the more minerals it contains, especially if it is made by cold pressing.

Orange

Chakra: sacral centre
Glands/body organs: reproductive organs, spleen, prostate
Action on: immune system, reproductive system, digestive system

This ray assists in the assimilative, distributory and circulatory processes of the body and is drawn into the body's system at the splenic centre. Orange links strongly with the reproductive organs of both men and women. The orange ray is also often called the wisdom ray as it combines the physical red ray and the yellow mental ray.

Orange is wonderful for removing our inhibitions and any feelings of repression, of being in a rut or fear of change. It helps us to cope with new ideas and become more flexible, and supplies us with the courage to cope with life, thus giving us emotional strength.

The US National Cancer Institute estimates that about a third of cancers are linked to bad diet, so what you eat may significantly help reduce your risk. Certain foods block the chemicals that initiate cancer. Antioxidants found in some vitamins and minerals, and in orange-coloured apricots and watermelons, have been found to can destroy oxidizing free radicals, the substances thought to make cells more susceptible to cancer, and some can even repair some of the cellular damage that has been done. Some foods, for example wheat bran, have also been shown to shrink pre-cancerous cells. Beta-carotene is one of the most studied antioxidants, found in deep green, yellow and orange vegetables, such as spinach, sweet potatoes and carrots. In studies in Harvard University, it was found to have a direct effect on toxic cells taken from malignant tumours. It also reduced the growth of lung cancer cells and altered the proteins needed for tumours to grow.

One hundred and seventy studies carried out in 17 nations revealed that people who eat the most fruits and vegetables have about half the cancer rates of those who eat the least. Ordinary fruits and vegetables have even been found to cut the risk of lung cancer caused by smoking.

Ailments Related to the Orange Ray

Asthma

If the asthma is chronic it can be treated with orange, but if the condition is acute and very painful blue is the better choice. Even if the asthma has a physical cause it is often found in shallow breathers who have emotional and mental problems relating to fear. These sufferers are breathing fearfully and need to be taught how to breathe powerfully. Deep rhythmic breathing is most important in order to free the body from poisons and mucus, and to enable the blood to circulate properly.

All mucus-forming foods should be cut out of the diet. These are mainly meat, eggs and dairy products. Replace cow's milk with soya milk. Avoid watery yin foods such as fruit juices, cold drinks and iced foods, as well as sugar. All warm orange, yellow or green herb teas are very beneficial; the permeating aroma helps soothe the throat and clear the lungs. Eat warm cooked foods, avoiding spicy or cold food. Garlic and ginger also help release mucus from the body.

Asthma is aggravated by humid conditions and dampness as well as air pollutants, so avoid these conditions if possible. Deep breathing with orange is very beneficial (*see* chapter 10, page 206), using a strong positive mental affirmation. Bronchitis and other chest troubles can also be helped in this way.

Enteritis (Inflamed Intestinal Tract)

Symptoms of this problem can include fever, diarrhoea and constipation, and are usually accompanied by abdominal pain. Anyone suffering from this condition should abstain from extreme foods in both the infra-red and ultraviolet range, such as salt and sugar. They should temporarily avoid all animal products, and their diet should concentrate on rice, millet, rye and grains other than wheat flour. Oily and greasy foods should be avoided, as should acid-forming fruits. Soothing white/green ray foods like buttermilk, curds, soya milk and yogurt can be taken, as they contain living bacteria that strengthen the intestines.

Male Impotence

Plenty of regular exercise and continued regular sexual activity are desirable in cases of impotence, as suffers need to connect with the body and revitalize the *chi* within our systems (as we all do). Certain psychological aspects should be considered, such as building up self-esteem and self-love.

Zinc-rich foods should be eaten, such as egg yolks, ginseng, golden seal (*Hydrastis canadensis*), pumpkin seeds, raw honey, sesame seeds and wheatgerm oil. These all fall under the orange and golden-yellow rays' energy. Pollen and vitamin E and F supplements are also recommended.

Menstrual Problems

Here orange energy imbalance needs attention, and foods from the magnetic colours of red, orange and golden-yellow should be eaten in abundance. Apricots, blackcurrants, blackstrap molasses, eggs, nuts, red grapes, red beets, prunes or cherry juice, and wholegrains are all excellent for sacral centre problems.

For menstrual cramps a warm bath containing a few drops of one or more of the following essential oils will bring relief: basil, bergamot, black pepper, camphor, cardamom, cypress, juniper, neroli, rosemary and sandalwood. These oils harmonize with the red and orange frequency, which releases and expands contracting muscles. Cypress and sandalwood are on the blue frequency and will help soothe pain.

Rheumatism

Rheumatism is a word that many people use to describe a whole array of ailments relating to pain in the joints, muscles, tendons and connective tissues. Many of these problems occur because of poor circulation and a build-up of calcium deposits around the joints. A diet rich in antioxidants is very beneficial, of which orange food is the best source.

Orange energy increases circulation without increasing heat in the body and so increases blood supply into the muscles helping to improve movement. Often rheumatism is brought on by damp, cold weather, and warming orange foods help remove the dampness from the body, gently energizing and warming us from the inside out. Many recognized anti-arthritis diets in use for many years are based on fresh raw food rich in vitamin C and beta-carotene. The regular intake of apple cider vinegar can also reduce and prevent calcification. Cereals, eggs and brewer's yeast (a blue-ray food), which supply selenium, are also beneficial in reducing inflammation.

Yellow

Chakra: solar plexus
Glands/body organs: liver, gall bladder, pancreas, stomach, brain
Action on: nervous system, digestive system

The yellow ray is associated with the solar plexus and is a very important centre for the whole nervous system. The connection between the solar plexus and the nerves is clear; as we all know, when we are nervous we often get butterflies in our stomachs and experience a feeling of constriction and pain in the chest and abdomen. Yellow controls our digestive processes, our liver and intestines, and the mucous membranes within the body. It is eliminative, so it is the purifier of the whole system and promotes secretions which fortify the endocrine system.

Yellow is the mental ray and stimulates the intellectual faculties: yellow foods nourish the brain cells and central nervous system. Yellow stimulates the logical mind and reasoning powers so while studying or undertaking any mental or scientific study we should eat as much yellow food as possible. In order to keep the 'electrolyte soup' of the brain in top condition we need to increase our potassium intake, and golden-yellow foods such as bananas, dates, mushrooms and nuts will help to keep our minds alert.

Citrus fruit possess a natural substance that neutralizes the powerful chemical carcinogens in animal-derived foods. Swedish studies found that those who ate citrus fruit daily reduced the risk of pancreatic cancer by half. Foods containing the yellow ray will purify the blood and are particularly good for the skin. (As a physical remedy, add yellow-ray apple cider vinegar to bath water 1 tbsp/30ml to alleviate itchy skin.) However, yellow-ray energy needs to be balanced with blue-ray foods. Yarrow and marjoram and violet are blue/violet herbs which can be made into teas which also help with skin troubles. When we have jaundice or hepatitis our skin turns yellow – we have a block in our eliminating process and have an excess of the yellow ray. The banana with its strong yellow energy can act as a regulator of the large intestine (*read* Dr H E Stanton's *The Healing Factor* for further details). Treatment with the yellow ray can be helpful in cases of nervous exhaustion, indigestion, constipation, liver troubles and diabetes.

Evening primrose oil has been used for centuries to treat complaints such as colds and mental depression, and problems relating to the liver, spleen and digestive system. This oil is made from the seed of the yellow evening primrose flower, which contains amongst other things gamma-linolenic acid (GLA). GLA is a vital chemical needed by all the body organs in order for them to function properly. It also helps form cell membranes through which food and oxygen flow into the cells and waste materials flow out. Evening primrose oil operates on the yellow colour frequency, strengthening the central nervous system, and by taking a supplement of evening primrose oil one can treat conditions as diverse as eczema, alcoholism, hyperactivity and diabetes, as well as prevent many more.

Ailments Related to the Yellow Ray

Alcoholism

There are many reasons why people become dependent on alcohol, and like all obsessive behaviour patterns one trigger is disharmony between our minds and our bodies. A good diet, such as one that uses the Colours for Life principles, will help to restore balance on a physical level, while the underlying causes should be addressed by counselling and psychotherapy. A colour-corrective diet can also be used to supplement the treatment. Both yellow and purple foods will be of assistance here. Yellow/green has a purgative action on the liver, and the purple energy contained in food will help balance the pituitary and glandular functions. Purple energy is especially good for redressing mental imbalances where there is a problem with obsessive behaviour and phobias.

Food cravings and diabetes

Often our cravings result from an imbalance in our diet. We may be overloading our body with either sweet or salty foods. If we have been eating too much salt (which is yang) we will try and compensate by eating sugary foods. As a result the pancreas, the gland situated behind the stomach, may fail to produce enough insulin – the hormone that regulates the blood-sugar level. Those suffering from full-blown diabetes should obtain medical advice and treatment, whilst remaining aware that troubles related to the pancreas, gall bladder and liver indicate a blockage in the yellow energy centre.

It has been found that when focused on the solar plexus, green light stimulates the head of the pancreas to produce insulin. This indicates that, in all probability, we can stimulate the pancreas with vital energy from golden, golden-yellow and green foods.

To restore balance and the body's natural processes, gentle regular exercise is recommended with a diet low in salt and high in fibre. Fibre-rich foods include almonds and spinach, and baked beans, bran cereals, jacket potatoes and wholewheat bread, which are golden-brown complex carbohydrates. These release energy gradually throughout the day, instead of providing one quick high, unlike proteins, especially those of animal origin, which take a great deal of body energy to digest, putting greater pressure on the internal organs related to digestion, and should be avoided.

Follow the yellow colour-corrective diet for a week before starting with the Full-Spectrum Colours for Life Diet. If you feel you need another week of the yellow diet, alternate this with the Colours for Life Diet until you feel in harmony and your cravings disappear.

Gallstones

Gallstones occur when there is too much mucus and fatty acids in the body fluids. Too much food in the ultraviolet range is a contributory cause; cold drinks, sugars, ice-creams, synthetic colourings and additives are all such foods. Bitter resentment built up over a period of time may be the underlying cause and these negative thoughts often turn into crystallized form.

As the foods which aggravate this condition are yin in nature – that is, from the blue to ultraviolet wavelengths – the body requires balance from golden-brown and orange foods. Pumpkins and squashes are very beneficial. Cooking with ginger also helps melt the stones. Orange-solarized water can be taken daily, and colour visualizations in which the stones are seen to dissolve also reinforce the melting action. Colour breathing with a golden-peach light has also been found to be most beneficial. Treatment by a qualified colour therapist using orange light over the kidneys and lower spine has been found to be most successful (*see Seven rays to Colour Healing* by Roland Hunt for more details).

Hypoglycaemia

Hypoglycaemia can result from prolonged stress, causing an imbalance in our energy system, from untreated diabetes, and from alcoholism, as excessive adrenalin is produced when anxiety is exacerbated by sustained alcohol consumption. Hypoglycaemia causes acute hunger, confusion and irritability. The brain cannot store glucose, the energy needed for all its functions, so it must get it from the bloodstream. If the bloodstream contains too little sugar, the sufferer becomes confused and sweaty, with a rising pulse, and if not treated many become unconscious; brain damage may follow. If you are hypoglycaemic, eat regularly to avoid wild swings in energy – typically a light meal or a snack every three or four hours. Avoid refined carbohydrates, eating wholegrains instead. Wholegrains are digested more slowly, thus maintaining a more stable blood-sugar level, and the complex carbohydrates will keep you going for much longer than other types of foods.

As with diabetes, sufferers have a malfunctioning yellow energy centre which is related to the nerves and the liver, gall bladder and pancreas. The liver stores glucose in the form of glycogen, releasing it again as glucose when required. In the case of hypoglycaemia, the liver requires stimulation as the flow of glucose is blocked. Yellow-green bitter salad vegetables like raw spinach, chicory and endive can help to stimulate liver functions and the other digestive processes.

Illnesses Requiring Treatment by X-rays or Synthetic Drugs

If we look at the electromagnetic spectrum we see that X-rays form part of the higher frequencies of ultraviolet light. X-rays can be very damaging to our health, especially as the effects are cumulative. That means that even though one is exposed to a small amount of radiation with each X-ray taken, the total exposure can damage healthy cells.

Both X-rays and synthetic drugs fall into the ultraviolet part of the spectrum, and so they give rise to a sharp imbalance of the violet/yellow energy levels in our systems. We need to combat this overstimulation of the violet energy centres by introducing a quantity of yellow energy into our system. This we can do by drinking lemon juice, or eating foods containing lemon peel. Lemon juice can be made more potent by solarizing a glassful in the sun for a hour before cooling and drinking. Experiments in some hospitals in which patients were given lemon juice compounds proved that this treatment was most helpful and allowed the patients to withstand much heavier therapeutic radiation without damage to healthy cells.

Jaundice

When the bile duct in the liver becomes obstructed, bile is absorbed into the bloodstream, producing a yellowish facial and skin discoloration. The blockage is caused by foods which are mucus- and fat-forming. For this reason all fried, oily or greasy foods should be cut out of the diet. All animal products, including meat, eggs and dairy products, should be avoided.

Fasting for two or three days is most beneficial if we wish to cleanse ourselves internally, but a fast should only be undertaken with the supervision of an experienced person, preferably a medical practitioner. For most people a day or two without solid food is sufficient. This is known as a liquid fast. Choose a weekend or a time when you can relax and recharge your batteries. Make yourself nourishing juices from fresh fruit and vegetables. Include juice from organically grown carrots, as it is high in vitamins B, C, D, E and K. Another widely used combination is asparagus, beetroot, carrot and cucumber juice. Cabbage juice is prized as a nerve tonic – particularly if you suffer from insomnia. Pineapple juice is valuable as it contains enzymes which destroy many types of acute infections. In addition to consuming fruit and vegetable juices, be sure to drink plenty of pure water and herbal teas.

Other types of fast should be accompanied by drinking blue-solarized water three times a day. Eat lightly cooked green- and blue-ray vegetables, plus some rice and lentils, until the system clears.

Parkinson's Disease

This disease is associated with degeneration of both the central nervous system and the muscular system of the body. This means that there is an imbalance of the yellow and violet energies. Yellow is associated with the nervous system and violet is associated with glandular functioning of the pineal and pituitary glands, as well as the central nervous system of the brain and spinal cord.

Organically grown golden-yellow food, like raw nuts, grains and sprouting seeds provide nourishment to both these systems. Yellow-fleshed turnips have been found to be especially useful.

Citrus juice mixed in with ½ rounded tsp pure gelatine has also been found to be beneficial (*see* the *Handbook of Natural Healing* by Dr Airola, PhD, for more details).

Stomach and Duodenal Ulcers

During the digestive process the stomach produces strong hydro-chloric acid, and if this acid secretion becomes excessive, ulcers occur. Mildly alkaline vegetables can cause the stomach to secrete pepsin, which helps regain the balance of the digestive juices. Strongly yin or alkaline foods, however, have the opposite effect and stimulate the secretion of strong acids in the upper stomach. If this occurs over a lengthy period the stomach lining becomes irritated and easily ruptures.

Duodenal ulcers are caused by an excess of acid or red-ray animal foods.

Fasting is recommended for both types of ulcers. Once food is reintroduced into the diet the following guidelines apply:

1 Food should be lightly cooked and mildly seasoned.
2 Salt should be used sparingly.
3 Eighty per cent of the diet should be golden-brown grains and cereals, lentils and beans: the remaining twenty per cent should consist of both green leafy vegetables and root vegetables like carrots, potatoes, parsnips, swedes and turnips.
4 Yogurt contains live bacterial culture and live enzymes so assists in proper digestion and elimination. It has been found to assist in cases of stomach ulcers (*see* Dr H E Stanton's *The Healing Factor* for further details). It also protects the body against infection.

The Colours for Life Diet should keep the digestion in balance.

Green

Chakra: heart
Glands/body organs: thymus, heart, arms, hands, breasts
Action on: circulatory system, parasympathetic nervous system, digestive system

The green ray rests in the cardiac centre. Green's psychological effects include bringing a feeling of new life, freshness and brightness, and relieving stress, emotional problems and tensions:

often when we have had a severe crisis, whether with a relationship or at work, we need to lower our blood pressure and relieve the tensions by surrounding ourselves with green. Green also alleviates headaches and other problems due to tension. Green links to the circulatory system and especially the heart, and green cold-pressed vegetable oils such as olive oil are now finding a place in the prevention of heart disease and high blood pressure. Green energy neutralizes disharmony of malignant cells, cysts, tumours and cancers. It also affects the digestive system and the para-sympathetic nervous system.

Chlorophyll, which gives plants their green colouring, appears to promote regeneration of damaged liver cells, and also increases circulation to all the organs by dilating blood vessels. In the heart, chlorophyll aids in transmission of nerve impulses that control contractions of the muscle. The heart rate is slowed, yet each contraction is increased in power, thus improving the overall efficiency of cardiac work.

Dark green leafy vegetables lower the risk of many cancers. Spinach, broccoli, kale and dark green lettuce are full of antioxidants, folate and lutein. Green vegetables are also high in biochemic cell salts essential for healthy body functions: lettuce, spinach and cucumber contain eight biochemic cell salts each, cabbage and asparagus six cell salts each. Cruciferous vegetables, such as cabbage, cauliflower, Brussels sprouts, broccoli, kale, mustard greens and turnips, eaten lightly cooked (so as not to destroy the vitamins and minerals) as part of a low fat diet, may reduce the risk of breast, stomach and colon cancer.

Green grapes have been found invaluable for re-establishing the appropriate acid–alkali balance in the body, which is why grape diets have proved very popular. The Colours for Life Diet does not encourage one-food diets; a cleansing and balancing diet based on different green, yellow and violet foods will have the similar effect without leaving the body stripped of essential minerals and vitamins.

Ailments Related to the Green Ray

Abnormal Blood Pressure (Hypertension or Hypotension)
Abnormally high or low blood pressure falls under the green ray because it governs the circulatory system of the body, keeping it in balance so that neither should occur.

High blood pressure (hypertension) is often found to be a secondary symptom of other problems related to the heart and circulation, so these should be looked into first. High blood pressure can result from eating too much food in the infra-red and red category. These are high in saturated fats and cholesterol, which clog up the arteries and arterial walls.

A balanced diet favouring green leafy vegetables, fruits and herbs, and omitting dairy and animal red-ray foods and cooked tomatoes can soon correct this imbalance. If these red foods are avoided, it is important that foods from the ultraviolet end of the spectrum, especially sugar, cool drinks and ice-cream, are also avoided, if balance is to be maintained.

Low blood pressure (hypotension) can be greatly relieved by a high intake of iron-yielding foods, especially green leafy vegetables like spinach, which have a high content of red-ray energy in them. Consider taking a mineral supplement daily as well as eating red-orange fruits and vegetables. There are about twenty-five mineral elements present in the body, in varying proportions. Some of them – such as sodium, calcium and iron – are essential elements, forming part of tissues or body compounds, and you may therefore wish to take these minerals in supplement form (although a sensible precaution might be to consult your doctor or nutritionist first). Most of the other minerals, known as trace minerals, are required in very small amounts and are likely to be present in the majority of foods, so that it is usually unnecessary to take them as supplements.

High-protein vegetable foods such as red kidney beans and red lentils, together with soya or tofu, will strengthen the blood and circulation. Drinking red-solarized water every morning will be excellent. Peppermint and parsley tea is stimulating and full of nutrients, and cooking with rosemary, thyme and mint helps raise arterial blood pressure. Once the blood pressure returns to normal, the Colours for Life Diet will maintain energy levels. Remember, it is common for the blood pressure of vegetarians to be about 10mm lower than that of meat eaters.

Colds and Influenza

Lemon juice in warm water is very soothing when you have a sore throat or suffer from congestion in the lungs. Pineapple juice also contains enzymes which destroy many types of acute infections. Garlic is a wonderful antibiotic and is a powerful antiseptic: cooking with garlic or eating garlic raw or in tablet form helps combat bronchitis and sinusitis. Golden-yellow honey is another marvellous agent for fighting bacteria and alleviates cold symptoms.

Cysts

It is very important to note where in the body a growth occurs and the organs that may be affected, because there are many emotional and mental attitudes that might be the underlying cause of the problem. The area of the body where the cyst occurs will give a hint of the type of suppressed emotions or negative mind patterns which need to be released and the area where energy is blocked in the system. Green has a beneficial effect on irregular growth of cells, neutralizing the unharmonious vibrations of malignant growths. It balances and harmonizes the body at the cellular level, giving the body time for the immune system to respond to the irregular cells, recognizing and destroying them. This insufficient response by the immune system to cells which are not obeying the rules of growth leads to cancer cells reproducing unchecked (*read* Dr Christine Page's book *Frontiers of Health* for more information).

Green leafy vegetables are a most important part of a corrective diet, for all types of growths. Eating fresh natural foods in season is one of the most important guiding principles of the Colours for Life Diet and is particularly important in these cases. To prevent cysts, eliminate toxins and foods that cause fat and mucus to collect around an organ. Drinking green-solarized water and green teas can be beneficial. For ovarian cysts, bathing in bath water coloured green by vegetables such as turnip tops is very soothing and healing. Alternatively, use can be made of green-ray aromatic essential oils such as geranium and palma rosa.

Blue

Chakra: throat
Glands/body organs: throat, thyroid, parathyroids, lungs, mouth
Action on: respiratory system

Blue is located at the throat centre and has a contracting and constricting action. It slows things down so that the body can combat infectious diseases in which there is a rise in temperature. It is an antiseptic, light and cooling, and astringent. It controls our self-expression and speech. Blue encourages transportation of oxygen to the tissues. If blue is deficient we will suffer from fatigue due to lack of oxygen in the system and brain cells.

Blue can bring peace and quiet of mind, especially where there has been over-excitement, or mental torture. Although it can be relaxing and calming, too much blue can become depressing, so it should be used in conjunction with its complementary colour, orange. If you serve a plate of blue foods, you could serve them either accompanied by orange food or on an orange plate.

Blue food can help alleviate throat troubles, fevers and children's ailments such as measles and mumps, inflammations, spasms, stings, itchiness and headaches as well as sunburn. It is useful after shock, insomnia and period pains.

The blue cast which distinguishes spirulina (a kelp) is phycocyanin. Phycocyanin is related to the human pigment bilirubin, which is important to healthy liver function and digestion of amino acids.

Ailments Related to the Blue Ray

Emphysema
Emphysema is a lung disease that results in diminished oxygen supply to the vital organs. In cases of emphysema, foods of the blue ray are soothing, antiseptic and antibiotic in effect. Supplement the diet with brewer's yeast and kelp. Honey is also extremely soothing and a natural antibiotic. Honey works on both the blue and orange ray, so it is cooling and at the same time relaxes tightness in the chest. Pacifying green-ray foods such as yogurt, curds, sour cream, garlic and comfrey are also excellent. Fruits that are helpful can be red, orange, yellow or violet, especially lemons, oranges, blackcurrants and rose-hips. These fruits contain a high level of vitamin C.

Bronchitis can be helped by breathing in steam from hot catnip tea. Slippery elm tea is also soothing as it heals from the inside.

Insomnia
The guiding principles of the Colours for Life Diet ensure that only pacifying foods are eaten during the evening, thus aiding sleep. If you eat a heavy evening meal rich in proteins and fats your digestive system will be put under pressure, making relaxation impossible. The mind must also be relaxed as it is

over-stimulated during the day. Time must be put aside before you go to bed to unwind and slow down mental processes. Reading poetry or listening to gentle music aids sleep, whereas watching action-packed videos or loud music will only get your adrenalin going with the result that you not only spend hours trying to sleep, but when you do you are bound to have nightmares and turbulent dreams.

A glass of warm milk, Milo or herb tea like camomile or valerian before you go to bed will be of great assistance. You might also take a warm (not too hot) bath before you go to bed, into which you have placed a few drops of any combination of the following essential oils: melissa, camomile, sandalwood, marjoram and lavender.

Thyroid Insufficiency

The thyroid gland is part of the endocrine system of glands and is particularly responsible for growth. Together with the para-thyroids, which straddle the vocal cords, it plays a very important part in the whole metabolic process. Chronic tiredness and depression often indicate an underactive thyroid gland. Other symptoms include weight gain, drying of the hair and skin, hair loss, constipation and intolerance of the cold.

Spirulina has a characteristic blue hue and has been found to boost the action of the thyroid. Either take spirulina tablets before meals, or include seaweeds such as kombu or wakama and kelp products in the meal which are rich in iodine. The rich source of essential minerals and other chemical nutrients in kelp make it harmonize with the thyroid, which is on the blue frequency.

Indigo

Chakra: third eye
Glands/body organs: pituitary, mouth, nose, ears, sinuses, left eye
Action on: skeletal system, bone marrow, pain

Indigo vibrates at our brow centre, just between our eyes, also known in Eastern philosophy as the third eye centre, which relates it to the ability to detach the mind from the emotions.

Indigo controls the pineal gland and is a purifier of the blood. The pineal gland controls the nervous, mental and psychic potential of man, so that the organs of sight and hearing also are under the influence of the indigo ray. Psychologically, this ray has a purifying and stabilizing effect, especially in cases where fears and repressions have produced a serious mental complaint. Like the orange ray, it helps broaden the mind and prevents the growth of tumours.

Because indigo is made up of blue with a small amount of red, it helps to broaden the mind and free it of fears and inhibitions. If you suffer from acne, eczema or skin troubles, indigo foods – like blue foods – will cool and soothe.

Curiously, given the connection of indigo with the third eye and the detachment of emotions, indigo light has been used by doctors in Texas to induce anaesthesia for minor operations. The patient in these operations remains awake but his or her mind appears to disregard signals from the body and they are not aware of pain. It is worth noting that ultraviolet light is used quite extensively elsewhere in orthodox medicine.

Indigo food can be used to treat all diseases of the eyes, ears and nose, as well as diseases of the lungs, asthma and dyspepsia. Foods vibrating on both the blue and violet rays contain indigo energy. Indigo does contain a little red-ray energy so eating blue foods alone will not provide a true reflection of indigo. By eating both blue and violet foods, you will be receiving indigo energy.

Ailments Related to the Indigo Ray

Colour Blindness

There are two main types of colour blindness. The first results in the person being unable to see the colour red. This can be caused by the over-consumption of red-ray foods. The second occurs when there is an inability to detect colours at the blue-green end of the spectrum. This type of colour blindness is related to a high intake of yin or blue/violet foods. The eyes are closely related to the liver function and sexual organs. The Colours for Life Diet should balance out both of these extremes, as long as other extremes in eating are avoided.

In cases of eye problems, exercises can be very helpful, as can a gentle massage on the temples and point of the third eye. Washing the eyes with indigo-solarized water helps to strengthen them.

Fevers, Itches, Stings and Skin Conditions

Indigo-solarized water is an excellent way of making use of the indigo ray. Cotton wool dipped into indigo solar-charged water can be applied to the lids of tired eyes. Apply it to soothe itches, stings and inflamed skin conditions. Gargle with indigo-solarized water to soothe throats. Taken internally it will have a cooling and soothing action for fevers or any inflamed conditions.

Menopausal Problems

As women get older many problems can develop as a result of hormonal imbalances. Today HRT treatments with drugs are gaining popularity, but there are many natural ways in which we can help ourselves through the menopausal years without experiencing the psychological and physical problems associated with this time of life. If you are menopausal, it is of utmost importance that you reduce or eliminate your intake of sugar and junk foods, especially sweets and cakes, as well as honey, which contains sucrose. These foods encourage water retention and block our body's ability to absorb essential minerals.

Salt reduction is also essential for the same reasons. If you desire a salty flavouring for your food try using soya sauce, which is rich in natural oestrogen. Other delicious salty flavours can be achieved by sprinkling blue-black nori (dried seaweed) on your food. Seaweed and spirulina are rich in iodine and help balance the hormonal functioning of the thyroid gland. Reduce or eliminate stimulants such as alcohol, coffee and tea, for these contain infra-red rays which can make symptoms worse. Instead, drink green tea, as they do in Japan.

The symptoms of the menopause can be greatly reduced by eating two servings of raw green salads each day. Green vegetables are full of natural enzymes which are destroyed if heated. It is not commonly known that we only have a certain irreplaceable number of enzymes in our body and that these decrease during our lifetime. In order to retain these enzymes we should eat as much natural plant material as possible. Plants contain their own enzymes, which aid digestion, thus saving our enzymes for better absorption of vitamins and minerals.

Osteoporosis

Osteoporosis is generally caused by vitamin and mineral deficiencies, but can also be the result of inactivity, menopausal imbalances and consuming too much meat. To address these deficiencies eat mineral-rich food.

Eating too much refined sugar for too long can complicate matters, as it results in the depletion of calcium in our bones and teeth. Contrary to popular belief, eating dairy produce will not build up calcium stores, for little is absorbed. In fact dairy produce can interfere with our magnesium absorption, and increase menstrual and hormonal symptoms later in life. So in order to increase our intake of bone-fortifying calcium, we should eat treacle, black molasses and dried figs. Indigo foods will have a beneficial effect on the skeleton.

The red ray will also build up new blood cells and strengthen the whole system as well. To absorb the red ray, eat blueberries, raspberries, beetroots and strawberries, and drink turnip-top juice.

Golden-yellow foods like barley, millet, oats and rice are strengthening and nourishing, as are lactic-acid foods like sour milk products and sauerkraut.

Tooth Decay

The minerals in our food and in our normal body reserve are usually sufficient to meet our daily requirements. If, however, we have been eating refined sugar regularly, our supply of minerals will be depleted until it is no longer sufficient for our needs and then the body must utilize the minerals stored deep within the bones themselves. This means that the teeth and bones become weaker and weaker, and eventually decay. If we do want to sweeten tea, coffee or other foods, a little honey or maple syrup can be used instead, although in excess this ultimately has a similar effect as refined sugar. Natural sweetening should come from fruits and spices. Raisins and currants, as well as spices like cinnamon and cloves, can flavour puddings and desserts.

Violet

Chakra: crown chakra, top of head
Glands/body organs: pineal, spleen, right eye, head
Action on: central nervous system, psyche

The violet ray has the highest vibration of all the cosmic rays. It controls the crown chakra, in the head, and is also linked to the pituitary and pineal glands and central nervous system. The pituitary is the centre of our intuition and spiritual understanding. The lymph system and the spleen are stimulated by the violet ray, as violet is made up of red and blue. Violet influences the endocrine, neurological and physiological processes controlled by the pituitary and hypothalamus.

Psychologically, this colour has the most wonderful healing effect on all forms of neurosis and neurotic manifestations, and nervous and mental disorders; physiologically, on neuralgia, epilepsy, sciatica and diseases of the scalp.

The violet ray also has a relaxing effect and encourages sleep. It has a soothing, tranquillizing effect on frayed nerves and for those of a highly strung disposition. Artists, actors and musicians often suffer from high anxiety disorders and would find the violet ray useful to restore their sense of peace and calm.

Physically, violet can be used to treat cerebro-spinal meningitis, concussion, epilepsy, kidney and bladder diseases, rheumatism, tumours and varicose veins.

Ailments Related to the Violet Ray

The Adverse Effects of Ageing

As we get older the number of neurones or brain cells decreases through natural attrition. The area of the brain which is central to learning, memory and emotion may lose up to 5 per cent of its cells in the later half of life. The pattern of loss is not the same for all people and some may lose more cells than others. Ageing alone does not necessarily wipe out that many cells but specific disease processes do. One of the worst degenerative diseases is Alzheimer's disease, which is the leading cause of senile dementia (loss of memory and reason). Other conditions that affect brain ability include Parkinson's disease and multiple strokes.

Diet, exercise, stress management and the psycho-social environment are all vital components of long-lasting good health.

Plenty of fresh air and exercise will help also boost levels of vitality, and periodic juice fasting using orange and green juices for a few days will cleanse your system from any toxins building up. Fresh apricot, papaya (pawpaw), pineapple, lemon and lime will all purify the body's system. Garlic, ginseng and brewer's yeast are excellent for keeping the body in tiptop condition.

The Colours for Life Diet is an excellent way of influencing longevity. It will improve the quality of *chi* in your system while maintaining colour energy balance over a long period of time. Eat plenty of purple and blue foods, as this food is particularly suitable for a mature adult. These foods nourish your system at a higher level, especially later in life. This will keep your body and mind strong, adaptable and protected from harmful vibrations, so you can enjoy a long, happy and healthy life.

Migraine

Migraines are often triggered by food allergies. It is well worthwhile to go on an elimination diet to discover the causes. Likely culprits include citrus fruits, coffee and tea, eggs, milks, nuts and wheat.

Migraines can also be helped by violet energy foods and oils. Try rubbing a drop of lavender oil on the temples to bring immediate relief. Peppermint or rosemary tea can also be effective. Violet flowers can be eaten and will help to balance the crown chakra.

Varicose Veins

Varicose veins often result from a sedentary lifestyle. A complete programme of exercise, such as walking, running, swimming or bicycling, must complement dietary colour treatments. Lying with your legs up higher than your heart or doing a headstand is also beneficial.

The complementary colours of violet and yellow work well. So the diet of varicose vein sufferers should include plenty of fibre for good circulation and elimination of toxic material; golden-brown wholegrains, nuts and seeds will do this very well. Carrots, pineapples and marigold flowers will also help the cleaning yellow ray. Rose-hips, blackcurrants and purple grapes will help to stimulate the blood circulation without inflaming the condition. Violet-solarized water is also highly recommended, to be drunk each day.

10 | More Ways of Healing with Colour

Breathing Colour Energy

Throughout this book we have seen how the air we breathe is permeated with the forces of light and colour, and that air contains *chi, prana* or bio-energy. So, as well as through the food we eat, we can take in *chi* into our systems through deep breathing. We also need to breathe deeply to feed the blood system with oxygen, which in turn feeds all our cells and tissues, especially our brain cells. This keeps us alert and full of vitality, and aids longevity. The capacity to extract oxygen and *chi* from the air helps us absorb the maximum goodness from our food and drink. We take very little *chi* into our body when we breathe in a hasty or shallow fashion and so, as most of us do not breathe deeply enough, very few of us receive the vitality and full benefit of the vital force present in air. No wonder we operate at half capacity much of the time.

We need to become aware of how shallowly we breathe much of the time, and how this affects our energy levels and ability to relax. We must also now realize that shallow breathing also starves us of vital light energy. In other words, if we do not learn to breathe properly we will suffer from a serious form of energetic malnutrition no matter how much food we consume.

Just as we can learn various forms of yogic breathing to maximize our intake of *prana*, we can also harness our thought vibrations to help us absorb certain colour energies from *prana*. This technique is known as colour breathing. Colour breathing can be used for many purposes. It can aid meditation and relaxation of the mind, and it can be used to treat many emotional, mental and physical ailments. As an example of its beneficial qualities, colour breathing has also been used very successfully to aid women during their pregnancy and when giving birth.

Colour breathing is invaluable aid in cases of trauma, shock or hysteria, as it is immediate, silent and requires no equipment or difficult postures. It can also be combined with a cleansing diet to purify the body of all negative vibrations and pollution. It can even be used as a beauty aid!

There are many ways to practise colour breathing, and it is a matter of finding out which way suits you the best. Of course, the more you understand about the quality and action of each colour energy, the easier it will be to know which colour to inhale. You can also select a colour or colours intuitively by choosing one that feels right for you at that time. The colour you are attracted to is probably the colour energy you require at that moment.

Simple Colour Breathing Exercises

Before you start any colour breathing exercise it is best to practise the cleansing breath.

The Cleansing Breath
1 Close your eyes and centre your attention on your breathing for a minute.
2 Breathe slowly and rhythmically.
3 Imagine a ball of white light above your head.
4 Breathe in the white light, imagine it pouring in through the top of your head.
5 Circulate the white light around your body.
6 Now focus on your out breath. Imagine the out breath as being a dirty grey colour.
7 Consciously breathe in the white light, and consciously breathe out all the negative, harmful impurities from your system. See how polluted this breath is.

As you continue to do this, you will find that as you continue to breathe out, the grey air you are exhaling will become lighter and lighter . . .

8 . . . until you are aware of breathing in white light and breathing out white light.

9 Breathe in the white light and breathe out white light into the space around you.
10 Do this a few more times, and give thanks to your personal helper or guide, or the spiritual master with whom you feel an affinity for the benefits you have received. Know that your system has been cleansed and purified.

Now you are ready to use colour breathing to balance the body, emotions and mind.

Colour Breathing

1 Close your eyes and breathe deeply and regularly, concentrating the mind only on your breathing to begin with.
2 Then begin to focus your awareness at the third eye centre, between the eyes.
3 Imagine a ball of coloured light above your head: look at this colour with your inner eyes. Now start to breathe the colour energy into your system through your crown chakra. See the colour flooding into your being and filling up your whole body. Make sure the colour reaches your fingers and toes.
4 When you feel the colour energy has pervaded your whole system, start concentrating on your exhalation. Imagine breathing out the colour into the space around you.

Colour Breathing to Heal the Body
You can use whatever colour you need with this technique. Imagine the magnetic colours as warming and energizing you, while the cool colours calm and cool you. Pink and green balance and heal the emotions.

1 Close your eyes and breathe slowly and evenly.
2 Now imagine you are surrounded by a brilliant coloured light. How you treat the light will depend upon its colour.
3 If the light that you see is one of the magnetic colours of red, orange or yellow, draw it up inside you from the ground through your feet.
4 Green and pink should flow through you horizontally into your chest and heart chakra.
5 Electrical colours of blue, indigo or violet should be absorbed down through the crown of the head.

6 Breathe in the colour energy required. Imagine it circulating around your body, permeating every cell and tissue.
7 Send the colour to the area which needs healing or replenishing.
8 Imagine the action of the colour energy healing and balancing that area.
9 Breathe out any impurities into the space around you, watching your out breath becoming lighter and lighter.

Colour Breathing for Pain Relief

Use this technique to relieve any type of pain. It is especially useful for women in labour, or if you have recurring pain from, for instance, arthritic joints or cramps.

Remember that pain is only a symptom and not the problem itself. Pain is sent to us as a messenger to tell us that we are out of balance and something in our system needs correcting and balancing. Our energy system has been distorted and needs harmonizing.

1 Close your eyes and try to concentrate on deep slow breathing.
2 Try to force your mind to hold its focus away from the pain . . .
3 . . . and onto the breath.
4 Imagine a ball of deep blue light above your head. Look deeply into the midnight blue and try to feel its texture.
5 Breathe in the healing blue light, deeply and more deeply.
6 See it flooding into the area where you feel the pain.
7 It immediately soothes and comforts the cells and tissues like cool water washing over you. Feel it cooling any heat or swelling; imagine the muscles relaxing and not fighting the pain.
8 As the muscles relax, breathe more deeply and slowly.
9 You may like to imagine the deep blue changing to violet.
10 The violet light will help regenerate and cleanse the affected area. See the cells regenerating and healing, bathed in the violet light.
11 Let the pain be gently washed and soothed away. See it as a stream flowing away from you leaving you still and untroubled.
12 Breathe out the blue or violet into the space surrounding you, forming a protective envelope around your body. Give thanks for the help you have received.

Colour Breathing to Balance the Emotions

Use this colour breathing technique for immediate emotional relief for yourself, or instruct someone else who needs help in it.

1 Close your eyes.
2 Start breathing deeply and slowly. Use your inner voice to say, 'Breathe in, breathe out, breathe in, breathe out.'
3 See green light surrounding you in a protective envelope, or imagine a green blanket wrapping around you.
4 Breathe in the beautiful grass-green. Feel how cool, soft and soothing it is. Send it to your heart, your lungs, to all of your body. Feel the soft, cool green soothing your mind and know that everything will be fine. It is all being taken care of and you will be looked after.
5 Imagine lying on soft green moss: let your body feel relaxed and heavy. You feel so tired and sleepy, you could lie here all day.
6 Sit or lie comfortably while the green blanket cares for you.
7 Breathe slowly and quietly until you are ready to move.

Colour Breathing to Balance the Mind

1 Close your eyes and start to concentrate on the pattern of your breathing.
2 Lift your shoulders upwards and let them drop back down.
3 Squeeze your face muscles and then relax them.
4 Try to let your eyes roll back in their sockets.
5 Start to focus the mind on your breathing, breathing slowly in for a count of four.
6 Hold the breath for a count of four and then exhale for the same number of counts.
7 When you can do this naturally and without effort, on the next inhalation breathe in the colour blue. It is a wonderful sky blue which allows you to breathe more easily and more deeply.
8 With the next set of breaths, imagine this sky blue changing to dark blue and try to hold the image of a deep blue ocean in front of you.
9 When you are ready, imagine you are surrounded by a circle of royal blue light. Circle yourself three times and when you are ready open your eyes.

Absorbing Colour Energy through the Skin

We take in the coloured light energy into our being not only through our eyes and the food we eat, but also through our skin. In physiological terms the skin is capable of registering pressure, touch, vibration, temperature and pain. In fact the skin is the gateway to the body, and has been used by ancient healing arts as a medium of treatment of most illnesses.

In that the skin 'breathes' it can be viewed as part of our respiratory system. In traditional Chinese medicine the lungs are linked to the skin and so the condition of the skin is deemed to reflect the condition of the lungs.

Colour is absorbed through the skin, affecting every cell in our body. It is by absorbing sunlight that our body makes vitamin D. As all cells are light sensitive, so colour vibrations affect their growth and behaviour. In fact we give ourselves colour therapy every day, by the different-coloured clothes we wear. Light is filtered through the cloth and the colour vibrations permeate our tissues, nerves and cells. How often have you gone to your wardrobe in the morning and been unable to find a thing to wear? This is not because you didn't have any clothes, but probably because you couldn't find the right colour that you needed to wear that day. Sometimes we may even buy something and end up never wearing it. This could also be a result of the colour of our purchase not suiting our inner colours; that is, its colour is unharmonious with our own colour vibrations.

The colours we wear to bed do also affect our sleep, as do the sheets and bedcovers. Curtains are important too as they filter light especially in the morning. If you can't wake up easily, try yellow, pink or peach curtains, which will emulate the dawn.

The Scent of Colour

Like colour, aromas are vibrations which travel through the ether and permeate matter. We all know how smells permeate cloth, paper and even the walls of buildings. Many places which are believed to be haunted or have ghostly visitors have a bad smell. When walking into a room in a medieval castle or an English country house where an evil deed has been known to have taken place, it is common to notice that the place feels exceptionally cold and that it seems to be pervaded by an awful aroma. Bad smells are very often associated with places where bad events have taken place.

As aroma is very closely linked to colour vibrations, essential oils are ideal to use in order to enhance colour energy taken in through the skin. Coloured oils can be massaged into the skin, or aromatherapy oils used on the chakras or acupuncture points, and also as a perfume. Aromatherapy is the sister therapy which makes use of vibrations to restore harmony to the body, mind and spirit.

Aromas are another expression of light vibrations, and different aromas have sympathetic rhythms to various colours. Aromas and colours vibrate in a harmonious frequency, and therefore complement and aid one another.

Here is a list of some aromas and the colour harmonies with which they correspond. If you are using essential oils, remember that these work on different levels of our being and that they often relate to more than one colour harmony. As an example of this, let us look at rosemary essential oil. This is a true top-to-toe oil which acts as a warming stimulant which corresponds to the red-ray energy. In addition to this, rosemary is a plant that protects the garden against destructive influences, and it can provide protection for us in a similar way. Because violet is the colour that provides protection, rosemary oil relates to this colour too. Violet also links to the head, and rosemary is an excellent plant to use as a hair wash and is often added to shampoos.

Some oils and all the herbs and spices can be used to correct colour imbalances by adding them to your cooking. Many make delicious herbal teas. In the lists that follow check which colour corresponds to which oil, herb, or spice, and use these to create the kind of meal or drink you require; only essential oils marked with a * can safely be used internally.

You will note that some oils fall under two groupings. This is because sometimes, as we have seen in the case of rosemary, oils work on more than one level and act on different parts of our being simultaneously. Essential oils derive their colour signatures from the part of the plant used to extract the oil and also sometimes from the colour of the oil itself. So although fennel harmonizes with the green ray for cooking, the oil itself is yellow, giving it a yellow vibration; sandalwood is connected to the orange ray and is physically warming, but it also contains blue energy, which helps to sedate the mind. Some oils are made from more than one part of the plant and these link to more than one colour.

This enables the oil to work on more than one level and act on different parts of our being simultaneously. Essential oils derived from herbs are used medicinally to balance and heal the body, emotions and mind.

While many essential oils are suitable for cooking there are others which are toxic if taken internally. Before using an essential oil it is best to consult a trained aromatherapist. (Often you can use the fresh herb itself.)

However you choose to use an essential oil, always choose a brand you can be sure will be of a good quality and that comes from a reputable supplier. Cheap brands are usually of a lower quality. Many oils can be used in your bath or diluted as massage oils, but you need to check if you have a sensitive skin.

Red Aromas

*black pepper	stimulating and good for the intense cold
camphor	stimulates the heart, low blood pressure, coldness, warms stiff muscles
*clary sage	for inflamed skin conditions, muscular aches and pains, asthma, cramp, frigidity, nervous tension. Do not use externally while consuming internally!
*ginger	promotes self-awareness and acceptance; warming and stimulating
jasmine	sexually stimulating, good for apathy, rigidity, secretiveness
*rosemary	for tiredness and apathy; a nerve stimulant

Orange Aromas

benzoin	this relates more to a peach colour, which soothes the emotions and is good for loneliness and sadness
*cardamom	for expansion and warmth
*carrot seed	detoxes the liver and kidneys, relieves stress, improves energy, increases red corpuscles
*cinnamon	aids the digestion
*coriander	an appetite stimulant
marjoram	orange/blue: see under blue
*neroli	refreshing, relaxing, especially good for stress and depression
*sweet orange	effective for lack of energy, stubbornness, selfishness

Golden/Yellow Aromas

*bergamot	nerve sedative and antidepressant
*fennel	aids digestion, weight corrective, counters headaches
*grapefruit	counters worry, bitterness, dithering

*lemon	refreshing and strengthening, promotes selflessness
*lemongrass	counters boredom and lack of interest
*lime	counters a sluggish system, promotes selfishness
*oreganum	vibrates with violet as well as yellow and is an aid for mental disease. also helps the digestion, by acting on the liver, spleen and stomach

Green Aromas

*bergamot	sedative, nervine, good for countering inflammations and anxiety, balances hypothalamus, antidepressant
eucalyptus	good for colds, flu and congested lungs
geranium	hormone regulator, tonic for nervous system, dispels anxiety and depression, good for treating PMS and menopausal problems
*palma rosa	calming, and uplifting for the emotions
*peppermint	restores and uplifts the spirits
*rose	balancing for the emotions, soothing, comforting
linden blossom	tonic for nerves, promotes sleep, good for high blood pressure, counters migraine, neuralgia, vertigo
*verbena	aids parasympathetic nervous system

Turquoise Aromas

niaouli	aids respiration, flu, stings, burns and cuts
petitgrain	sedative to the nervous system, tonic for the skin, mild immune stimulant, refreshes and revives the body, relieves pneumonia and laryngitis

Blue Aromas

cajaput	antiseptic, good for the respiratory tract, reduces sweating, counters laryngitis and earache
*camomile	calming, soothing and healing
cypress	astringent, helps calm those who are too talkative
*marjoram	(orange/blue herb or oil) calms nerves, relieves anxiety, grief and loneliness, warms emotions, promotes good health, rheumatic aches and pains and swollen glands, aids circulation
sandalwood	for problems of the throat, good for dreamwork

Indigo Aromas

*clove	provides pain relief
tea-tree	anti-bacterial, anti-fungal
*yarrow	acts directly on the bone marrow, stimulates blood renewal, has a healing effect on varicose veins

Violet Aromas

frankincense	rejuvenating, restores subtle bodies, counters panic, instils confidence
*juniper	purifying and protective
*lavender	soothing, relaxing, purifying, protecting, effective for hysteria, palpitations, insomnia, migraine, depression, tonic action on the heart, lowers blood pressure, relieves epilepsy
*Spanish sage	a herbal gargle for sore throats
violet	sedative for the mind, calms anger and anxiety, an aphrodisiac, good for the kidneys and respiratory tract

Magenta Aromas

*clary sage	warm, uplifts spirit, effective for treating PMS, exhaustion and addiction
roso otto	sensual, purifies at all levels, good for treating allergies and addictions
ylang-ylang	calms anger, counters guilt, builds confidence

Some essential oils and their use in cooking

red	jasmine	chicken, eggs, cheese, rice, desserts, pastries, breads, cakes, yogurt, fruit
red	black pepper	meat, fish, chicken, eggs, vegetables, pasta
red/orange	ginger	meat, chicken, eggs, vegetables, desserts, pastries, breads, cakes, yogurt, fruit
red/pink	rose	chicken, eggs, cheese, rice, desserts, pastries, bread, cakes, sorbets, yogurt, fruit, vinegar, drinks
red/violet	sage	meat, chicken
orange	cardamom	fish, cheese, vegetables, rice, pasta, desserts, drinks
orange	coriander	chicken, fish, pasta, desserts, bread, cakes, fruit, drinks
orange	mandarin	meat, chicken, fish, vegetables, rice, pasta, desserts, pastries, bread, cakes, sorbets, yogurt, fruit, drinks
orange	nutmeg	meat, chicken, eggs, vegetables, rice, pasta, desserts, pastries, bread, cakes, sorbets, yogurt, fruit, drinks
orange	orange	meat, chicken, eggs, rice, pasta, desserts, pastries, bread, cakes, sorbets, yogurt, fruit, oils, drinks

yellow	cinnamon	meat, chicken, rice, pasta, desserts, pastries, breads, sorbets, yogurt, fruit
yellow	cumin	meat, chicken, fish, cheese, vegetables
yellow	dill	fish, vegetables, rice, pasta, bread, fruit
yellow	grapefruit	chicken, fish, rice, vegetables, pasta, desserts, pastries, bread, cakes, sorbets, yogurt, fruit
yellow	fennel	chicken, fish, cheese, vegetables
yellow	lemon	chicken, fish, eggs, cheese, vegetables, rice, pasta, desserts, pastries, bread, cakes, sorbets, ice cream, fruit, vinegar, oils, dips
yellow	star anise	fish, vegetables, rice, bread, fruit
yellow/green	basil	meat, fish, chicken, vegetables, bread, rice, pasta
green	geranium	eggs, cheese, rice, pasta, desserts, pastries, bread, cakes, sorbets, yogurt, fruit, vinegar
green	lime	meat, chicken, fish, vegetables, rice, pasta, desserts, pastries, bread, cakes, sorbets, yogurt, fruit, oils, dips, drinks
green	melissa	chicken, fish, eggs, cheese, vegetables, rice, pasta, sorbets, yogurt, fruit
green	parsley	meat, chicken, fish, eggs, vegetables, rice, pasta
green	peppermint	vegetables, desserts, pastries, cakes, sorbets, yogurt, fruit
green/pink	palma rosa	meat, chicken, eggs, rice, pasta, vegetables, pastries, cakes, sorbets, yogurt, fruit, drinks
blue	marjoram	meat, chicken, fish
blue	thyme	meat, chicken
blue/violet	rosemary	meat, chicken
indigo	clove	meat, rice, pasta, desserts, bread, cakes, sorbets, fruit, drinks
violet	lavender	meat, chicken, fish, cheese, vegetables, rice, pasta, desserts, cakes, sorbets, yogurts, fruit
magenta/pink	ylang ylang	chicken, rice, pasta, desserts, bread, cakes, yogurt, fruit

NB Only essential oils marked with a * can safely be used internally.

Conclusion

Now that you have come to the end of this book, you are probably well on your journey to optimum health and well-being. Let us look at the steps that have brought you to this point.

Whenever we look at our state of health we have to remember that we are partly a product of our genetic make-up, and partly a result of environmental factors. It is therefore a mistake to blame ill health or eating problems on either inherited factors or lifestyle alone.

By looking at your physical frame and personal colouring at birth, you have discovered your inherited colour bias, and you can use this information to help you develop your strengths so that you can protect yourself against any potential physical weakness.

By heightening your awareness of your own eating habits and attitudes you will also be able to assess whether you are eating emotionally or intellectually and whether your diet is controlled by social and cultural constraints. When we understand the difference between 'want' and 'need' we can discover the right amount of food we require. It is about re-educating our minds as much as our bodies. The aim is to reach the point at which we can eat freely as much as we need, without worrying about our health or our weight.

The Colours for Life Diet is perfect for maintaining balance in all parts of our being. The key is variety and balance. If any colour is missing from our regular diet, we will experience problems in the corresponding area of our being. Here is a summary of the colour recipe for health:

- Red food gives us a good appetite and builds up stamina
- Orange food gives us physical energy and mental strength
- Yellow food feeds our mind and nervous system
- Green food balances our entire system, and helps us connect to nature and to love
- Blue food helps us to relax and promotes restorative sleep

- Violet food balances our psyche and connects us to the spirit

Following these guidelines, it is easy to create a delicious and healthy diet by making sure you eat a high proportion of fresh locally grown fruit, vegetables and herbs, together with pulses and legumes, and if you are not a vegetarian some fresh organic animal products. These foods should reflect primarily the orange, yellow and green rays, although you will also need some red and blue food, subject to your colour bias. Purple foods provide a good balance of red and blue as they are made up of these rays. So, although they are stimulating, purple foods are not too 'hot'.

Whenever possible ask your local greengrocer or vegetable grower to include some older varieties of Rainbow foods, such as different coloured potatoes, onions, peppers, squashes, herbs and lettuces. These are strong varieties which are better suited to local conditions and contain more vital light and earth energy – the staples of the Colours for Life Diet.

The Colours for Life Diet is a perfect way of creating a way of eating, tailored to your personal needs and lifestyle. The proportions of the Rainbow colours to include in our diet depends on your innate colour bias but also on your lifestyle and immediate needs. So if it is a cold winter's day or you are feeling particularly tired and run down, you can use a single-colour food to boost your energy levels. If you are experiencing particular emotional, mental or physical problems a special coloured diet will act as a catalyst for your own internal healing mechanisms.

If you lead an active life or have a fast metabolism, you will require more yang/stimulating food, whereas if you are less active you will find the purifying and cleansing actions of yellow and green food beneficial. For those of you who, like me, lead a quieter and meditative life, a light diet of predominantly blue and purple yin food is the perfect choice. These yin colours help us to develop our sensitivity and are spiritually uplifting.

Although our body has inbuilt ways to cleanse impurities from our system, we should not forget that we also need to get rid of toxic vibrations from our minds and emotions. We can do this by practising purifying yogic breathing exercises and meditation. Simple colour breathing exercises are excellent for all of us, helping us absorb *chi* from the air, as well as food and water more effectively.

Once you feel the benefits of the Colours for Life Diet and colour exercises, you should introduce colour energy into other areas of your life. We take in light energy through our eyes and skin, as well as through our food, so wearing certain colours or surrounding ourselves with a particular colour reinforces the healing action of that colour.

There may also be times when it is difficult to eat the right colour food, for instance when you are visiting someone or travelling. This is the perfect opportunity to find other ways of absorbing the light energy you require. A green scarf draped over the back of your chair or pillow will relax your mind and soothe a headache, while a soft pink rose quartz crystal makes an ideal necklace if you need emotional stability. The colours in your kitchen, dining room and bedroom will also have a profound affect on your well-being, so look carefully at these, making sure they are beneficial to you.

I hope that this book has opened your eyes and heart to a new and exciting way of looking at colour and food. Use it as inspiration to take colour into other areas of your life so you can look towards a bright and radiant future.

Further Reading

Airola, Dr Piavo, *How to Get Well: Dr Airola's Handbook of Natural Healing*, Contemporary Books, Chicago, 1984

Batmanghelidj, F, *Your Body's Many Cries for Water*, The Therapist, Worthing, 1996

Biggs, Matthew, *Matthew Biggs's Complete Book of Vegetables*, Kyle Cathie, London, 1997

Bovey, Shelley, *The Forbidden Body: Why Being Fat Is Not A Sin*, HarperCollins Publishers, London, 1994

Charles, Rachel, *Food for Healing*, Random House UK, London, 1995

Chopra, Deepak, MD, *Perfect Health, The Complete Mind/body Guide*, Transworld Publishers, London, 1990

Cowmeadow, Oliver, *The Art of Shiatsu: A Step-by-Step Guide*, Element Books, Shaftesbury, 1994

Davis, Stephen and Alan Stewart, *Nutritional Medicine: The Drug-Free Guide to Better Health*, Pan Books, London, 1987

Hanssen, Maurice with Jill Marsden, *E for Additives*, Thorsons, London, 1988

Heline, Corinne, *Healing and Regeneration Through Color*, Devorss & Co., California, 1987

Lacy, Marie Louise, *Know Yourself Through Colour*, HarperCollins Publishers, London, 1989

Laver, May, and Margaret Smith, *Diet for Life: A Cookbook for Arthritics*, Pan Books, London, 1993

Le Tissier, Jackie, *Food Combining for Vegetarians: Eat for Health on the Hay Diet*, HarperCollins Publishers, London, 1992

Mandel, Peter, *Practical Compendium of Colorpuncture*, Energetik-Verlag, 1986

Page, Dr Christine, *Frontiers of Health: From Food Combining to Wholeness*, C W Daniel & Co, Essex, 1992

Reader's Digest Association, *Foods That Harm, Foods That Heal*, David & Charles, Newton Abbot, 1996

Robert, B Tisserand, *The Art of Aromatherapy*, C W Daniel Co., Essex, 1977

Stewart, Maryon, *The Phyto Factor*, Hutchinson Publishing, London, 1998

General Index

acidity/alkalinity x, 34, 51, 193, 194
additives 41–5
ageing 202–3
ajoene 131
alcohol 45–6
alcoholism 189
animal kingdom 36, 182–3
anthocyanidins (anthocyans) xi, xii, 34
anthoxanthins xii
antioxidants x, xii, 50, 183, 185, 187, 194
appetite and hunger 17–18
aromas 209–14
asthma 186
astral (emotional) body 6–7
aura 6–8
  photography 38
automatic eating 19
Ayurvedic medicine 32

beta-carotene 34, 54, 58, 59, 61, 185, 188
bio-energy 13 *see also* light energy
bioflavonoids *see* flavonoids
biorhythms 15
  diet and 75–9
Bircher-Benner, Dr 52
bladder 8, 24, 73, 74, 79, 182
blood pressure 184, 194–5
blue
  aromas and essential oils 212, 214
  /blue-violet cosmic rays 3, 4, 7
  bodily correspondence 8
  complementary colours 24, 117
  and daily energy cycle 73, 74, 79, 81
  energy imbalance 138, 144
  foods ix, x, xii, 34, 41, 69–70, 216
  healing treatments 181, 196–8
  herbal teas 57

herbs and spices 56
inherited bias 27, 31
intellectual eating 21
and seasonal energy cycles 73
solarized water 118
in surroundings 125, 126
yin-yang energy ix, 36
body
  balance with mind and soul 2, 5
  and etheric body 6
  feeding 9–11
  healing with colour breathing 206–7
body organs
  and colour 7–8, 181
  and daily energy cycle 74–9
  and seasonal energy cycles 73
breathing
  and asthma 186
  colour 204–8
Buddha 14
butter versus margarine 47–8

calcium 55, 137, 195, 200–1
cancer x, xi, 30, 39, 41, 50, 59, 128, 131, 132, 133, 183, 185–6, 188, 194, 196
carbohydrates 52, 53, 57–8, 59, 60, 123, 130, 131, 132, 134, 190, 191
carotenoids x, xi, xii, 34
carrots 58–9
cell salts 183, 194
chakras 7–8, 30, 34, 136, 138, 181
  base 8, 182
  crown 7, 8, 32, 145, 170, 201
  heart 8, 30, 170, 193
  sacral 8, 141, 185
  solar plexus 8, 30, 188
  third eye 8, 53, 70, 198
  throat 8, 31, 181, 196

flavonoids (bioflavonoids) xii-xiii, 50
food(s)
  to avoid 45–50
  colour groups and nutritional value
    ix-xiii, 34
  combining 134
  cravings 24–5, 122, 147,
    189–90
  to enjoy 50–64
  fresh versus processed xiii, 38–45
  relationship with colour vii-viii, 40–1
  types 22–3
  and the yin-yang scale 35–8
free eating 22
free radicals 10, 39–40, 185
fruit 51–2

gall bladder 8, 30, 73, 78, 79, 142, 188
gallstones 30, 190–1
gamma-linolenic acid (GLA) 54, 189
Gandhi, Mahatma 14
garlic 131, 195–6
Gerg, Dr Wolfgang 127
gold
  bodily correspondence 8
  and daily energy cycle 73, 74, 76, 81
  foods 34, 170
golden-yellow *see* yellow
Gordon, Dr James 13
gout 184
green
  aroma and essential oils 212, 214
  bodily correspondence 8
  complementary colours 24–5, 117
  cosmic rays 3, 4, 7
  and daily energy cycle 73, 74, 76, 78,
    79, 80, 81
  energy imbalance 143–4
  foods ix, x, xi, 34, 40–1, 52–5, 68,
    147, 215
  healing treatments 193–6
  herbal teas 57
  herbs and spices 56
  inherited bias 27, 30–1
  and seasonal energy cycles 73
  social eating 20–1
  solarized water 118
  in surroundings 126
  yin-yang energy ix, 36, 37
green tea 50, 128, 129, 133

haemoglobin 52, 183
Hay diet 134

healing
  with aromas 209–14
  colour absorption (skin) 209
  colour breathing 204–8
  first step 11–12
  properties of colour 135
  special diets 134
  specific ailments 181–203
heart 8, 12, 24, 29, 68, 73, 74, 77, 79,
  193
  disease x, xii, 10, 47, 55, 59, 128, 194
herbal teas 50, 57, 128
herbs 54–5, 56–7
hormones xii, 5, 53, 200
hypoglycaemia 191
hypothalamus 5, 53, 136

ideological eating 21–2
immune system x, xii, 10, 29, 53, 54,
  59, 61, 66, 117, 137, 147, 184, 185,
  196
impotence (male) 187
Indian diet 133
Indian philosophy 22–3
indigo
  aromas and essential oils 212, 214
  bodily correspondence 8
  complementary colour 117
  and daily energy cycle 73, 74, 78, 79,
    81
  foods 34, 70
  healing treatments 198–201
  ideological eating 21–2
  inherited bias 27, 31–2
  solarized water 118
  yin-yang energy 36
influenza 195–6
infra-red 34, 35, 45, 50, 125, 182, 186,
  195
infusions 57
insomnia 192, 197–8
insulin 190
intellectual eating 21
intestine 30
  large 24, 74, 76, 79, 189
  small 73, 74, 77, 79
iron 50, 52, 55, 62, 76, 174, 195
irradiation 39–40
isoflavones xii

Japanese diet 133
jaundice 182, 192
Jesus Christ 14

Recipe Index